What the reviewers said about the 1993 Lambda Award nominee, *The Romantic Naiad:*

"*The Romantic Naiad* gives an evening of light reading on sexy lesbian themes. And a few of the stories are so exceptional that even at a price of almost $15, this collection is worth every penny."

Tee A. Corinne
The Advocate

"*The Romantic Naiad* is the latest anthology in what I hope will be a continuing series of short pieces by Naiad writers. It is an impressive collection indeed.... Ranging in tone from sweet to steamy, the stories in this anthology will provide unmixed delight."

Deborah Peifer
Bay Area Reporter

"A follow-up to *The Erotic Naiad,* this collection of romantic stories includes plenty of sex, too."

Diane L. Coleman
The Washington Blade

"Twenty-seven authors from the Naiad stable offer contributions varying from the saccharine to the succulent ... [and it's] not surprising that the mystery writers are second in number only to the romance."

Marie Kuda
Booklist

"Of all the feminist presses, Naiad Press stands alone in its consistency.... The women of Naiad are proud of this predictability, of course, as evidenced in their early slogan 'Lesbians always know: if it's a Naiad book it's a book they want to own,' and their choice of titles for their short story collections."

June Thomas
Lambda Book Report

"*The Romantic Naiad* is a good collection of short stories in the romantic line. This publisher continues to provide the bulk of lesbian romance and mystery novels that are available and most are well done. This work is no exception."

The Letter

"Flights of fantasy, they leave a ring of light around the edge after the inside image disappears.... Love scenes, though veering toward the graphic, are not vulgar, and if love interests turn up in the scenery (or around every grocery store aisle) it only proves that proximity can play a major role in kindling a romance.... This book will appeal to many readers only too anxious to gobble up love stories from the variety of authors included here."

Lisa Nussbaum
Library Journal

"Editors Forrest and Grier have gathered together twenty-five new stories by some of Naiad's most satisfying and successful writers of lesbian love. Sometimes steamy, sometimes touching, often wry and wonderfully funny... if you didn't find this under the tree this past Christmas, despair not. This collection is worth having waited for."

Cleve Boutell
Small Press Magazine

THE MYSTERIOUS NAIAD

Love Stories by Naiad Press Authors

EDITED BY

KATHERINE V. FORREST
AND BARBARA GRIER

THE MYSTERIOUS NAIAD

Love Stories by Naiad Press Authors

EDITED BY
KATHERINE V. FORREST
AND BARBARA GRIER

THE NAIAD PRESS, INC.
1994

Printed in the United States of America on acid-free paper
First Edition

Cover design by Bonnie Liss (Phoenix Graphics)
Typeset by Sandi Stancil

Library of Congress Cataloging-in-Publication Data

The Mysterious Naiad : love stories by Naiad Press authors /
edited by Katherine V. Forrest and Barbara Grier.
        p.   cm.
    ISBN 1-56280-074-4
    1. Lesbians—United States—Fiction.   2. Detective and mystery
stories, American.   3. Lesbians' writings, American.   4. Love
stories, American.   I. Forrest, Katherine V., 1939– . Grier,
Barbara, 1933– .
PS648.L47M97   1994
813.009′35206643—dc20
                                                                94-15980
                                                                CIP

ABOUT THE EDITORS

Katherine V. Forrest

Author of the novels *Curious Wine* (1983); *Daughters of a Coral Dawn* (1984); *Amateur City* (1984); *An Emergence of Green* (1986); *Murder at the Nightwood Bar* (1987), which has been optioned by film director Tim Hunter; a short story collection, *Dreams and Swords* (1987); *The Beverly Malibu* (1989) (Lambda Literary Award winner); *Murder by Tradition* (1991) (Lambda Literary Award winner); and *Flashpoint* (1994).

Articles and book reviews have appeared in a number of publications, including *The New York Times* and *The Los Angeles Times*. All book-length fiction has been published by The Naiad Press, Inc., Tallahassee, Florida. She is co-editor, with Barbara Grier, of *The Erotic Naiad* (1992), and *The Romantic Naiad* (1993).

Fiction editor, Naiad Press.

Member, PEN International.

Jurist, Southern California PEN fiction award.

Katherine V. Forrest was born in Canada. She has held management positions in business, and since 1979 has been a full-time writer and editor. She lives in San Francisco.

Barbara Grier

Author, editor, bibliographer, writings include *The Lesbian in Literature, Lesbiana, The Lesbian's Home*

Journal, Lavender Herring, Lesbian Lives as well as contributions to various anthologies, *The Lesbian Path* (Cruikshank) and *The Coming Out Stories* (Stanley and Wolfe). She is co-editor, with Katherine V. Forrest, of *The Erotic Naiad* (1992), and *The Romantic Naiad* (1993).

Her early career included working for sixteen years with the pioneer lesbian magazine *The Ladder*. For the last twenty-one years she has been, together with Donna J. McBride, the guiding force behind THE NAIAD PRESS.

Articles about Barbara's and Donna's life are too numerous to list, but a good early overview can be found in *Heartwomen* by Sandy Boucher (N.Y., Harper, 1982).

She lives in Tallahassee, Florida.

TABLE OF CONTENTS

THE
MYSTERIOUS

NAIAD

Love Stories by Naiad Press Authors

EDITED BY
KATHERINE V. FORREST
AND BARBARA GRIER

Tied Up at the Moment
Karin Kallmaker

Drew Dorfman was not much bigger than me, but he had biceps the size of footballs.

Twisting, I managed to avoid the blow he was aiming at my midsection. Instead, his fist slammed into my left breast. Tears started in my eyes as a hot needle of pain shot through my sternum and shoulder. But I could still breathe.

I spun away from the impact and kept my balance. Concentrate . . . arms out . . . strike . . . and follow through. My left heel snapped his head back. As

1

I swung back to face him I saw him wobble and fold to the floor.

I had won the fight, for the moment. I'd taken karate to protect myself, not to apprehend thieves. Already I was regretting that I hadn't called the police, rather than follow Dorfman in here to catch him dead to rights. My boob throbbed with fire. The bruise would be a long time healing.

I was being paid to find out who was lifting inventory at A&M Manufacturing. I'd been hired by A himself, in great secrecy. I don't think M, the silent partner, even knew. Our contract did not cover the molten pain still radiating from my breast. Or the likelihood that Dorfman and I would come to blows again when I did try to call the police. I could hope that a cruising patrol car would notice the lights on in the middle of the night. If so, it would save me another punch and rescue me from my own stupidity.

I'd been keeping an eye on the employees by posing as a shipping clerk. A nice, easy job, but after a week I knew that day surveillance wasn't going to turn up anything. More goods had disappeared three nights ago when there were supposedly no employees on the premises. And with no signs of forced entry everything pointed to an inside job. So the last two nights I had been staking out the entrance. I was surprised that it was Dorfman, though. He had the collective brain power of a turnip — he had to have had help.

I knelt with my knee on Dorfman's throat to immobilize and intimidate him. I might as well see if I could get any information from his tiny brain.

"Who hired you?"

He glared at me. His breathing was raspy and he'd had corned beef hash for dinner. He managed to spit out two words that rhymed with "duck view."

I put a little more weight on my knee and his eyes bulged slightly. "That's not very nice," I said, conversationally. "I know you're not in this alone, so why take the fall all by yourself?"

He spluttered another unimaginative invective and I mentally sighed. My breast felt like it was going to fall off.

I started to bear down with my knee on Dorfman's throat, but I heard a deadly click behind me.

"Put your hands in the air," a no-nonsense voice said.

"If I put my hands in the air I'll crush his windpipe."

Dorfman grunted as though to confirm the fragility of his windpipe.

There was silence, then cautious footsteps toward me. Every hair in my body stood up as the barrel of a gun pressed into the side of my neck. A booted foot came down on one hand.

"Put your other hand in the air. Now move your knee." The gun barrel moved away and I took a deep breath. It felt good to be breathing.

The voice was starting to sound familiar. A woman's voice, deep and calm. The boot was at the end of a khaki-panted leg. Not Dorfman's accomplice, I realized. A cop, Marysville Sheriff's office. Relief made me giddy — I lost my balance and fell on my rear.

At that point I got a good look at the cop. Long, trim legs. Curve of waist accentuated by the bulky leather gun belt. An upper body with broad, strong shoulders that Botticelli would have fainted over. Prominent jawline, broad cheekbones, brown hair. The gaze from topaz-colored eyes conveyed my status as a lower form of insect.

Damn.

Liz Crocker. Full name Elizabeth Cady Crocker.

We had a history of sorts.

The last time we'd met she'd wanted me charged with obstruction, but the Marysville D.A. wouldn't go along. Her complaint to the licensing board had put me up for review of my investigator's license, though — and that had been a spiteful thing to do. Maybe I shouldn't have asked her in front of the other deputies if anyone ever called her Betty. Still, her actions had been all out of proportion with the incident. Most probably her spite had to do with the first time we met.

"Well, well. If it isn't Lucretia Eliot, Private Investigator." She smiled far too sweetly.

"I have permission to be here from the owner," I answered, just as sweetly. "I'm investigating missing inventory." Slowly, but deliberately, I slid away from Dorfman who was just as slowly sitting up. "He's the one doing the breaking and entering since he works day shift only."

Dorfman croaked out, "She hit me for no reason at all."

"I've got a bruise the size of Alaska that says you're a liar." I put my arm over my aching breast.

Dorfman leered knowingly. Crocker said, "Save it for the judge." She stepped back and pointed the gun

at Dorfman. "On your stomach. You know the drill."
She read him his rights, he grunted that he
understood them, then she slipped handcuffs out of
her belt.

With Dorfman under control I decided that I
should get up off my rear. I was three-quarters of
the way onto my feet when Crocker swung back to
me and barked, "Stay on the floor."

Dorfman was stupid but not slow. My mouth was
only half opened to warn Crocker when he undercut
her legs with a swipe of his own. She fell heavily and
her service revolver skittered across the floor.

All three of us lunged for the gun, but Dorfman
blocked Crocker and she blocked me. Dorfman ended
up with it.

"Both you broads freeze." He tried to look tough,
but it didn't work. His eyes were bulging with
tension and fear. He was just a small-time thief, not
a killer. In Marysville we had lots of the former but
very few of the latter. He had probably never
intended to hold a gun much less on a cop.

Crocker must have seen his fear as well. Her
voice was calm and she made no threatening moves.
"Use a gun, go to prison. If it's your third trip, you
go forever. Put the gun down and slide it over to
me."

For a moment I thought he would do it.

"This is the rest of your life," Crocker went on.
"You determine your entire future right now."

"Shut up," he snapped. "I gotta think."

We'd be here all night. I almost said it aloud, but
I decided at the last moment that perhaps I should

be a good girl and keep quiet. After all, I had distracted Crocker and that was why we were both looking at the gun. I was old enough to know better.

"You don't have time," Crocker began. "I have to radio in."

"Shut up!" He pointed the gun, not very expertly, at her midriff.

"Give it up," I couldn't help saying. "If this goes any further every cop from here to the Oregon border will be looking for you."

"Shut up!" He was yelling now. "The both of ya!"

We let him think. It took a while. Eventually, Dorfman gestured at me with the gun. "Over there." I obligingly stood over in one corner. He backed away from Crocker a little, then said, "Put the cuffs on the ground and kick them this way."

She did. He picked them up, never taking his gaze off Crocker. I inched forward, unsure of what I could do, but he immediately sensed my movement and blurted, "Don't move or I'll shoot her. I really will."

He wasn't convincing but I decided not to risk it.

Dorfman awkwardly cuffed one of my wrists. It was loose, but not loose enough to drop off, darn it all. He motioned at Crocker and then cuffed her so we became a two-woman chain gang. He took the nightstick that hung from Crocker's belt and her keys.

"Outside."

With one hand he locked up the back door of the building and even set the alarm again. Crocker's patrol car was visible, although parked some distance away — I hadn't heard her arrive. My own car was down the block where I'd left it after seeing Dorfman pull up in a white, hard-paneled van. Dorfman pointed us to the van. Digging a length of nylon rope out of the back, he proceeded to tie Crocker and me together, face-to-face.

Crocker was shoving herself away from me as hard as she could. Unlike the first time we met, I apparently repulsed her now. Dorfman was cinching the ropes and she was wasting energy trying to make sure our breasts didn't touch. At least that was what it seemed like. It was also fine with me. Normally my boobs would like being squashed against another woman's ample bosom, but Dorfman's punch had put me completely out of the mood.

Dorfman finished tying the last of about a hundred granny knots. He opened the left door of the van and easily toppled us inside — no small feat. Together we probably weighed two-fifty. He slammed the door and I heard what sounded discouragingly like a hasp falling in place and click of a combination lock. His footsteps crunched to the cab. Moments later the van was headed out of the A&M Manufacturing parking lot.

We wiggled and grunted until we were on our sides. The floor of the van was corrugated metal and it was very cold. There was almost no light. I was too old for this — why hadn't I left the arrest to the professionals? Stupid, Eliot, stupid.

Crocker relaxed and I realized that the ropes were a lot looser. Then I felt the fool — she hadn't been trying to keep from touching me, she'd been buying us a few centimeters of loose rope. If I had helped we might have had enough slack to get free, but no,

I had been too busy thinking about the first time we'd met. Her body wedged up against mine made it all too easy.

We turned right and I couldn't stop myself from rolling on top of her. We turned right again almost immediately and I rolled all the way over her, landing with a grunt on the other side. I felt lucky not to have hit my head.

Her voice, ever calm, whispered across my ear. "Are you okay?"

"Just dandy," I said. "Never been better."

"Nice attitude." Her voice sounded like steel. "If we keep our heads, we'll get out of this in one piece."

"Whatever you say, miz deputy sir." Way to go, Eliot. Do you think if you tried you could sound more childish?

She pulled back her head so she could look me in the face. Even in the darkness, it was too close. With a thump, I was back in the bar where we'd met. Her arms were around me and we were dancing. Just barely.

I had seen her several times before. I'd gone to the bar because it was the one women-only place between Sacramento and Portland. She was always with a possessive-looking blonde, so shared smiles had been our only contact. Friends told me she was a cop and that she was icy, but I found that hard to believe. She had a slow smile that went from cool to provocative whenever she caught me staring. One night she'd been alone and I couldn't stop staring. She didn't stop smiling. So I asked her to dance.

That dance was something I'll never forget. We began a genteel distance apart and when the music slowed and the lights dimmed a little, we moved closer together.

The way she looked, smelled — everything about her — was like lighter fluid and I was a lit match. I felt drunk though I'd only been drinking soda. We moved closer and I decided her neck looked good enough to bite. Without a thought, I nibbled.

She melted against me like honey in the sun. We were hardly moving. I was pulsing, my head was spinning and I kept kissing her neck.

The music changed, went up-tempo with a vengeance. We moved even more slowly against each other.

When her lips nuzzled my ear lobe my knees buckled. She tightened her arms and held me up and without a thought I pulled my head back, stared intently at her lips, and I swear it was she who kissed me.

She kissed me all the way through *Vogue*. I kissed her through *We Are Family*. We kissed each other through the song after that. Or songs. Or days.

I had felt as though I were sunbathing on the first sunny day after a cold, bitter winter. She was the hottest, longest, headiest day of summer I'd held in years.

"Are you sure you're okay?"

With a shudder, I snapped back to the present. Off and on I'd been thinking about her since that night. I remembered those long, breathless kisses far more vividly than the scene her from-that-moment-on-ex-girlfriend made, pulling us apart. Then it had been humiliating but now I only remembered her kisses. And that she'd never approached me again.

About a year later, she'd tried to have my investigator's license revoked. She obviously blamed me for the break-up, but she was the one who had accepted the offer to dance. It had seemed to me that night that we were headed for the nearest bed. I don't do one-nighters, certainly not with women committed elsewhere, but I was ready to with her. If I wanted to be honest with myself, I was still ready to, a fact which disgusted my ego and accounted for my childishness.

I swallowed and looked away. "I'm fine. A little worried."

"Can you get a hand into my right back pocket?"

"Now that's a unique come-on." Damn it, all I had meant to say was a simple yes.

Her voice was like ice in my ear. "I am not and will never again come onto you."

"You've made that quite clear."

"Answer my question."

"Yes, I think I can."

"Good. My spare handcuff key is in there."

The van turned a corner and she rolled on top of me. We both swore.

When we settled on our sides again, I could hook one finger in her pocket, but I couldn't get any deeper. "Hold me closer to you and I might be able to get my arm all the way around."

She wriggled her arms until there was no air between our bodies. I could touch the key, but not get a grip on it.

"Can you move up?" I asked.

"Up where?"

"Let me get my knee between your legs."

"I don't see how that will help."

"Can you shimmy up while I keep the ropes down around me?"

She got the idea. Inch by slow inch she worked her way up my body. She'd gain a fraction and I would pull the cords back down. My hands cramped several times and circulation was going at my knees and shoulders where the ropes were tightest. The cold floor was leaching my body heat and the arm pinned under us was almost useless.

"I think I can get it now," I said.

My cheek was smashed against the buttons of her shirt. I worked my hand into her pocket and could now grip the key firmly.

"Wait," she said abruptly. "I think my foot is almost free." She struggled for a moment, then swore. "Almost. Another couple inches." She squirmed and though I couldn't see very well I could tell her breasts were level with my suddenly very dry mouth.

I told myself to concentrate on something else. So I traced the movement of her pelvis up my stomach. Inappropriate.

"Almost. . . ." She was panting as hard as I was from the exertion and discomfort. "Almost. . . ." She kicked violently.

"That's my shin!"

"Sorry . . . almost . . . hah!" With a restrained shout of triumph she freed one leg, then the other.

We were able to untangle my legs and awkwardly move to a kneeling position. The damn nylon cord didn't want to slide over our clothes so we each began inching the slightly loosened cord up from our hips. The goal was to be bound at just our waists.

Circulation was returning with pins and needles, but my knees were killing me. Still, I was acutely aware of her hands sliding and flexing around my hips. She had strong fingers.

I was having less success with the cord around her hips. Abruptly I realized the problem. "It's caught on your holster. Can you unhook it?"

She sighed and began working her arms from around me to between us. "I can't get my elbows out. Can —"

The van slewed around another turn and we toppled over. She was on top of me and her thigh was hard against my pelvis.

Pain in dozens of places won out over a throb of pleasure in one. "Get off me," I managed to say.

"Put a sock in it," she snapped. "If he gets to where he's going before we get loose —"

"My elbows are trapped, too. What do you want from me?"

"Let's try to stand up."

"Yeah, right."

She made an exasperated sound and then rolled off me. We were up against one side of the van.

"If we use the wall we should be able to stand up."

I didn't think that it would work, but I cooperated. It worked.

She pinned me against the wall. Her thigh was between my legs. The cords were just loose enough that she could slide her arms around me again.

For a moment I was back on the dance floor and

I wanted to kiss her again. While we were dancing, I'd wanted her to pin me against the wall and unbutton my shirt — put her hands inside — touch me —

"Pull my belt around till you can reach the buckle," she ordered.

Behave, I told my libido. It was as successful as telling a cat to fetch.

With her leaning hard into me I could shift her belt around. The holster tangled with the cords even more tightly, but I was able to cinch the buckle open and get it off her waist. We went round a couple more corners but managed to keep our balance.

It was hard going to get the cords over both our hips, but we managed it. As we struggled the light improved slightly. Sunrise, I thought. The ropes were loose and I felt the cord across her back slip. Suddenly, we could move inches apart, then we were shrugging the ropes off our shoulders. Then we were free. She unlocked the cuffs, retrieved her holster belt and tucked the cuffs in their accustomed pouch.

I sank down, rubbing my arms and legs.

She was at the doors without a pause, seeing if we could open them from the inside. Her precisely enunciated curses told me it was no go.

She lowered herself to the floor and stared at anything but me.

The silence got very long. Very heavy.

"Where do you suppose we are," I said finally.

She looked at me and I couldn't read her expression. Bitterness, resignation, anger? "I'll just get out my Bat-scanner and tell you."

"You *do* have a sense of humor," I said, nastily. "Sarcasm isn't great humor, but it does count. Irony counts for more, though." We'd been on the road about forty minutes by my watch and now that we had conquered the ropes my anxiety about what would happen when Dorfman stopped the van was gaining the upper hand. I wanted reassurance, not sarcasm.

She caught her upper lip between her teeth and said nothing.

The van made a long, slow curving turn and picked up speed. I stood up. "We're on a freeway. He must have headed for Sacramento." I checked my watch again. "The timing's about right. If I'm right, we're headed . . . north on I-Five."

She stood up too. The ride had smoothed out and she paced. I leaned against the wall behind the cab and watched her dark form moving back and forth. I was responsible for our being in this mess.

"I'm sorry," I said eventually.

"For what?" She looked at me in the dim light and her gaze cut me — it was steel. And it was hot.

I couldn't breathe for a moment, then managed, "For everything."

She turned away. "I can't think about it right now. You're a civilian. I'm responsible for you." She paused and then spoke so quietly that I don't think she meant for me to hear. "I can't think about . . . what happened then."

I was abruptly angry. "I understand that right now, but what about the last two years? Did you think about me at all? I thought — it wasn't casual to me. I'm sorry about . . . her."

She clenched her fists and closed her eyes. Her lips were stiff, as though she didn't want the words to break through them. "I've thought about you too much. Way too much."

Surprise turned off my anger. "You have? Then why —"

"Because of Sarah. Our relationship was over. We'd been sleeping in separate beds and she was looking for a place of her own. But she hadn't released me from the commitments I made and I shouldn't have been dancing with you. Doing what we were doing — ready to do what we were going to do. It was . . . dishonorable. Maybe that sounds antiquated, but that's the way I am." Her spine was straight, her fists clenched.

I pushed away from the wall and walked toward her. "So you've been refusing yourself the thing that got you into trouble. In fact, trying to get rid of the thing that got you into trouble."

She crossed her arms, looking down at the floor. The light was getting better — I could see her cheeks stained red with embarrassment. "Something like that. It didn't work. I'm sorry about your license. I had really hit bottom." She shied away from my approach. "Don't. I'm on duty. Dammit, I'm responsible for you."

"And I'm responsible for you," I said. "You're not the only one with a sense of honor. I got us into this because I thought I could apprehend him myself. I should have called for help the moment I saw him go inside."

"Goddamn amateur," she muttered.

I touched her shoulder with one fingertip and a shudder ran through me.

"Don't," she said again.

"Kiss me," I said. Our situation had faded from my mind. I was intent on her lips.

"We could be on our way to our deaths and you want me to kiss you?" She tried to be stern, but I could see that she was breathing hard. Her voice sounded as though she was having trouble swallowing.

"Precisely. Because we could be dead any moment you should kiss me. We don't . . . I just have to know if it was my imagination."

"It wasn't."

I put my hands on her shoulders and pulled her to me. Maybe the time tied together had shown us how to fit into the curves of each other's bodies. We fit and she kissed me.

I was at once and irrevocably at sea in her arms. Like before, she rocked my senses and just with her lips on mine. Her lips on other parts of me — good God, what would that do — I'd be lost in a place only she could find me.

She gasped against my mouth and I felt tears on her face, on my face. It was excruciatingly sensual and honest and real. Though I had been with other women in love and in lust, nothing compared to the way she felt against me.

My arms were twined around her neck, her hands under the waistband of my jeans. I was trembling, moaning against her.

She suddenly raised her head. "We're getting off the freeway."

"Woodland, do you think?"

She shrugged. "Maybe." She pushed me away. "We need our wits."

I had to support myself against the side of the

van. "I'm sorry," I said. I was crying and my teeth started to chatter. "I think it's just reaction. I'm scared. Scared of where we're going." Scared of you, I could have said.

"We're going to get out of this," she said firmly. She had no right to look so calm.

The road worsened and then turned to gravel. We were slowing to a crawl and then the van stopped. The engine rumbled to a stop.

"We're here," Liz whispered.

We stood behind the right-hand door and waited. After a few minutes we heard voices. An argument. Someone called Dorfman a moron — someone knew him well, obviously. I took a deep breath and it steadied me.

"No, you can't make me take care of this. You shouldn't have brought them here! My wife's gonna wake up, you idiot!"

"I'm not taking the fall." Dorfman was practically growling. "You're Mr. Big Money. You can buy your way out of this."

I heard the rattle of the lock, then the hasp grated. The left door swung open and Dorfman stuck his head in.

Liz kicked him brutally and jumped on him as he staggered backward.

"Get her off me," Dorfman shrieked. Sounds of struggle reached me and I took the chance that Dorfman's accomplice had gone to his aid.

The smallish man in the bathrobe never saw me coming. I finished him with an incapacitating kick to the groin.

As I turned back to help Liz I saw Dorfman struggling to get Liz's service revolver out of his belt.

I landed half on her, half on him, trapping his arm. Liz kicked me, unintentionally I hoped, but I went sprawling and Dorfman's arm started to come up. We both leapt at it, hoping to trap the gun against the ground. Our heads collided. I saw stars.

When my vision steadied I could see that Liz looked as dazed as I felt, but she was hanging doggedly onto Dorfman's arm. He was thrashing and wasting energy calling us both names. I heard the groggy groan of the other man and realized he was getting to his feet.

I remember vividly everything that happened next, but it seemed as though it was all happening to someone else.

I kicked behind me, knocking the other man back to the ground. Liz lost her grip on Dorfman's arm. I saw the gun pointing at me, I saw Dorfman's finger tightening. Liz lunged across his body, yanking the gun away from me — and toward her. Her future — my future — a future we might share stretched out in ribbons of time as his finger tightened again. I kicked Dorfman as hard as I could in the neck, not caring if I broke it, and watched with shocked detachment as his hand spasmed.

The gun didn't go off.

Liz got him in a choke-hold and I pried the gun out of his nerveless fingers. Between the two of us we cuffed him to the trailer hitch on the van. He was bloody and half-unconscious and the other man was groaning. I got my first good look at him and recognized him from a picture in the office of A&M Manufacturing. This was Mr. M.

All in all, the entire fight took maybe thirty

seconds. I had dust in my mouth, bruises up and down my arms. My knees were killing me.

Liz got up, dusted herself off and held out her hand for her gun. I gave it to her. Mr. M. readily agreed to lie face down on the ground when she asked. She then calmly read them both their rights. I plunked down on the ground without meaning to and just stared at her.

The sunrise was pink and orange and it lit her brown hair into a shimmering glow. Her shield glinted, seeming at that moment what it had once represented — a knight's pledge to protect the weak and wield might for good. She looked like the embodiment of justice. My body hurt nearly everywhere and I wanted her more than ever and she looked so goddess-like she scared me and I couldn't breathe.

A door slammed and a middle-aged woman ran wildly toward us while screaming over her shoulder for the kids to call 9-1-1. She came to a sudden halt as she took in Liz's uniform and badge and then every ounce of color drained out of her face. I thought she was going to faint and I felt sorry for her. She obeyed without a murmur Liz's calm command to sit down.

Liz flicked a glance at me, then fixed her gaze back on her prisoners. But the glance was enough. For a moment, the goddess of right had softened. Her lips had curved in a way only I would notice. Curved in what in other circumstances might have been an invitation to dance.

In the distance I heard the welcome wail of a siren.

Charon's Crystal

Jaye Maiman

The first thing you need to know is that I don't believe in the occult. Pure and simple. I believe in good food, straight talk, and friends who make you laugh so hard your ribs hurt. K.T. Bellflower and I have been together only a few months, but already she knows this about me. Maybe that's why she decided to spring the news on me as we dined in her Greenwich Village restaurant with two of my closest friends and the baby girl they had just adopted.

"From what Lurlene said, I knew this psychic had

to be mighty convincing. Now Lurlene feels she has to leave town, and she won't go without me," K.T. said, barely glancing at me. "I'm telling you, she knew things about the past that were uncanny. And she asked to see *me* specifically. Said something like, 'the woman who saved your life once will do so again.' So I went to see her and right away she tells me I'm Lurlene's only source of strength, ever since my mom took her into the family. And she insists the only way Lurlene will go is if *I take her.* Which is probably true."

To be honest, I was only half listening. I'm a private detective and my work offers me all the mysteries I can handle. Right then, my focus was on the meal K.T. had personally prepared for me. Mesquite-grilled red snapper with a citrus vinaigrette, served with a side dish of roasted eggplant and garlic. I forked a piece of garlic and said, "Honey, I'm glad your chef's on vacation. The guy can't hold a candle —"

"Robin Miller," K.T. said, interrupting my rapture. "You're impossible."

On the other side of the table, Beth and Dinah stifled giggles. They knew me better than K.T. did. Give me a choice between eating fine food and chatting about K.T.'s high-strung friend Lurlene and some flimflam fortuneteller, and there was no contest.

K.T.'s dander was up and it made her face as pink as Chinese roast pork. "Are you listening to me?" she said. "This Charon Centauri has convinced Lurlene that if she doesn't leave town, her entire life could be ruined." To Beth and Dinah she explained, "She's been working as a photographer's assistant for her boyfriend. Well, Charon says Brian Fritzl,

Lurlene's boyfriend, is the problem. Lurlene is crazy about him, but she thinks the sun rises and sets with Charon. All I know is Lurlene's so confused she's starting to sound suicidal. So today I booked two flights to Hawaii. I know if I can get Lurlene out of town —"

I dropped my fork. The clatter woke little Carol, who let loose a royal howl. Beth swept the baby into her arms, but no amount of shushing was going to make Carol quiet down. Dinah self-consciously scanned the restaurant. An elderly woman with Texas-sized hair glared at our table from across the room. Beth and Dinah exchanged knowing looks. They packed up like experts. The next thing I knew, K.T. and I were alone and my snapper was stone cold.

"You're planning to fly down to Hawaii with Lurlene just because some damn psychic says so?" I clenched my teeth together so tight I thought I heard enamel crack.

"I don't know if this psychic's for real or not, Rob, but I know what Lurlene needs. And right now, she needs to get away from here."

I asked impatiently, "Wouldn't it make more sense for me to look into this Brian before you help Lurlene screw up her life for no good reason?"

K.T. leaned over the table and snapped, "Don't you think that thought might have crossed my mind? I asked Charon if I should hire a private eye to check out Brian and she said the tactic would only backfire by making Lurlene more defensive. And when I thought about it, I realized she's right. Besides, you and Lurlene don't exactly see eye-to-eye."

"Right now," I said, squeezing a meshed half-moon of lemon so hard the juice shot across the table, "I'm not seeing eye-to-eye with you either."

"You don't really care what happens to Lurlene, do you, just as long as you don't have to question your precious sense of reality!" K.T. scraped her chair back hard.

Suddenly I felt panicky. I didn't want K.T. to leave. I grabbed her by the wrist and said, "K.T., real psychics don't prescribe methods for altering the future. This woman's just a con artist." As soon as the words were out of my mouth, I realized I had taken the wrong approach. The more I pushed, the more resolved K.T. became in her defense of Charon Centauri.

"Charon doesn't dish out whitewashed fortunes. She believes people can change their own fates." She shook off my hand. "And if she's such a con artist, why is she chasing one of her best clients out of town? Answer that, Sherlock."

I leaned back in my chair and took a deep breath. "Will you at least let me meet her, before you make a final decision?"

It wasn't until the next night, when we parked outside a dilapidated brick-faced commercial building suitable for drug deals or the occasional terrorist meet, that I realized K.T. had orchestrated my responses like a maestro. Here I was, in the heart of lower Manhattan's meat-packing district, sitting in a six-by-six waiting room painted jet black. K.T. went in first, leaving me with a kiss on the cheek and a victorious wink. As soon as the door clicked behind her, the room plunged into darkness. I sank down into a cracked vinyl couch the color of wet ash.

Maybe it was my imagination, but the still, cool air of the anteroom smelled a little like raw beef. After a few seconds, I stood up and crossed to the door leading into the fortuneteller's den. I pressed my ear to the cold metal door, but the damn thing was dumb.

A faint twinkle along the ceiling pulled my gaze upward. A pale-green plastic re-creation of the constellations glimmered a few feet above my head. I groaned out loud. What the hell was I doing here?

A breeze fluttered across the back of my neck and I whirled around, expecting to find the door open. Only it wasn't. I narrowed my eyes and palmed the walls deliberately. There had to be air vents planted in the walls at strategic locations. I knew any minute I'd hear an eerie yodel of a moan straight out of the Vincent Price archives.

I searched for a good twenty minutes, but couldn't find the vents that kept sending sudden bursts of icy air down my back. I gave up after crashing into a plaster pedestal and dislodging a massive crystal that rested on it. The crystal rammed into my stomach like a boxer's fist. I fumbled with the sharp-edged obelisk, then stopped short. An electric hum, audible only because of the room's unsettling quiet, emanated from the object resting between my hands.

All at once, I flashed back to the tragic accident that has haunted me my entire life. I was three years old again and a gunshot reverberated in my ears. The gun unwieldy in my tiny hand, I stared across the dark closet and watched my sister's eyes flash wide open, the cry from her five-year-old body wrapping around me like a net, the gun smoke searing my nostrils, her blood splattering my cheeks, my upper lip.

I jolted myself out of the memory by slamming the obelisk onto the pedestal, gratified by the sound of chipped plaster raining to the floor. The room was too small, too dark, and I was suddenly too upset to worry about the niceties of confidential psychic readings. Madam Charon Charlatan was about to meet her demise in the form of one fed-up lesbian detective.

I spun on my heel and stomped toward the door. It swung open just as my fist sliced through the air. Only chance kept me from clobbering the fortuneteller in the center of her broad forehead. Although the corners of her mouth angled down in a tight grimace, her cocoa-brown eyes were smiling.

"Not terribly patient, are you? Come in," she said, bracing the door open with one foot.

Charon was far younger than I had expected. She couldn't have been more than twenty-one. And she was too damned good-looking. Ruggedly good-looking. Shorter than me by less than an inch, she had the musculature of an Olympic swimmer and wore the garb of a bronco buster, complete with fringed shirt and riding boots. Her hair was thick, wiry, and black. She wore it tied in a ribbon and slung over her left shoulder like a boa.

"I'm twenty-two, in case you're wondering." Her gaze didn't waver as she added, "Psychic abilities are not defined by age."

I shot her a withering glance, then scanned the room calculatedly. The decor recalled depictions of Mars in sci-fi flicks of the fifties. Cement block walls gleamed a high-gloss midnight blue. Around the perimeter of the room massive boulders painted a dark, bloody red appeared to erupt like volcanic islands from the rough cement floor. Crystals dangled from the ceiling on near-invisible wires. All of a sudden I became aware of a mechanical whoosh that ebbed and flowed at regular intervals.

Three halogen spotlights hung over the center of the room, where Charon had positioned two vermillion bean bags and a slab of shellacked, petrified wood. K.T.'s butt was firmly ensconced in one of the bean bags, her denimed legs crossed at the ankles, her palms planted on her thighs, elbows angled out defiantly. I twitched my eyebrows at her teasingly, but the fire in her eyes seared my confidence. My honey was mighty pissed.

"Charon Centauri and I are not finished yet, Robin," K.T. said, enunciating each word a little too carefully.

I was about to defend myself when Charon touched my shoulder lightly and said in a composed voice that belied her years, "Enough K.T. You know what you need to for now. I trust your spirit. We will talk again before you leave. But right now, this one, this one needs time. Please."

The two of them shared a knowing, strangely intimate look that further irritated me. K.T. rose, shook herself like a wet pooch, and walked past me without a word. I turned to follow her, but Charon's next words stopped me as if she had landed a blow to my head.

"Your sister grieves for you."

Her voice was so small it could have belonged to a hummingbird. I froze, watched the door close behind K.T. A tremble rocketed up from my toes.

When it reached my lips, I was ready to explode. If K.T. had revealed my secrets to this goddamn con artist . . .

I spun on my heel and crossed back to where she was standing. Instantly, she sank into the bean bag. Towering over her I said, "How much do you charge for this shit?"

One eyelid twitched as she answered. "This *shit,* as you call it, is a precious gift —"

"How much?"

"Please, sit —"

"How much?"

"Three hundred dollars, but only —"

I laughed, feeling strangely relieved.

"One day, I hope to do this for free, but right now I must charge. This work provides my only income. You must understand. Great musicians don't perform for free. Neither do I."

I noticed she had a slight accent. Possibly Mexican. "You're not from New York?" I asked suddenly.

The question threw her. "No. New Mexico. Tijeras. But I don't see what —" She stopped herself and closed her eyes. When her body began to rock, I wanted to laugh again. But for some reason I didn't. Instead I sat down opposite her. Okay, I thought. Might as well see the whole act.

I don't know how many minutes passed before I felt a little electrical shock in my buttocks. Oh, this is good. The bean bag must be wired.

"K.T.'s friend Lurlene is in grave danger. She flies like a finch into the brutal clutch of a hawk. This dark man she so foolishly loves will crush her spirit." Her eyes sprang open. "She will fall into a sleep that doesn't end, unless you and K.T. can save her. This is the message I must make you believe. Her life is in your hands."

"Is this what you told K.T.?" I asked.

"Yes. And much more. Her spirit is very strong. As is yours. But you've spun a web around your soul and it will take much work before it can fly."

"Goddamn," I said, standing abruptly. "You're taking advantage of people's fears."

She rose quietly, scanning me all the while with a look of puzzlement. "You're a detective," she said at last.

I'm sure she wanted me to be impressed. I wasn't. I asked, "What makes Brian so dangerous?"

She touched her eyes, her patience starting to fray. "My powers are great, but they're still young. Imagine looking through a telescope that's just slightly out of focus. You can determine shape, color, but not definition."

I shrugged off her explanation and asked abruptly, "What's in this for you?"

One corner of her mouth lifted in apparent amusement. "You really don't know what to make of me. Have you ever met a psychic before?"

I turned my back on her as if to dismiss the question. In actuality, I was checking out the room. All of a sudden, I felt a hand press against my lower back. I pivoted around. Charon had not moved.

"Nice trick," I said, hoping the sudden twitch above my eye wasn't visible.

Again she smiled. "No tricks, and no illusions. I cannot make you believe if your mind is closed. All I can ask is that you don't stand in Lurlene's way. She needs to leave town, and K.T. must go with her."

I narrowed the space between us. "Don't you want your money?"

"Your friend has paid for all this in advance."

I rubbed a palm across my eyes. Six hundred dollars. For an hour of poetic warnings and special effects. "I expect you to return every goddamn dime. Otherwise you may find yourself facing a pack of very unfriendly visitors from the NYPD."

"Don't threaten me," she said, her tone sounding a hell of a lot less ethereal. "I will not return what I've earned. Despite what you think, I am not a fraud." She held her hands up, revealing palms that were surprisingly rough and crisscrossed with deep lines. The breeze that swept over me this time was warm, cloying, like a blast from a clothes dryer. The woman belonged in Hollywood.

Her gaze fixed on a spot somewhere over my shoulder. "You have not asked about Carol."

My mouth went dry. "Dinah and Beth's baby?"

"No," she said matter-of-factly. "Her namesake. Your sister. The one you killed."

The air was zinging around my head. How dare K.T. reveal my secrets to this charlatan! "My sister is none of your goddamn business." With those words I stormed toward the door.

"She says it's time to make peace. Especially now. With your mother so ill."

Another electrical shock crackled through me as I touched the doorknob. Without turning I said quietly, "My mother will outlive us both."

"You have not talked to her in over a year. But your brother has. Still, even he does not know. Your mother will find out tomorrow. She has cancer, and Carol —"

I yanked the door open, said, "The show is over,"
and stepped into the anteroom. A single overhead
bulb flickered on.

K.T. was sitting on the couch, her leaf-green eyes
beseeching me for understanding. I ignored her and
walked straight outside. It was late March and in the
stiff wind rushing toward us from the Hudson I felt
both the sting of winter and the caress of spring.
The sulphur-yellow glow of street lights spotlighted
garbage cans lying on their sides, long-tailed creatures
scurrying between them like shadows. At the far end
of the block, a man wearing an olive-drab uniform
rammed his fist against a corrugated metal garage
gate that rattled in response, then rose smoothly. I
didn't speak until I reached the car, then I snapped
open the passenger door and said, "Thanks for
keeping my confidences."

She looked genuinely perplexed.

I raised one eyebrow. "My sister? Or are you so
determined to make me believe in Charon that you're
going to deny telling her?"

Her lips parted. Even in the sulphur yellow glow
of the street lamps, I could see her skin flush. "I
swear, Robin, I never," she sputtered. "Not even to
Lurlene."

Our eyes blazed at each other. Finally I walked
around to the driver's side. I turned the ignition and
waited for K.T. to get inside. I drove her home in
silence. When I told her I needed to be alone that
night she didn't argue, although I knew she wanted
to.

Twenty minutes later, I was back on Charon
Centauri's block.

Using a dumpster as a shield, I stood across the

street and examined the building that held her business. Sandwiched between a meat-packing factory on one side and a loading dock on the other, the soot-stained edifice had four stories. The windows on the third and fourth floors were boarded up, and the second floor's were dark. I watched them for movement, then crossed the street and rammed my finger into the rusted doorbell. No answer.

I leaned against the door jamb and drummed my fingers against the metal in time with the warning beep of a truck heading down the street in reverse. I waited for the truck to disappear before making up my mind, then I scampered over to my car and dug out my leather pouch of lock picks.

As I selected a pick bestowed upon me by my brother, an ex-burglar who now owns a locksmith shop on Staten Island, I marveled at the lack of building security. Either Charon had not lived in New York long enough to become properly paranoid, or else psychics like her didn't need Medeco locks and electronic alarm systems. In any case, breaking in was obscenely easy.

I entered the anteroom for the second time that night, the scent of beef stronger now than it was earlier. Sweat trickled down between my shoulder blades and a thrill ran through me.

As much as I hate to admit it, I love breaking the law. But only for the sake of justice. I know that sounds like a contradiction, and maybe it is, but after turning thirty I stopped believing people are rational beings. As I sliced through that dark room, every nerve in my body blazed. It was like the instant before making love, my senses heightened, my body tense and its animal instincts exquisitely exposed.

I opened the second door and paused, struggling to hear any sound other than the pounding of my own pulse. From a floor above me came the murmur of acoustical guitar. Scott Moulton's *Tropical Dreams*. So Charon was still in the building. That raised the ante. I hesitated half a second, then entered the second room. No cool breezes now, no electric shocks. Just a yawning gloom.

I located the bean bags and oriented myself. Earlier I had noticed another door at the far left-hand corner. I headed in that direction. A floorboard creaked loudly under my feet. I halted mid-step. From above me, I heard something slam into the floor. The music paused. I issued a silent challenge: Can you sense me here, Charon? It seemed like an hour passed before the music resumed. Quickly I crossed to the third door.

The knob resisted. Surprised to find an interior door locked, I knelt down to inspect the door frame. Again, no alarm. I snapped the lock with a pick and stepped inside. Light spilled in from a narrow barred window. I smiled grimly. Next to me stood a desk bearing a 486 Dell Computer, complete with a CD ROM drive, modem and fax. Clearly, Charon was a high-tech psychic. Oh, this was going to be fun, I thought.

Before searching the desk, I circled the room once. The music seemed louder here. In the far right-hand corner, a wrought iron staircase spiraled toward the ceiling, terminating in a mustard-brown steel door. Standing at the base, I felt as if I could hear Charon breathing on the other side. I stared at the door, half-expecting her to swing it open, a look of expectancy on her smooth olive face. When nothing happened, I felt strangely disappointed.

I returned to the desk. On the top shelf was a collection of CD ROM disks I knew well from my work as a private eye. I fingered the spines. National address directories, business listings, street atlases, a New York occupational license listing, and an encyclopedia. Sweat had begun beading down my forehead. I wiped the back of my hand across my brow and sat down. A typewritten list was taped onto the fax. Charon had subscriptions to more database services than my agency.

Without thinking, I flipped on the system. The screen flickered, counted off bits of memory, then blinked at me. I typed in a few commands, scanned the directory listings, then felt my breath catch in my throat. Name after name scrolled over the screen. Charon's client database had to exceed seventy. KTBELLFL.076 flashed by. So did LURLENEH.042 And then ROBINMIL.079. I leaned forward and typed in the eleven digits. The son-of-bitch listed my name, occupation, birth date, parents' and siblings' names, and a single note. *Sister Carol killed at age five in a firearms accident. Key incident. Investigate!*

Why had K.T. betrayed me? My fingers hesitated over the keyboard. Something made my head turn to the right. A scampering sound. I stared into the dark corner near the staircase. I could make out a filing cabinet, milk crates filled with magazines. As quietly as possible I rolled the desk chair backward. Again I approached the staircase. The music had stopped. I leaned against the railing, afraid to breathe. This time, I was positive that Charon was upstairs, waiting on the other side of the door.

Time to exit, I warned myself as I sidled back across the room. I flipped off the computer just as my eyes settled on two black-and-white photographs pinned to the corkboard above the desk. In one, Charon Centauri perched on a gnarled tree limb, the leaves providing a gauzy, surreal backdrop. Her arms draped casually around a limb, her dungaree skirt hiked seductively over her knees, she stared at me with a confidence that belied her years. But it was the second photograph that made my breath catch. Dressed in the same outfit, Charon was leaning into the arms of a man I had met just once. Brian Fritzl, Lurlene's photographer boyfriend.

Suddenly Charon's urgent warnings to Lurlene made perfect sense. I had to give her credit. When it came to removing a rival, Charon was downright ingenious. I unpinned the picture and slid it into my jacket pocket. Just then the overhead light flashed on. I shrugged to myself and turned. Wearing only a man's oversized flannel robe, Charon descended the staircase slowly, without comment. Since she wasn't screaming for the police, I decided to make my way to the exit.

"Suddenly in a rush?" she asked. I stopped and faced her. Her tone unnerved me. It held an edgy quiet, the tense respite of a hurricane's eye. She ran a hand through her tangled wet locks and asked, "Where's the photograph?"

I patted my pocket and said, "I'm borrowing it, if you don't mind."

With a studied languor, she loosened then retied

the robe's belt. "As a matter of fact, I do." With her head lowered, her voice was practically a whisper. "But I don't suppose that matters much." She seemed so young just then that my resolve faltered. Almost as afterthought she added, "I could call the police, you know."

I ran a hand over the keyboard and said, "True. But that probably wouldn't help either of us."

Anger flashed in her eyes. "You really don't understand. The computers are a tool. That's all."

"Do your clients know how much of your *insight* comes courtesy of Information USA?"

She sat down on a step, wrapped her arms around her knees, and shook her head, murmuring quietly. If there was a conversation in progress, it didn't involve me. At length she said, "My mother skipped town when I was eight," then looked up at me, her eyes at once angry and tired. "After that, my father became an alcoholic. He was never violent, though. Matter of fact, I preferred him drunk . . . it was the only time I saw him laugh. When I was seventeen, we were in a bad car accident. That night, he had picked me up from a friend's house."

She paused to drape the robe over an exposed knee before continuing. "I woke up from a coma three weeks later. My father was dead and I had these strange headaches, as if there were voices in my head. You ever hear a radio station drift? It's almost like that."

I sat down in the desk chair and watched her pick lint off the robe.

"In college, I majored in computer science. I thought a discipline like that would help ground me. But the interference grew stronger. Finally, I went to a psychic myself. She also happened to be my astronomy teacher." A private smile flickered over her lips. "She helped me to understand what a gift I have."

All at once her body language changed and she again resembled the woman I had met earlier in the evening. Confident, slightly affected, and defiant. "The computers help me make sense of the psychic messages."

I pawed an instruction manual for an electronic credit reporting service. "You rip people off, Charon."

Her eyes narrowed. "On occasion. But then our professions aren't so different, are they?"

Remembering the way she had hurled my sister's name at me, I blurted, "Not quite. *I* don't pretend to carry messages from the dead."

A wave of hot air swept over me as she stood suddenly. "What exactly do you want?"

I rolled the desk chair closer, as if I were ready to mow her down. Maybe I was. "Can't you read my mind, Charon?"

She hesitated, circled the chair nervously. "You want to know about Brian. Fine. I came to New York City less than a year ago. A friend introduced us. He gave me a few modeling assignments. I fell in love."

Maybe I was getting a little psychic myself, because just about then I realized why Brian was so important to her. "He was your first, wasn't he?"

For the first time, she looked surprised. "Yes. Maybe that's why I had such a hard time understanding the messages."

"Messages?"

"I don't know what else to call them . . . two months ago, they broke through. Anyone involved with Brian is destined for pain. It nearly killed me to stop seeing him. And then Lurlene walks in, at *his* recommendation, and blithely catalogs the beginning of their affair." With increasing agitation, she strode over to a wood crate, flipped the lid back and retrieved a blue velvet pouch. First she held it to her chest as if contemplating her next move, then in one motion she pulled the drawstring, extracted an object, and knelt before me. She pressed an amethyst shard into my hands, then circled them with her own. Her palms were on fire. "Press this crystal to your forehead and concentrate. You'll know then I speak the truth," she whispered urgently. "She *is* in danger. I don't know why, all I know is she must leave him. As I did. No matter how much it hurts." A teardrop splattered onto my lap.

I extricated my hands, letting the crystal fall to the floor. Charon was rapidly becoming unglued. Since I'm a sucker for bawling women teetering on the brink of disaster I decided it was time to hightail it out of there before I fell for her con. I kicked the chair back. "I don't know if you're crazy or just a skilled liar. Either way, I'm warning you to leave Lurlene alone. I plan to tell her about you and Brian, and I pray she doesn't blow this relationship on your say so."

As I opened the door to leave, she flinched as if I had struck her. I said, "If you ever contact any of us again, I promise you I'll make you pay. And pay dearly," then scrambled before she remembered that I had put my own career on the line by breaking in.

The first thing I did when I got home was call K.T. Even *I* could hear the triumph in my voice. K.T. barely took a breath until I finished, then she apologized profusely. I cut her off. "You were protecting a friend. I can understand that. What I can't understand is why you betrayed my trust."

"Betrayed your —" she started, then stopped. "Robin, I told you . . ."

"Don't." Her denial hurt more than her disloyalty. "Look, tomorrow I'll put the photograph in the mail. I know you'll be able to turn Lurlene around. But as far as we're concerned . . ." I swallowed hard. "I'm going to need some time off."

I thought I heard her sob. Covering my mouth with a damp palm, I said, "Don't say anything more, K.T. Please," then hung up quickly.

I spent the rest of the night struggling to distract myself. I played music constantly, read and reread the day's mail, ate half a box of Oreos, then finally crawled onto the couch between my two cats and slept. Around eight in the morning, the phone rang. I untangled myself, then turned up the volume on my answering machine.

As I listened to my greeting, I hunched forward and shoved my hands deep into my jean pockets. "Hey Rob, it's Ronald." I squinted at the phone. A phone call from my brother is a pretty rare event. Just then I felt something prick my right thumb. "I know you're up. You're the sister who never sleeps. Pick up, it's real important."

My stomach turned over as I grabbed the phone. There was blood on my fingertip. "What's up?" I asked as I dug back into the pocket.

"I just heard from Mom. She's got cancer."

Slowly I opened my fist. There, gleaming in the palm of my hand, lay Charon's crystal, one pristine point dotted with a bead of my blood.

Only the Good
Die Young

Pat Welch

"I'll kill the son of a bitch myself! I'll tear his heart out, I'll cut him into a million pieces!"

Helen had been sitting quietly in the hallway outside the conference room of the Northeast Branch of the Berkeley public library when the angry words burst out, penetrating the thin walls. She jumped from her chair as a loud bang shook the wall where she'd been resting her head. What the hell was going on in there?

Mrs. Norment, the aging librarian, heaved her huge chest in a tired sigh and shook her head. The expression behind her cat's-eye glasses told Helen she'd heard this before. She squeezed herself out from behind the desk piled high with books and waddled down the corridor, brushing past Helen. Mrs. Norment rapped on the door smartly, her plump fist dislodging the sheet of paper taped there. Helen picked it up from the floor and read, GAY TEEN RAP GROUP, SATURDAYS 4 TO 5:30 PM, WELCOME FRIENDS.

The door flew open, and Helen looked into the startled white face of Diane Bates. Helen had never seen her old friend so upset. The therapist's usually placid countenance, framed with soft white hair piled high over her round face, was creased with tension. "I'm sorry, Mrs. Norment," she said in low tones. "We'll try to keep it quiet."

"There are other patrons in the library, Ms. Bates!" the older woman hissed.

Helen ignored the whispered conversation and peered over the librarian's shoulder into the small room. They hunched in the child-sized chairs around a low table covered with the cutouts and glue used by the library's youngest visitors the day before. One young woman was standing near the door, still grasping the chair she'd banged against the wall moments ago. Her red face glowered beneath a very short haircut, and her bulky body shivered with rage under the loose shirt and black tights. The others cowered in their seats, looking away from the scene at the door.

Diane glanced at Helen before closing the door. Mrs. Norment went back to her desk as Diane said, "We're almost finished, Helen." Before the door shut Helen heard her say, "Please just sit down and relax, Heather."

Helen leaned against the wall and looked down at the list of names Diane had given her earlier that morning. There it was, Heather Thompson. Helen's eyes were drawn to the middle of the list, where the name of Sarah Maxwell had been crossed out in a firm black line. It was Sarah's death, Helen knew, that they were discussing in the library's conference room. Two weeks ago, only a few feet away from where Helen now stood, Sarah's body had been found by a janitor. Glancing at her watch, Helen saw that it was nearly 5:30. She itched to get into the room where Sarah had died.

The door burst open, slamming against the wall. Heather stomped out and glared at Helen. "You're that private eye, right? Helen Black?"

"That's me," Helen said, forcing a smile.

Heather rubbed a hand across her tear-stained cheek. "We don't need any private eye to solve this one," she sneered. "Check out the football star. He's the one that did her." Heather's eyes filled with tears and her face screwed up in pain as the other kids silently filed out of the building. "He killed her 'cause she loved me!"

Diane was behind her, patting her shoulder and leading her out of the library. Mrs. Norment let out another sigh and prepared to lock the door behind them.

"Could we have just a few minutes, Mrs. Norment?" Diane asked, hurrying back to the main desk. "I wanted Helen to see the utility room."

"Suit yourself." Mrs. Norment led them back down the corridor to double doors marked EXIT, turning off lights as she went. "I don't know what you think you'll find," she wheezed. "The police have been all over here for days. They didn't find a thing."

The overhead fluorescent light revealed a dim gray interior, lined with dusty metal shelves, large trash bins, and posters in stacks. A plastic-covered sign stood opposite the doors on a tall metal stand, the sign's surface cracked in a neat diagonal line. Helen saw her own short square body reflected in it. The streaks of gray just beginning to show in her hair gleamed in the plastic under the harsh light.

Mrs. Norment clucked and gestured at the sign. "They still haven't replaced it!" she moaned. "It was supposed to go out two weeks ago."

Helen looked closely at the sign. It announced the sad tidings that the library would be cutting hours next month due to lack of funds. "They think Sarah knocked it over when she fell," Diane said, failing to hide the catch in her voice.

Helen saw Diane's hands tremble. "Mrs. Norment, could you let us have just a couple of minutes? I promise we won't be long," Helen said with her sunniest smile. The librarian just managed to keep from rolling her eyes in exasperation as she left them there.

Diane fought to keep from giving way to sobs.

"She came here after the group session. They think she must have met someone, got into a fight, and then —" Diane broke off and moved away from Helen's arm around her shoulders. "Whoever it was hit her on the head with one of these," she went on, holding up a decorative brick similar to the ones that lined the walkway in front of the building.

Helen crouched down to look at the pile of stone arranged haphazardly in the center of the room. She picked up one of the bricks. "They're not very heavy," she remarked, hefting one in her hand. "Anyone could have done it, as long as they hit hard enough." She tried a door half-hidden behind some shelves. "Where does this go?"

"Outside. There are some garden tools, the meters, things like that."

The door was locked. Helen turned back to see Diane weeping.

"I'm sorry, I just can't help it. Sarah was so young, so alive. And so confused, too."

Helen made her slow way back around the room, stopping to look at a stack of bookends heaped on the shelves. "What do you mean, confused?"

"Well, she'd just broken up with her boyfriend, and she wasn't sure —"

"The football star?"

Diane's face froze. "That's right. John Freeman. She was a cheerleader, president of her sorority, making plans for college, when everything happened."

Helen leaned on the shelves. "And what about Heather? What role did she play in all this?"

Diane took off her glasses and wiped them, averting her eyes from Helen. "I guess there's no point in hedging about it. I think Heather had an unbelievable crush on Sarah. It was Heather that talked her into joining the group."

"And how was she in the group? Did she participate, or hang back?"

Diane's face and voice softened. "She was just getting to the point where she was opening up. They're really a great bunch of kids, you know — very supportive. All of them are up against an awful lot, coming at them from all sides —"

Helen interrupted, "Do you know if Heather and Sarah saw each other socially?"

Diane sighed and suddenly looked exhausted. "They know they aren't supposed to, but I'm sure Heather was pushing Sarah. Much too hard."

Helen nodded. They walked out to where Mrs. Norment was waiting, then outside into the October evening. Winter was coming early this year. Helen shivered in her shirtsleeves and saw Diane into her car, and then went off to meet Manny Hernandez.

Her ex-partner was in an unmarked car a block away, parked near Telegraph and Ashby. Helen sank into the front seat with a sigh as she reached for the coffee he handed to her. "Where did Heather go?" she asked as he pulled into the traffic on Telegraph.

"Looks like she just walked home, all by herself." He steered up the steep hill on Ashby that led to the freeway. "How's your friend?"

Helen recognized the note of caution in his voice. "Yes, I saw the same thing you did. Diane was a little too interested in Sarah Maxwell."

"You think that's why she called you in? Over the protests of Berkeley's finest?"

Helen shrugged. They entered the Caldecott Tunnel and sped toward Orinda. "Maybe just easing

a guilty conscience. Maybe she thinks there was
something else she could have done." As they
emerged on the other side of the tunnel, Manny
tossed something at her.

"Take a look at our girl."

Sarah smiled at the camera over the fluffy
pom-poms she bunched at her chest. The long
honey-colored hair fell over thin shoulders and set off
huge brown eyes. A cheerleader's short skirt emphasized her slender figure, but the cheekbones were too
sharp, too fragile. Anorexic?

As if reading her thoughts, Manny said, "A very
unhappy young lady, it seems. Parents divorced just
last year, dropped from being a straight A student to
getting all C's. She started refusing to eat right
before she hooked up with Diane and the support
group."

Helen studied the face, wondering what
possibilities Sarah might have had. Had she in fact
been a lesbian? Or was it just exploring? No one
would know, now. The real question was whether or
not homophobia had had anything to do with her
death.

Helen looked up as Manny pulled off the freeway.
"Where the hell are we?"

Manny smiled as the car stopped beside a huge
green playing field. "Welcome to suburbia. How about
a little male bonding?"

In the distance, behind a chain-link fence, young
men in dirty white uniforms bashed each other madly
or thrust themselves against padded barriers, grunting
and groaning and shouting curses. The high school
rose behind them. In the bleachers nearby a handful
of die-hard fans, mostly young girls, watched the

display of muscle with great intensity as the sun slid down the sky.

As they got out of the car Helen hesitated. "Manny, you know this is all very unofficial. Are you sure I ought to be here?"

"We're not doing anything wrong! Just watching a little football practice. Won't even talk to the guy. And speak of the devil, there he is over by the goal post."

Helen watched the three teammates carrying on an intense conversation. From their gestures she decided they were arguing over how to execute some intricate maneuver on the field. "What about Sarah's parents?" she asked Manny as the tallest of the three punted an imaginary football.

He snorted. "Shit, I think they're just happy their dear sweet thing is not going to grow up to be a lesbian. Better dead than gay." He kept his face turned away from Helen as he spat out the words.

Helen felt the familiar fury course through her. Poor Sarah.

A sharp wind whipped across the field and the tall punter ran over to where they stood at the fence.

"Hey, John," Manny said. "What's shakin'?"

John Freeman ripped off his helmet to reveal a round, plump baby face. Yes, Helen thought. Those big blue eyes and the thick blond hair cut stylishly short along the sides, the broad shoulders — the all-American boyfriend. Sarah must have been the envy of most of the girls in school. The only blemish Helen could see was a single reddish pustule that peeped out from the side of his neck.

"What the hell are you doing here?" he blurted out. With a backward glance at his cohort, who remained close, he squared his shoulders, propping his helmet against his hip. "I already talked to you guys." He glanced over at Helen, unsure of her importance. Should he sneer at her, too, or simply ignore her?

Manny spread his hands and gave him an innocent smile. "Just thought I'd see how good the team was this year. Got a game tonight?"

"Tomorrow. This is Orinda, not Berkeley. You can't do anything to me here." He relaxed a bit, looked at his buddies with a smile, then turned back to Manny. "Why don't you go arrest someone? Start with that dyke who kept following Sarah around, whatsername, Heather?"

The others snickered at the name. Apparently Heather was a big campus joke. Helen felt her rage coming back, but she folded her arms and let John do the talking.

"Sarah did this to herself," he was saying. "She's the one who started hanging around with all the fags. I tried to stop her, to —"

"John! Who is that you're talking to?" Manny and Helen wheeled around to see a slender blonde making her way to them across the graveled parking area. Her dark blue suit was cut to show off her perfect figure, and the hand that swept a loose hair from her neck back up into the French knot was beautifully manicured. Her face was a slimmer, feminine version of John's, and Helen knew the woman had to be his mother before Manny muttered the name to her.

"Lieutenant Hernandez! This is a surprise." The peach-colored brow wrinkled in concern as she glanced at her son. "Do you have any news about Sarah?"

"Not yet, ma'am. Just wanted to say hello to John here, see how he's holding up."

Mrs. Freeman looked at him thoughtfully for a moment. "Well, we're all very upset, still," she sighed. "It's been a horrible shock for John. For all of us, really. We all loved Sarah. It must have been the divorce, I suppose?"

Manny looked at her blankly. "What do you mean?"

"That made her think she was gay. All that upheaval! Young people need stability more than anything else, don't you think?" She looked expectantly at Helen. Getting no response, she continued, "I know Dick and Charlotte well. They're both so broken up over their daughter...." As her voice trailed off, she looked once again at her son. "Run along, darling, get cleaned up. We're supposed to be at the Masons' tonight after dinner."

John blushed in mortification at the endearment, then trotted off to the locker room, followed by the two boys who'd stayed in the background. Mrs. Freeman asked, "Do you have children, Lieutenant?"

"Yes, ma'am. Two boys."

"Then you know how difficult it is these days to raise them!" She turned sincere blue eyes on them both, and an earnest plea entered her voice "The schools have no money, drug dealers everywhere, it's so hard to find good schools. Why even that little library out there where Sarah died, having to cut its hours! Sometimes my husband and I just wonder what's going to happen, especially with that fool in the White House. I worry about my Johnny, facing a world full of horrible things."

Manny pointedly looked from her to her gleaming

beige Mercedes, to the elegant houses nestled in thick
greenery lining the road in front of the high school,
to the clusters of pink-cheeked, well-fed students
lounging over their shiny sports cars and wearing
expensive clothes. He looked back at Mrs. Freeman,
taking in the rings and the perfect teeth. "Yes,
ma'am, life is sure tough for some folks."

"Do you have any idea who would have done such
a thing? Was it one of those poor troubled children
Sarah got mixed up with? Maybe it was drug-related.
I'm sure that's a real problem with those kinds of
children."

Helen could tell without looking at him that
Manny had had enough of Mrs. Freeman. He cleared
his throat and said, "We're working on it, ma'am."

Moments later John rushed out of the locker
room, his hair slicked back and his face shiny from
the showers. He slung his duffel bag in the back seat
of the Mercedes and slumped down in the front,
waiting for his mother. Mrs. Freeman again graced
them with a sigh. "What is that saying — only the
good die young? So very sad." She picked her way
with delicate steps back to her car, calling out over
her shoulder, "Do let us know when you find out
anything."

Helen and Manny watched the Mercedes disappear
into the shadows. "Ready to puke yet? Jesus, what a
woman." He began trudging back to his car, then
stopped when he realized Helen wasn't following him.
"Yo, sport. *Vamos.*"

"Manny, can we go back to the library? There's
something I want to check out. Something I want
you to see."

Helen was silent during the ride back to Berkeley,

while Manny let out bits and pieces of information about John Freeman.

Sarah had started dating him last fall. "They became a big item around campus — you know, cheerleader and football player."

"So what happened? She suddenly realized he wasn't the right type?"

Manny shrugged. "From what I've picked up from the other students, the word is she was always kind of interested in Heather. John was just a cover. He's not talking, but some of them think he must have caught Sarah and Heather together, making out or the modern-day equivalent. Anyway, he's alibied, he was at football practice that night."

As they drove back through the tunnel that led to Berkeley, Helen felt a wave of sadness, remembering her own high school years in Mississippi. After being caught with a girlfriend, she had been beaten and kicked out of her home. "Poor Sarah," she said quietly.

"I know."

They had reached the library, and Manny used keys that had been made available to the police to go back into the darkened building. "What's up, Watson?" he asked as Helen fumbled her way through the stacks to the corridor leading to the utility room. He opened the doors and they were standing again in the place where Sarah died. "Come on, what's the tour about?"

"Just look around." The cracked plastic on the poster, the dusty shelves, the dull sheen of trash barrels. Helen stood still, a cold chill of certainty settling over her. "I was right. Shit."

Just then something darted across their line of

vision, heading for the door that led outside. Manny was on the other side of the room before the figure could open the door and slip away. Heather tried to jerk away from him, but his hands clutched her arm in an iron grip. "Get the fuck away from me!" she yelled.

"How the hell did you get in here, Heather?" Manny demanded, trying not to hurt her as she struggled against him. In answer she tried to twist her head around so that she could spit in his face, but the effort was too painful.

Helen went to the back door. Sure enough, in spite of the lock, it was possible to play with the knob and force the door open. "Damn," she breathed. Helen used her body to hold the door open, and light from the utility room spilled over the stacks of decorative bricks that lined the tiny paved area. Looking up, she saw the parking lot through the thick tangle of overgrown shrubbery that edged the yard. Yes, it all fit — after dark, with everyone gone home, no one would see what had happened in this dark spot.

Helen went back into the room where Manny still struggled with Heather. "Come on, Heather. What are you doing here?"

"Nothing!" Heather burst into tears, collapsing against him with her considerable weight. "It was all my fault! I should have left her alone, but I loved her so much! I couldn't stand what that fucker was doing to her!" Manny relaxed his hold briefly, but it was all Heather needed. She broke away from him and fled outside.

"No, Manny, let her go."

"But she just said —"

"Never mind what she said. We've got to get going. Now."

He stopped protesting and listened to what she had to say, asking one or two questions as they got into his car. He drove quickly while she talked, breaking his silence only to radio for a black-and-white to join them.

The journey ended abruptly, Manny pulling up before a three-story house on a wooded lane. Light poured from the house in a golden glow that lit up the entire road. Helen leaned against the car as Manny knocked on the door, flanked by uniformed policemen.

John Freeman's muscular figure filled the doorway. There was no trace of belligerence in the pouting features as he took in the official presence on his doorstep. Manny murmured a few words to him, and he took a step back. Before Manny and the others could enter the house, Mrs. Freeman appeared. She was dressed for the evening in a short, shimmering gold dress that accentuated the smooth lines of her figure and made her hair shine with reflected light.

"No!" she shouted at Manny. "Get off my property now! My son is a minor, our attorney —"

"Mrs. Freeman, we're not here for your son."

Her face froze in ugly fury. "Mom," John moaned. "Mom, they know."

"Mrs. Freeman, you have the right to remain silent —"

That was as far as Manny got before Mrs. Freeman started screaming. "That little bitch would have ruined my son! She deserved to die, like all the rest of those sick perverts! I'm glad she's dead, I would do it all over again to save my son!"

Helen shuddered as Mrs. Freeman was handcuffed and pulled, still screaming, into the patrol car.

The screams echoed in Helen's ears the next morning as she led Diane back into the utility room to explain how she'd known that Mrs. Freeman had killed Sarah Maxwell.

Helen gestured toward the cracked sheet of plastic in the metal frame announcing the new hours of the library. "She said something to us about how the library was cutting hours. She's over in Orinda, with no reason to be back here in this room. And Mrs. Norment said yesterday that they'd never had a chance to put the sign out for the patrons to see."

Diane shook her head. "So she was out here waiting that night?"

Helen jiggled the outside door until it opened onto the paved yard. "See those trees? It was closing time, already dark. She parked her car around the corner and waited. Apparently she called Sarah over to her, wanting at first just to talk to her."

"But how did it happen? How did she — I mean —"

"John wasn't giving up on Sarah. It was affecting his grades, meaning he might not get into an Ivy League school. Mrs. Freeman couldn't believe Sarah would turn down her son. I think she was hoping Sarah would be persuaded to keep on dating John, at least until they graduated. No one would be embarrassed that way."

Diane's eyes filled with tears as Helen went on. "She grabbed one of these bricks, and Sarah took off.

She made it back into the utility room, as far as that metal stand." Helen stopped when she saw Diane's face. "There was a full confession. Hard to say what will happen to her, though."

"I loved her, Helen," Diane whispered as they walked out into the sunlight.

"I know. She seems to have inspired a lot of strong feelings in a lot of people. She was a very special person."

Diane took a deep breath and dried her eyes. "Well. I have some other very special people to take care of."

"Like Heather?"

"Like Heather — like all the other kids in the group. I just wish I could help them find a safe place to live, to just be themselves." She smiled wryly up at the sky. "Do you think we'll ever find it?"

Helen had no answer. She waited in front of the library, leaving only when Diane's car had become a dim blur of blue winding through the quiet Sunday morning.

Fire Burns

Penny Mickelbury

Warm, fragrant night air swirled gently around
Mimi and Gianna, thanks to the little red Karmann
Ghia convertible that was in no hurry to cover the
miles from Garrett County back to Washington, D.C.
and work.

Mimi had bought and lovingly restored the classic
1969 Ghia for trips just such as this, and she
delighted in sharing the experience with Gianna who,
until she began the relationship with Mimi a year
and a half ago, knew nothing of this part of

Maryland, the far Western part, on the other side of four mountain ranges — the Allegheny, Appalachian, Blue Ridge and Catoctin Mountains — and far enough away from major urban centers to discourage hordes of weekenders and day-trippers.

Mimi had been introduced to the area ten years ago by her best friend, Freddy Schuyler, who was at the time a star offensive tackle for the Washington Redskins. A loner, even in college, Freddy was always looking for a way not only to avoid the crowds that came with celebrity, but to be his homosexual self away from prying eyes. A mountain cabin six hours from D.C. was just the ticket.

But few of Mimi and Gianna's friends could fathom their willingness to endure such a long haul just for a weekend, even if it was the three-day Memorial Day holiday. Mimi, for her part, would rather spend four hours in a car that was moving than the two hours of sitting and waiting always required to cross the Chesapeake Bay Bridge on any given weekend between May and September. Besides, like Freddy, she never wanted to be going to the same place as that many other people.

Pale yellow moonlight provided the only illumination other than Mimi's headlights on the two-lane black top road. Not that Mimi needed light. She knew the way. And she was in no hurry. It had been months since she and Gianna had spent time alone, and she wanted to savor it until the last second. Who knew when another miracle would occur, giving them three whole days of solitude. Gianna had taken the time simply because she hadn't had more than a day off in three months. Mimi had the time because, even though she was a top investigative reporter, she was on temporary assignment to the city desk. During the summer months, when the investigative units slowed their productivity, investigative reporters frequently filled in for general assignment reporters who were on vacation, and the city desk shift she was working allowed her the three-day weekend. Mimi had surprised herself by enjoying the change of pace. She was tired of spending weeks, sometimes months, uncovering wrongdoing and sending miscreants to jail.

Mimi had met Gianna during one such investigation and now it seemed a miracle that their relationship had survived the pressure. Mimi smiled inwardly as she remembered meeting the icy, controlled Lieutenant Anna Maglione, head of the Washington, D.C. police department's Hate Crimes Unit, and her amusement increased as she contrasted the intense police lieutenant of that time with this woman who now sat next to her holding her hand, relaxed and calm and humming along with Pointer Sisters' "Slow Hand."

Indeed, thought Mimi, leaning into the kiss that Gianna was bestowing on her right ear, and then squirming when she felt her tongue.

"You're going to cause an accident."

"That's not what you said a few hours ago."

"That's because a few hours ago my hands were on you and not on the steering wheel, as you might recall."

"Oh, I recall," Gianna said softly, and they sighed in unison, in shared regret that the three days of swimming and boating on placid Deep Creek Lake, and sleeping and love-making, had so soon, too soon, come to an end.

The road shifted suddenly, curving dangerously and climbing steeply, and Mimi needed both her hands to downshift and guide the car into the hairpin turn. An orange glow in the sky appeared ahead and to the south. She frowned. The last vestiges of the sunset had disappeared two hours ago, and besides, the sun had set behind them. They were driving east.

"Is that a fire?" she asked, noticing that Gianna, too, had come to attention and was focused on the hill they were about to crest.

"It sure looks like it . . . Mimi!" Gianna's scream reached Mimi's brain at the same time the white streak came barreling over the hill, well in excess of the speed limit. And on Mimi's side of the road. She leaned on the horn and yelled at the top of her lungs. Then did the only possible thing. Ran the car into the ditch to avoid the collision that surely would have killed them.

The Pointers were silenced as the Ghia crashed to a halt, knocking over several feet of a wooden fence so weathered that no evidence remained that it had ever been whitewashed.

Gianna reached for Mimi, took and held her shoulder. "Darling, are you all right?"

"I'm fine," Mimi growled, "but that son of a bitch!" She pounded the steering wheel and turned to see red taillights already disappearing over the hill, then turned back to Gianna. "How about you? Still all in one piece?"

"I think so," Gianna replied, anger creeping into her voice, replacing her relief.

Mimi opened her door and got out of the car to inspect the damage.

"Great Christ Almighty!"

"What?" Gianna tried to open her car door. It was wedged against the fence. "Mimi, what is it?" She scrambled across the tiny car and exited the driver's side, aware that Mimi was running up the road. Gianna reached back into the car and grabbed her purse—which held her 9mm Glock Automatic—and took off after Mimi, who was now twenty yards up the road.

"Jesus Christ," Gianna whispered when she saw the fiery spectacle. "Jesus Christ," she said again, and halted in awe of the sight before her, a sight from a history that she had never dreamed could actually be repeated, despite the fact that she earned her living investigating the proliferation of hate crimes. A cross was burning in the yard in front of a farm house, and behind it, a barn was engulfed in flames.

Drawing abreast of Mimi, she was moved to tears at the emotion etched into her face: Pain, fear, anger, horror—all vying for some means of understanding what was before them. Then Mimi's face changed, and she pointed and shouted and began running again, down the steep, brush-covered hill, toward the flames. Gianna saw two figures running around the barn, and she, too, left the paved road and crashed through the brush down the hill, a hand inside her purse with a hold on the Glock. Just in case . . .

A man and a woman in their mid-fifties directed high-powered water hoses at the flaming barn, though clearly it was wasted effort, wasted water. But it was just as clear that it was their barn and no expenditure of time or effort or water was useless. The fire in their eyes burned and crackled as hot as that other fire which was devouring the ancient wooden relic of a time past.

The man looked over his shoulder and let out a groan. "Oh, Lord," he said almost to himself. Then he yelled out, "Go back inside, Mama! Go back in the house!" Then, to Mimi, he said, "Miss, would you go help my Mama get back inside?"

Mimi peered through the thickening smoke. A tiny figure dressed in white and leaning heavily on a cane was making her way toward the barn. Mimi nodded and trotted off toward the old woman. Gianna, wondering whether to join the fire-fighting effort or to join Mimi, had her dilemma solved.

"Her medicine is on top of the refrigerator. She'll say it's not time to take it, or she already took it. Ignore her." The man returned his attention to the task of battling for his barn.

"Have you called the authorities?" Gianna asked, and took a step backward as if she'd been physically pushed, so powerful was the look the woman gave her.

"They won't come for us," she spat. "Besides, one of them probably lit that cross." The woman's voice broke on the last words and the tears rolled down her face.

"The police'll come. But not until the fire is out," the man said matter-of-factly.

Gianna, weighted down by an overwhelming sadness, crossed the yard to the farm house, the familiar argument waging its always unwelcome battle inside her head: could it be true that the authorities would allow the barn to burn because the people who owned it were of a different race? The answer, of course, was yes. Then came the next questions: Why? How? And for those questions, there were no answers. None that had ever made any sense. Gianna felt an instant of total helplessness, and was immediately surprised at herself, for in that instant she'd actually forgotten that she was the law. Not, perhaps, here in Washington County, Maryland, in whatever town they were in, but she was, nonetheless, the law, and she was not helpless. Comforted by that realization, she opened the door to the farm house and entered the peaceful beauty that had been so suddenly shattered by hatred's ugliness that night.

Gianna followed voices down a polished hallway past a formal living room into an old-fashioned parlor, a gentle, relaxed room with three overstuffed chairs, each with its own footstool. There was also a couch, a wide-screen television with a VCR on the shelf beneath, and a state of the art music system. These people were rural but not isolated. Bookshelves filled an entire wall, and books occupied every inch of available space. This was a home of avid and active readers. Indeed, the room was a home of active, involved people. Cut flowers stood in vases on virtually every surface, as did framed photographs of several generations of family.

Mimi perched on the stool adjacent to the chair in which the old woman sat. Gianna was able to study her quickly: the woman was old, yes, and apparently needed a cane to walk and medicine to control an illness of some kind. But she was the strongest woman Gianna had ever seen. She exuded strength and life and energy. Sensing Gianna's presence, she turned bright, sparkling brown eyes to her, eyes magnified by wire-rimmed spectacles.

"I'm Elizabeth McCray. That's my boy, Hubert, and his wife Gladys out there trying to save the barn."

Gianna said, "I'm very sorry about what's happened tonight."

"Never thought I'd see that again. I had nightmares about fiery crosses until I was a full grown woman with a house full of babies. Night riders and burning crosses. Thought all that was over and done with."

"You've seen it before?" Mimi asked quietly.

"Yes, indeed," Elizabeth McCray said, "and they're just as cowardly today as they were seventy years ago, the land-grabbing bastards!"

Mimi couldn't mask her confusion. "Land-grabbing? This is about land? Not race?"

"Same thing," the old woman snapped. "We're the only Colored still own land around here. Rest of 'em sold out. Took the money and ran. But not the McCrays. We been here a hundred years, and we'll be here another hundred."

"Who wants the land now?" Gianna asked.

"Damnfool developers! They built some ski resorts up in the mountains. Then they built some golf courses down in the valley. Then they started building houses but they ran out of land. The two hundred acres of the McCray farm is standing smack in the middle of their plans." The old woman looked so pleased with herself that Gianna almost laughed.

She said, "Your son asked me to make sure you took your medicine..."

"Already took it," the old woman said quickly, and Gianna couldn't stop herself from smiling.

"He said you'd say that. Which way is the kitchen?"

The old woman gestured with a curt nod to a doorway to the left. Gianna was almost to the door when Hubert and Gladys McCray entered the room, covered with soot and smelling of smoke, followed by a uniformed officer whose shoulder patch read *Washington County Police.*

"Who are you people?" he asked with barely disguised hostility.

Because Gianna had turned to ice at the officer's tone, Mimi answered for them, explaining where they'd been and the circumstances of their accident and their seeing the fire. When she began to give a description of the vehicle that had run them into the ditch—a white Range Rover—she saw the cop's eyes narrow and he quickly switched gears.

"You girls been drinking?"

"I beg your pardon?" Gianna was so angry her words came out a whisper.

"Just answer the question before I decide to run you in for a breath test."

Hot bile rose in Gianna's throat making it impossible for her to speak. She'd never known hatred born of helplessness and it was choking her, cutting off her breath.

"We're not girls and we haven't been drinking." Mimi raised her stare from the officer's name tag and met and held his eyes, not bothering to conceal her contempt. "Do you want a statement from us, Officer Bowen, as we may be material witnesses to a crime?" He held her stare for a long moment, as if deciding what to do. Then he reached into his pocket for his notebook.

"Give me your licenses, one at a time. You first," he said, pointing at Gianna. She hesitated a long moment before reaching into her purse, a moment during which Mimi knew she debated whether to present her police badge. But her hand emerged holding her wallet from which she extracted the license. She gave it to Bowen and watched in silence while he wrote. Then he followed the same procedure with Mimi. Nobody spoke until he was done. Then he said, "If I decide I want a statement from you I'll let you know." And with that, he turned and left the house. The five people in the room stood still as statues. Gladys McCray broke the silence.

"I told you. Didn't I tell you? If he didn't set the fire, he knows who did." Hubert put an arm around her, holding tight.

"I know, too. Damnfool developers," Elizabeth muttered.

Hubert McCray went to his mother, patted her hand, and then asked Mimi and Gianna how they came to be in his yard at ten o'clock on Memorial Day night. After they explained, in more detail than they'd given Officer Bowen, Hubert offered to lend Mimi and Gianna a car to drive home in—an old but very well-cared-for Buick station wagon. He promised to haul the Karmann Ghia out of the ditch and into his garage first thing in the morning—like every farmer everywhere he had a four-wheel drive pick-up with a hitch—and have his own mechanic give it the once-over. Mimi and Gianna exchanged names and phone numbers with the McCrays and for reasons that they could not articulate, did not reveal to these gentle people that they were, respectively, a journalist and a police lieutenant.

"Are you all going to be all right?" Mimi couldn't hide her concern.

"We'll be fine, thank you," Hubert McCray said, the conviction in his voice tinged with sadness. "This isn't the first time they've tried to burn us out, although, in truth, I thought I'd seen the last of this kind of thing. Fiery crosses," he said, almost mumbling to himself.

Elizabeth McCray mumbled to herself, too. "Evil is a fire. Hatred is a fire. Greed is a fire. And just like fire, they all burn, burn up everything in their path. And what's left after the burning usually ain't good for much. Except starting over." But there was more anger than sadness in her words.

For the next week, Mimi and Gianna waited to hear from Officer Bowen or any other member of the Washington County police, despite a dour prediction from Freddy that the Second Coming was a more likely occurrence. Freddy had a passing acquaintance with the authorities in all five of the Maryland counties between D.C. and his cabin in the woods, based on his status as a former star offensive tackle for the Washington Redskins and most cops' fascination with jocks. Freddy opined that either the cops had already found out who had burned the cross at the McCray's and destroyed their barn, or they didn't care and didn't intend to pursue it. Neither circumstance would warrant a call to D.C.

When Mimi called Hubert McCray to check on her car, he had good news and better news: her prized vehicle had suffered no structural damage, and the ruptured tire, broken headlight, and dented fender had already been repaired. Then Hubert, sounding almost shy, made Mimi a proposal: he and Gladys would drive the Karmann Ghia to Washington in exchange for an introduction to Freddy Schuyler. Hubert said that Gladys had a fit when she realized who Mimi's friend in Garret County was, and not only did she want to get away for a day or two, but, well, she'd die for the chance to meet a Redskin.

Mimi and Gianna did better than that. They treated the couple to a night on the town — dining and dancing at Freddy's night club, the hottest, trendiest spot in D.C., where Gladys met half a dozen current and former Redskins, Bullets and Capitals. While Hubert and Gianna burned up the dance floor, Gladys couldn't decide whether she was more in love with Freddy or with Freddy's lover, Cedric, a published poet and a literature professor, and it didn't bother either of them in the least that they'd spent the weekend with gay men and lesbians.

Over Sunday brunch, Hubert and Gladys confirmed Freddy's prediction: they'd heard nothing more from the police and they didn't expect to. Instead, they'd taken turns sitting up nights guarding their property with a shotgun until their youngest son, a long distance trucker, had arrived two days ago. His presence made their trip to D.C. a possibility, and now they'd return and get on with life. Yes, they'd keep in touch with their new D.C. friends. Yes, next time they'd bring Hubert's mother with them. And they'd take Freddy up on his invitation to visit him at his cabin. Mimi led them to the entrance of the Beltway and they watched and waved until the Buick wagon was out of sight.

Mimi did not recognize the car blocking the entrance to her garage, and she struggled to stifle a curse. It was late and she was tired and only an idiot would park like that!

"Calm down, babe. I'll check it out." Gianna was already out of the car and closing the door. She slung her purse over her shoulder and sidled over to the offending vehicle, cop style, which would have been a good thing, Mimi realized, had the danger been inside the car. She saw the shadow emerge from the dense hedges that separated her yard from her neighbors'. She flung open the car door. "Gianna!" she screamed.

Then too many things happened at once. The shadow was firing a gun, Gianna was firing back and yelling for Mimi to get down, but Mimi wasn't about to get down until she determined that Gianna was allright, but a burning jolt to the head knocked her to the ground. The buzzing was much too loud and the flashes of light much too white, but then the light changed, to an orangy glow—to a fiery cross—and then darkness descended.

* * * * *

"They shaved my head?" Mimi screeched and grabbed her bandaged head, wincing with pain as she did so. Gianna pried Mimi's hands away from her head and locked them in a vise-like grip.

"They did not shave your entire head—"

"Oh, great. I'll look really lovely with half a shaved head. How could you let them do that to me?" she wailed.

"Be grateful you've got half a head to shave." Gianna's irritation covered her fear. The bullet had only grazed Mimi, just above the left ear, but Gianna would never forget the sight of Mimi's blood-covered, unconscious face.

Gianna's words sobered Mimi quickly. "I am. And I'm sorry. Gianna, what happened? That was no random robbery or street shooting."

Impressed as always with Mimi's instinctive response to crime and criminals, Gianna explained that their attacker was a Baltimore resident who'd apparently come to D.C. specifically to kill them, since he had both their names and addresses written on a piece of paper hidden under the floor mat in his car.

A shudder ran through Mimi, followed immediately by a prickling excitement. "How were our names written, Gianna?"

"What do you mean?" She felt Mimi's sensors on alert.

"Were they written 'Gianna Maglione' and 'Mimi Patterson' or 'Giovanna' and 'Marilyn,' like on a driver's license?"

"Bowen, damn him!"

In their professional lives, Gianna was Anna and Mimi was M. Montgomery and absolutely no one ever referred to them by their given names. By their legal names. Only a stranger would write their names as Gianna had seen them on the paper in the would-be assassin's car.

"So some asshole cop in Washington County hired a Baltimore hit man to take us out?" Mimi's skepticism was running unchecked.

"I don't think so," Gianna said, her brain whirring. "I think Bowen passed on our names to the jerk who ran us off the road, the jerk who set fire to the McCrays' barn."

"The developer," Mimi said, remembering old Elizabeth's pronouncement.

They sat in silence. Mimi knew that Gianna, a decorated police professional, approached crime-solving by the book. And Gianna knew that Mimi, an award-winning journalist, relied on instinct and a wide network of off-the-record sources, and never did anything by the book if she could help it.

"Bowen's a dirty cop, and I hate dirty cops," Gianna said.

"The developer's a coward, and I hate cowards," Mimi said.

And they shook hands, not needing words to articulate the tenuous agreement they'd just reached.

"By the way," Mimi asked, "what happened to the shooter?"

"In a coma," Gianna replied, much too calmly, adding even more force to the impact of those few words on Mimi's psyche. Gianna, who'd been a cop for twenty years and who took pride in the fact that she could count the number of times she'd discharged her weapon, had taken someone to the edge of death.

Mimi grabbed her, pulled her in close, and held

her for a long time. "Do you want to talk about it?" she asked.

"No," Gianna said slowly, "not yet. Right now I just want to find who sent him."

Between themselves, they called it The Cross Burning Thing, and they worked it, secretly, whenever they were able to find or create free moments from their normal duties, which was easy for Mimi since she was shamelessly exploiting the sympathy of her editors at the paper. She'd been shot, after all. It was more difficult for Gianna, since the police department didn't think much of an out-of-town hit man targeting one of its lieutenants, and she'd had to spend an entire day reviewing past and current case files for investigators searching out a reason for the attack.

Under the agreement by which they parceled out the work—as much for efficiency as to guarantee that they didn't get on each other's nerves—Gianna handled the official part of their investigation, and Mimi the unofficial part. Mimi obtained from Hubert and Gladys every document and piece of paper from the developers, including the original prospectus, and Gianna ran a check on every principal listed. None of them had ever had so much as a traffic ticket. Mimi's media check of the developers bore similar fruit: nothing but good press. It was a well-known and well-respected group which had built resorts in Colorado, New Mexico, Arizona and Florida.

The white Range Rover that ran them off the

road was proving a more difficult matter. They were sure only of the truck's color and make, which wasn't enough to run a check on. "Can you run a check on Officer Asshole Bowen? Is there some kind of national cop registry where you can check him out?"

"No, you silly . . ." Gianna stopped suddenly and Mimi waited, feeling the intensity from the other end of the phone. "Mimi, have you touched your driver's license since Bowen gave it back to you?"

"Dammit, Maglione, you're brilliant!"

"I know. Meet me at Suzanne's in an hour. I'll buy you lunch since I'm confiscating your wallet."

Grady Bowen was an ex-Baltimore City cop who'd quit the force three years ago rather than withstand the scrutiny of an Internal Affairs investigation into his lavish lifestyle. He'd left Baltimore and returned home, to Washington County, at about the same time his older brother, Riley, was released from prison on drug charges. The still-comatose hit man was a Baltimore low-life with a criminal record as extensive as his ties to mid-level drug dealers. The only thing that didn't fit was the McCrays, and Mimi and Gianna were greatly relieved when a check revealed that the family, every one of them in four Maryland counties and three other states, was cleaner than church on Easter Sunday. So why burn their barn? Why burn a cross in their yard? What was their tie-in to Washington County's crime ring?

* * * * *

While Gianna was uncovering the Baltimore drug connection, Mimi spent hours in the library poring over the history of the Ku Klux Klan and the phenomenon of night riders and cross burnings. She was surprised to learn that not only was their activity unrestricted to the Deep South, but that Maryland once had one of the most virulent and active Klan organizations. Interesting as it was, however, the information raised more questions for Mimi than it answered. Cross burnings were meant to intimidate, to frighten, to control, to maintain the sense of inferiority in the newly freed slaves. Since it was illegal during the Klan's heyday for persons of color in the South to own land and property, the night riders rarely burned houses and barns; and by the time enough Blacks owned enough land for greedy whites to want to steal it, they usually didn't waste time burning crosses. In addition to being cowards and idiots, Mimi thought, the cretins who'd burned the McCrays had also mixed their metaphors, as it were. They should have burned one thing or the other but not both.

Unless ... Mimi snatched up the phone and punched in Gianna's number.

"We should go see what's in the McCrays' barn," she said without preamble when Gianna answered.

"Off-hand I'd say the charred remains of the late Eldon Lee, along with a cache of automatic weapons ripped off from the stockade at Fort Meade a couple of months ago."

"How the hell do you know that?" Gianna had stolen her thunder and Mimi was pissed and didn't mind showing it.

"Our would-be assassin is awake and making a

joyful noise. Aren't you glad I'm not a killer?" Gianna meant to be funny but Mimi felt her relief. She'd shot a man, yes; but killed him—no.

"What's making him sing the song of the week?"

"He thinks his pals set him up," Gianna said gleefully. "Sent him to take out a D.C. cop and a newspaper reporter. He couldn't wait to stick it to them."

Mimi let herself fully enjoy the moment, even though she wondered again what mutual but unspoken message had prompted them to conceal their identities from the McCrays and Bowen.

"Who's—who was—Eldon Lee?"

"Riley Bowen's former cellmate. He tried to cheat Riley in a deal to trade guns for drugs. So much for honor among thieves."

"What kind of fool steals from the Army?" Mimi asked, not really expecting a rational answer to an irrational question.

"What put you on to the barn?" Gianna asked, ignoring Mimi's question.

"Logic."

"Like hell!" Gianna sputtered. "There was nothing logical about this whole business."

"Exactly," Mimi said smugly. "It made no sense to burn the cross *and* the barn if the objective was to harm the McCrays. Ergo, there was another objective. Did you notice Hubert and Gladys's brand-spanking-new barn out in the middle of the field? That old one was nothing but nostalgia, so burning it didn't really harm them. Burning the cross, with the emotional and historical impact that brings, shifts the focus. Everybody forgets about a useless and empty barn. Unless it wasn't so empty."

"I'm glad you're on the side of the angels," Gianna said with more feeling than she'd intended, "because you have a brilliantly criminal mind."

"If that's a compliment," Mimi said lightly, "thank you."

"In a way I'm glad," Gladys said quietly.

"Glad they burned the barn?" Elizabeth was incredulous.

"No, Mama, not that. Glad that burning the cross didn't mean to them what it used to . . ."

"How can you say that, Gladys?" Hubert was so indignant he almost raised his voice. "Those boys knew burning that cross would upset us! That's why they did it!"

"No, Hubert. At least not like in the old days. They wanted to upset us to keep us away from the barn. They weren't trying to run us off the land. You see what I mean?"

And Hubert did see. And so, grudgingly, did Elizabeth, who finally allowed herself to be convinced that Officer Bowen had not only been fired from the Washington County force, but had also been charged with murder and very likely would go to prison.

Then, with a gentle caress of each of their heads, Elizabeth absolved Mimi and Gianna of their sin of omission: of failing to confess their true professional identities. She then sauntered into the kitchen and whipped up two of the best apple cobblers Mimi and Gianna had ever eaten. That was after they'd stuffed themselves on the best fried chicken, potato salad, string beans, and corn on the cob they'd ever eaten.

Then, when they were too stuffed to move, Gladys said she had a surprise for them, if they'd follow her, which they did—out the kitchen door and across the brick patio and down a stone path and past a fish pond into a clump of high grass, in the middle of which was pitched a yellow tent. Gladys unzipped the flap and held it open. Inside were two sleeping bags, zipped together, two air pillows, a can of mosquito repellent, and a flashlight. Mimi and Gianna were speechless.

Gladys was not. "Figured we had to make it worth your while if we expected you to stay here with us instead of going on to the lake. Enjoy," she said, and headed back to the house. In just a few seconds, she was no longer visible. In fact, no sign of the McCrays or their house or their barn was visible.

"You ever slept in a tent, Mimi?"

"Nope," Mimi answered, as she stooped to enter the yellow dome. "Kinda cute and cozy in here."

"The ground is hard," Gianna said.

"These sleeping bags are really soft," Mimi said, as she closed and zipped the tent flaps.

"Can bugs and things get in here?" Gianna asked.

"Not when it's zipped up tight," Mimi responded calmly.

"Then why is this bug spray in here?"

" 'Cause Gladys is a right on Sister," Mimi said, unbuttoning her shirt and kicking off her sandals. She watched Gianna inspect the tent seams as she unzipped and shimmied out of her jeans. When

Gianna completed her inspection and turned to Mimi, she found her quite naked.

"The mosquitoes will eat you alive," Gianna predicted darkly.

"Not if you beat them to it," Mimi said, grinning wickedly.

Sorting the Mail

Lauren Wright Douglas

Vegetarian magazine keep, sportswear catalogue, throw out, cat toys brochure keep, *Ferret* magazine, throw ... Wait. What in hell is *Ferret* magazine, Allie O'Neil wondered. She certainly didn't have a ferret, and neither did Jean. They had cats. Eleven of them. So who had subscribed to *Ferret*? Was this some piece of baggage from one of Jean's earlier "living situations"? Narrowing her eyes, she plucked the magazine from the trash.

Dear Mrs. O'Neill:

It's time to renew your subscription to Ferret, *the bi-monthly magazine dedicated to helping you ferret out the squalid little secrets everyone believes they've successfully hidden. In the hope that you've found our publication indispensable, we've included a subscription renewal card and a postage-paid envelope. But do hurry. Our charter subscriber rate of $21.95 is being extended to you as a courtesy, so a timely response would be appreciated.*

Sincerely,

Ellen Rourke
Subscription Department

A timely response, eh, Allie thought, noting with irritation the misspelling of her name (it's O'Neil with ONE "l", Rourke) and the misstating of her marital status (that's Ms. O'Neil to you, pinhead). She vaguely remembered winning a subscription to this rag as a raffle prize at the Dinah Shore Golf Tournament last year, but for the life of her she couldn't recall having ever read a single issue. I'll give you a quick response, Rourke, she snorted.

Dear Mrs. Rourke (sic):

Hoping the folks at Ferret *can take it as well as dish it out, I'm writing to tell you that I have absolutely no intention of renewing my subscription to your second-rate rag. I mean, you misspelled my name, married me to Mr. O'Neill (whoever he is), and thoroughly pissed me off. And you want to give me advice on ferreting out information? Dream on.*

Less Than Satisfied in Salem

Allie O'Neil

She pulled the page out of the typewriter, stuffed it into the postage-paid envelope and tossed it into the basket she and Jean used for outgoing mail.

And then she forgot all about *Ferret.*

Until an envelope arrived in the mail three weeks later.

"Here's something for you," Jean called from the kitchen, tossing Allie a large brown envelope which Allie caught as she passed through on her way to the couch. "Mailman brought it right to the door. Must be important," Jean said.

Curious, Allie carried it into the living room. No identifying marks. Not even a return address. How intriguing, she thought. Ripping it open, she held it upside down and shook. A single piece of paper wafted out.

Dear Ms. O'Neil:

It's from those lamebrains at *Ferret,* she realized, wondering why they'd bothered to write back. Probably an apology, she thought.

It was with great disappointment that I read of your decision not to renew your subscription to Ferret. *However, we do hope that you will reconsider and in anticipation of this event, we are extending our charter rate of $287.40.*

Whoa! What happened to $21.95?

to you for the next year. We know that you will find the information in Ferret *to be useful. Why, we number among our subscribers the investigators at Pinkerton's, many corporate security forces, and even a few government agencies. Techniques used by these people (techniques learned from* Ferret*) are similar to those which turned up your own torrid weekend tryst with Felicia Farr at last year's Dinah Shore Golf Tournament, a tryst you enjoyed while your present partner Jean Daniels worked overtime at the post office.*

Allie felt faint.

Among the techniques you will learn are the finer points of surveillance and photography, skills which enabled us to acquire the enclosed 8" by 10" glossy of you and Ms. Farr at the Whispering Winds Motel in Palm Springs.

Stifling a scream, Allie looked inside the envelope. Sure enough, there was the print in question, showing a particularly sharp and well-focused photo of her and Felicia in an ambitiously athletic and undeniably compromising position. Damn.

We do hope, Ms. O'Neil, to be able to once again count you among our satisfied subscribers and will hold our offer open to you for the next five business days. We look forward to receiving your check in the amount of $287.40.

Sincerely yours

Ellen Rourke
Subscription Department

Allie dived for her checkbook, realizing with a sense of growing horror that the amount *Ferret* was requesting was precisely the amount she had been filching from the grocery money for almost nine months and squirreling away in her sock drawer for a reprise of the lost weekend with the ingenious Felicia. Well, not precisely. Her stash amounted to $287.69. After paying *Ferret,* she'd have twenty-nine cents left over. Of course, she thought, of course.

The Dream Breaker

Robbi Sommers

The phone rings. *Hello? Hello?* I linger in empty silence until I hear the disconnect click. I know it's Sabina. Every night between nine and ten she calls. I've come to expect the sharp ring of the phone, but even so, it still startles me. I grab the receiver and listen, hoping this time she'll favor me with the sound of her breath, a simple sigh or a single word. A click and the dial tone are all she offers and I'm left to struggle with the perverse pleasure of her disturbing intrusion.

She won't leave me alone. She haunts me. Her torturous persistence suffocates yet excites me. A tap on my bedroom window sometime after midnight and I lie in bed breathless. Listening. Waiting. I want her to retreat but am desperate to hear her tap again. If only she'd leave me alone, I'd be free. If only she'd come through that window, I'd be free.

Eyes closed tight, I wait. Heart beating recklessly, I wait. I sense her at the edge of my bed. Her fragrance surrounds me like a desert sand storm and a whirlwind of memories ignites my passion. Thrashing through a flurry of dream fragments, I battle my way to the bed-stand light. Can I catch sight of her before she disappears?

Hello? I sit up in bed. *Hello?* I switch on the night light. She's a master of illusion, elusion, delusion. This I know.

Early morning dawn creeps through lace curtains. She's been here during my sleep. I can feel her. In my house. In my room. In the night. Spinning her web, filling my dreams with silky entanglements. She leaves nothing untouched. Camouflaged in shadows that come with the dark, she steals into my room, touches my things and tampers with my dreams. Perhaps if I wait for a full moon in Scorpio, I'll see the glimmer in her eyes when she slinks across the room?

I wonder what it's like to come and go as one pleases. Sometimes I slip into masquerade. I creep around my room and pretend that I'm her. My pearl earrings on the bureau, I roll between my fingers. I swirl antique perfume flasks beneath my nose and luxuriate in the exotic scents. Into my lingerie drawer, snooping through my journal — I become her, an outlaw, a dream breaker, a thief of hearts. There's a sense of power, a sense of intimacy that I'm certain she draws as she goes through my things, and I envy her.

She won't leave me alone. She's everywhere. She peers from behind curtained windows, hides behind closed doors. When I undress, subtle creaking betrays that she's somewhere between the walls, watching. On occasion, her silhouette flickers in the mirror. Vague, a mere whisper, she shadows me. Her breath heats my neck, her hands rest lightly on my shoulders. I turn to confront her but she's gone.

I light candles before retiring. In bed, I visualize white light surrounding me. A small velvet pouch filled with smooth, tiny rocks is tucked under my pillow. Will hematite and rutilated crystal keep her away? Will rose quartz bring her to me?

She speaks to me in every song. No matter what radio station I select, an orchestrated message from her snakes through the melodic words then wraps around my heart until I can hardly breathe. I can't go anywhere without her trailing in the shadows or peering at me through the walls.

And if she stepped from the gray and made her presence known? Oh Sabina, sweet Sabina — in bed, late at night, I wait feverishly. Dressed in black, she'd climb through the window. Bathed in silver light from the moon, she'd stand before me and whisper my name . . .

"Nora . . ." Even in a murmur, her tone is deep.

"Sabina!" The sight of her ignites me. Anger and excitement twist hard in my belly.

"I'm sorry that I —" Sabina gestures toward the window and shrugs. "I've missed you. I can't seem to —" She steps closer.

Her thin build is deceiving. I'm well aware of her strength. Her muscles are easily discerned when she's naked, when she's above me, when she lifts my ass and fucks me deep.

"You have to leave." My voice is harsh. I want to sound tough. I want to sound certain. But above all, I want her not to care.

"Do I?" The sarcastic edge to her words thrills me. She combs her fingers through her short blonde hair and rocks back slightly on her heels. Her hands are partially tucked in the front pockets of her tight jeans. My attention slips to her crotch. Is she wearing the strap-on? I strain to see the outline in her pants. Under those 501s, beneath the boxers she's probably got on, does she have a special gift for me?

Staring at the place that the dildo would be, I simply nod. My blanket lightly grazes my naked breasts. If I move, even slightly, the thin coverlet would surely drop. Already, just from the sight of Sabina, my nipples have contracted into tight knots. Sabina loves how stiff, how purple, my nipples get. She's said this again and again. I decide to taunt her. The blanket falls away.

Sabina's focus quick-shifts to my breasts then back to my face. She takes another step. "Then stop me, Nora. Stop me, if you want me to leave." The hint of a smile flickers on her thick lips.

Then stop me. The moisture between my legs drips. I lean forward and feel the dampness on my sheet. I'm ready for her, crazy for her. Will she flip me over and take me from behind? On my hands and knees, ass raised and ready, I'd give her what she wants.

She reaches the bed. A dirt smudge on her T-shirt — did she climb through the rose bushes to get to me? Crawl on her belly to get to me? Her fingers gently trace my cheek, then slide to the plum-colored tip of my breast.

"Nice, Nora. Very, very nice." She twists the erect nipple and it stands purple-hard. Her other hand slips to my waist and she grips me tight. "On your knees, baby." Without waiting for my reply, she coaxes me onto my belly.

I bury my face in the pillow as she climbs on the bed, as she raises my hips, as she presses against me. The zip of her pants is loud in the silence. She struggles and I know that she's dragging the large dildo from her boxers.

An eternity of seconds passes and the cool latex finally rubs against my ass. "Then stop me," she mutters. "Then stop me," she demands.

My face is buried in the pillows. I have nothing to say.

She slices the dildo between my cheeks. I force my ass higher, even higher and spread my legs. *Come on, come on, come on,* my pussy pleads.

Sabina swirls the tip against my slit. I'm greasy and oily and ready to go. I imagine the bulbous head, slippery against my pleated opening. Blindly, I reach for the vibrator stashed under the bed.

"Oh yeah." Sabina laughs. She pushes my arm aside and leans past me. I'm sure she's grabbed the vibrator for me. "Oh yeah, baby, oh yeah. Fly on this."

She plants the vibrator in my hand and I put it to my clitoris. The vibrator wildly hums. My entire body has become my clit — hard, bulky, erect. The bed, the room, the universe has become my clit. I'm riding an earthquake. I'm straddling a volcano. Hot lava seeps from my pussy and runs down my thighs.

Sabina wastes no time. She pierces the dildo into my ready cunt. The smooth, fat head separates my sex and penetrates deep. Big. Thick. Ribbed — and she jams it. She slams it. She rams it. There's nothing but the pounding vibrations. There's nothing but the sensation of in and out. I am electric, magnetic. I am energy unleashed. I teeter on the vibrator. I'm balanced on pleasure and nothing else.

"Sabina! Sabina!"

Then stop me. Then stop me. Then stop me.

I rock like a pony as she goes on and on. Up and down, I slide on her latex extension. Back and forth, I race with the speed of light. Oh Sabina. Sweet Sabina.

Late at night, I glance at the window. I sleep with rose quartz and whisper her name.

Heather went there with Jane. Jane confided to Polly. Polly is best friends with Carey and Carey called me, last night, as soon as she'd heard. In the city, in a part of town that we just don't go, a withered old woman does magic. *Eerie* is the word that Heather had used. *Macabre* was Jane's.

Heather's grandmother had a friend who knew the woman from the old country. She spills smoothed bits of bones from a tattered pouch and then peeks

into the future, steps into the past, resolves hopeless
dilemmas, unravels tangled knots — for a negotiable
fee, she does all this and more. If the moon is right,
if the spirits are willing, if a crow hasn't landed on
the street where she lives, then yes, after nine on
Friday nights, she's willing to listen to a seeker's
woes.

I decided to go. I had no choice but to go. Long
nights I'd endured, velvet-wrapped stones clutched to
my breasts. I'd bolt up in bed to an empty room —
the candles long extinguished, the bedroom black as a
hopeless heart. Was that a tap at the window or a
branch in the wind? Wishing her gone yet fancying
her here, I'd sit in the darkness of another hollow
night. There must be a spell, a charm, a chant to
make her come forward. I'd will her through the
window. I'd compel her to emerge from the walls.
Into my room, into my bed — there must be a potion,
an oil, a ritual, to force her to leave me once and for
all.

I want her to stop yet pray she'll be outside my
window late at night. It's convoluted and distorted.
I'm trapped in a crazy labyrinth of desire and
distress.

On a whim Sabina left me. Rode from my life on
a cloud of gray. Too confined, she said. Can't
breathe, she said. Surely she misses me. Certainly she
cares. After all, she comes every night, goes through
my drawers, peers from the curtains and tampers
with my dreams.

If only I could ensnare her before she fades. I'd
make her remember, force her to remember — grab
her wrist, not let go — until she remembered.
Sabina? I'd say. *Sabina!* I'd insist. I'd stay there,

grasp her and not back down. But she slips through my room with the slightest breeze, nudges me from dreams — whether day or night — only to evade me before I have a chance to convince her to stay.

Carey said she'd meet me at the service station on Market and Van Ness at eight forty-five. It was now nine-fifteen — Carey wasn't at home and she still wasn't here. I had already packed in a Kit Kat and a bag of chips. We had agreed on this gas station, hadn't we? Was she sitting in her car somewhere else, eating chips and waiting for me?

I used the pay phone to check my answering machine. Nothing from Carey although there was one hang up . . . Sabina. I bought a bag of pretzels in the mini store and went back to my car, back to the clock, back to the wait.

Nine-twenty. Nine twenty-five. At nine-thirty I tore into the pretzels. I could either head home to another night of Sabina's torment or proceed as planned — *to that side of town, to that kind of woman* — alone.

I stuffed the last pretzel into my mouth. If I didn't go tonight, I'd have another week's wait. I started the car, popped a CD in the deck and turned out of the gas station. It was now or never. To the other side of town I drove. The street lights became less frequent as I ventured closer to my destination. I scanned the deserted sidewalks. Where was everyone? Hiding in alleys, watching my lone car travel further into the black? Did they whisper as I passed? Did they plan what they'd do when I slowed at the stop sign?

I pushed the door-lock button again, as if repeating this gesture every half mile would afford me added security. I turned up my CD. Farther from the service station, the lit streets, the crowded sidewalks, I journeyed. Ten o' clock. Ten oh five.

Her street was actually a narrow alley. Under my vague direction, my car inched reluctantly into the darkness. Several knocked-over trash cans, scattered on the sidewalk, marked her driveway. I pulled along the curb and parked. I hoped that the creatures digging through the garbage were simply harmless cats just having a Friday night out, although I suspected they were rats.

I contemplated the dim, yellow light that illuminated the address, then focused on the *Welcome* sign propped inside the grime-covered window. *Eerie. Macabre.* The garbage marauders were looting the debris without a care. I lowered the car window enough to stick my head out. "Scat!" I called to the shadows. "Go on, get out of here!" Like I had some sort of say, some kind of authority, I brandished my clenched fist. "I said go!" They didn't bother to acknowledge me.

Exactly how hungry were those rats? If I opened the car door would they come after me, sharp, shiny incisors bared? Sabina knew how I felt about rats. Had she heard about this visit to the magic woman, got here first and pushed over the trash? Was she watching from a darkened alcove? This was Sabina's work, all right. She'd do anything to maintain control.

I wadded the snack wrappers into a tight ball and threw it out the window toward the scavengers. Although ineffectual, the feeble action toughened me. "So there," I muttered. I sneaked out of the car and hurried past the toppled cans to the stoop. My heart thumped. My breath was quick. Three knocks — were the rats behind me? Three more knocks — *C'mon. Open. Open. Open!* The door creaked and an old woman, shriveled and bent with age, stood before me. Her attention skimmed past me to the garbage. "Damn rats." Her teeth looked unusually yellow in the porch light and her face, wrinkled and drawn, had a pasty pallor.

Was there a polite way past the woman and into the safety of her house? "I'm looking for —"

"I know what you're looking for, child." She grabbed my wrist and guided me into the musty studio.

A spontaneous impulse to break away from her clammy, clasping hand and escape to my car gripped me. The room seemed too crowded, too dingy, too dreary. Lit candles covered a table pushed into a corner where stacks of newspapers leaned dangerously close. Shelves were cluttered with books, jars, figurines. An array of black velvet portraits — Jesus on the cross, a mournful Jesus, a thorn-crowned Jesus — hung haphazard and crooked on the walls. The place was a mess. More light would surely brighten things. With some bleach and hot water, the soiled gray curtains could be whitened. A complete scrubbing from ceiling to floor would add a little cheer. Didn't she notice the cobwebs? Didn't she care?

"You come for the dreams?" Her eyelid drooped to

partially cover her left eye but the colorless right eye was remarkably direct.

"The dreams?" I said vaguely. Uneasiness fluttered through me. With a fast turn, I could be out the door, past the rats and heading home.

She released my hand and shuffled across the room. Her crumpled housecoat hung loose on her body. She was not tall, maybe five-three, with large breasts and a full build. Her wavy hair was thick, almost completely gray, with occasional streaks of black. Embroidered barrettes pulled the hair back from her face.

She smiled at me, in an odd sort of way, then sat in a rocking chair. Arranging the housecoat around her knees, she motioned for me to join her. She resembled a little old grandmother — harmless, eccentric and a bit absent-minded.

There was no reason to leave. I had come this far. Sabina's torture had led me to this and there was no turning back. "Well, yes, the dreams ... I suppose." I crossed the room and sat next to her.

"As I said." Not looking at me, the woman began to slowly rock in the chair.

Sabina woke up with a start. Cramped next to her on the sofa, LeAnn still dozed. Pins and needles prickled hard in her hand and her neck ached. Each loud tick from the mantel clock triggered a sharp throb in her head. "Jesus, what ya do to me, baby?" Sabina whispered.

Irritated that she had drifted into sleep after sex, Sabina untangled herself from LeAnn's embrace and

sat quietly on the edge of the couch. The ticking of
the clock reverberated loudly. The sharp numbness in
her hand still tingled. She massaged her palm, then
gently rubbed her temples. The clock began to chime
again and again. Fiery darts of pain raced fast circles
in her head. Eleven? Midnight? There were too many
clangs to be certain. It didn't matter, she was
leaving.

She had no desire to wake LeAnn, no desire to
chitchat, no desire to do anything but get in her car
and go. Her clothes were in a crumpled pile on the
floor. Head pounding, dizzy, she compelled herself to
stand.

"Sabina?" LeAnn mumbled.

"Sorry," Sabina, half-dressed, turned toward
LeAnn. "Tried not to wake you."

"Are you leaving?" Groggy, LeAnn sat up. She
pulled her tumbling curls away from her face and
wove them into a makeshift braid Her zinc-colored
eyes contrasted intensely with the purple-black of her
hair. "Are you upset about something?" She rose
from the sofa. Her breasts were small, soft curves.
Her waist flowed into full hips. Dark curls covered
her sex, although a provocative hint of pink flesh
dangled from the down-pointing tip of the silky
triangle. The pale-rose tint of her areolas matched
the color of her plush mouth.

"Why would I be upset?" Sabina tucked her shirt
in her jeans. "I had a headache and thought I'd head
home." *But the headache and dizziness had subsided,
hadn't they? There was no reason to go now, was
there?* She glanced at the clock. It was only eleven.

"Want some aspirin?" LeAnn stepped in closer.
The sweet scent of her pussy radiated from her like

intoxicating perfume. "I'll bet I could make that headache go away." Her seductive words flowed like hot, thick cream.

"Think so?" Sabina was beginning to melt. *There was nowhere she had to be, was there?*

"I know so," LeAnn cooed. She ran her hands across her breasts and her seed-like pink nipples bloomed into hard, red buds. "C'mon, honey. Let me help you forget that nasty headache."

"No, really —" Without thought, Sabina backed from LeAnn. "Really . . . Gotta go." She grabbed her jacket and headed out the door, not looking back.

Sabina started the car and backed out of LeAnn's driveway. As if she had smoked a joint, she felt giddy and high. Her intention had been to go straight home but once behind the wheel, she was struck by the unexpected desire to drive by Nora's house. She hadn't seen Nora, face to face, since the breakup and wasn't interested in making this the night for any semblance of a reunion. Yet she *did* feel a compulsion to turn left instead of right on Lombard and cross the Golden Gate Bridge.

The night was clear. Stars glittered promises from the velvety sky. Who wouldn't want to see the bay from across the bridge? People came from all over the world to revel in the beauty of this view. And while she was there, so close to the freeway exit, so near to the town where Nora lived — *what harm, really, would there be to merely drive by her house?*

Sabina turned left on Lombard. *Star light. Star bright.* Over the Golden Gate, she traveled. *First star I see tonight.* Past the view. To the exit. *I wish I may. I wish I might.* And on to the street where Nora lived.

When they first met, Nora had an unevenness, a curious edge, that had held Sabina's interest. Nora worked this energy like most women do exotic perfumes. She teased with its uniqueness, taunted with its seductiveness and enthralled with its intriguing allure.

It was after the first month that Nora began to change. Minor incidents escalated into reckless accusations. *You've been in my house while I was out, haven't you? Been in my drawers. Gone through my things. Read my journals.*

Why no, Sabina had first laughed, then insisted and finally had stormed back. Why would she steal through Nora's things? Did Nora have something to hide? Well did she? *Did she?*

Sabina turned off the headlights — it was best to remain undetected during a questionable enterprise. Slowly, she cruised past Nora's house. When she reached the end of the street, she doubled back. One dim light lit the porch, otherwise the house was dark. Sabina pulled onto the cross street and drove around the corner. As though she had performed this very act a hundred times before, she parked, tugged a dark knit cap over her blonde hair, and like a tomcat, zigzagged through backyards until she reached Nora's place.

The shade in the bedroom window was down, but no light illuminated the edges. Impulsively, Sabina tapped the window, then ducked. No sound from within, no light clicked on. Nothing. Was Nora not home? Sabina tapped again, this time with increased intensity — still no light.

Intrigued, Sabina crept to the side of the house, to the wooden step, to the hidden key. *What harm would there be in simply looking around?* She clicked on the small flashlight that hung from her key chain and unlocked the door. "Nora?" She stepped inside the kitchen. "Nora?" No answer.

Sabina snaked down the hall, the thin beam of light her only guide. The door to Nora's room was partially closed and creaked when Sabina pushed it open. "Nora?" she whispered. "Nora?"

How very much like Nora this room was — the deco vanity with its large circular mirror. The lace white curtains. A collection of beaded antique handbags and an array of colored perfume bottles. Everything seemed to glitter magically under the flashlight's direct beam. Sabina lifted a pearl earring from the bureau and rolled it between her fingers. There was something about touching Nora's things that elicited a sense of intimacy and completion.

She chose the purple perfume flask and dribbled it onto her wrist. *Nora. Nora. Nora.* She ran her finger across the mirror's smooth glass — had she left a smudge? The lingerie drawer slid right open. The lacy black panties fell into her hand. She stood there, not moving, relishing the feel of satin and lace. And the journal, as Sabina knew all too well, would be tucked under the pillow, along with the small velvet pouch that was filled with stones.

It is almost midnight when I pull into the drive. The sensation of exhilarated exhaustion still whirls around me. The old woman has taken care of things once and for all. In a tapestry pouch, embroidered with the same design as the woman's barrettes, are the charms. She told me not to open the pouch until absolutely necessary, but I do catch a glimpse as she dropped in the amulets. There are crystals and bits of ivory or bone — hard to be sure which. She sprinkled a palmful of tiny black and gold beads, then small twigs and finally some things that I couldn't discern. A heady scent of spice and pine emanates from the woven bag. I press the bag between my fingers. Nothing can stop me now.

It was the unknowing that made me so crazy — feeling Sabina in the walls, in the mirrors, having the eerie sensation that she would come into my house and go through my things. Finally, I'd pull her from the slippery cloak of illusion that she so cleverly hid behind and hold her accountable.

The darkened house awaits me and the light I will bring. I open the door, switch on the living room lamp. Not ready to sleep, but tired just the same, I decide to lie in bed, hold the pouch and wait for Sabina to tap.

I toss my coat on the couch — and it is then that I hear it. A noise somewhere. Quietly, I slink down the hall. How odd that the scent of my perfume hangs heavy in the air. Had she been here? Come to the window? Gone through my things?

I hold the pouch to my chest. *Come forth, Sabina* — the woman's magic words race through my mind. Will it work? Can I make her come out, at long last?

"Come forth, Sabina," I whisper.

I click on the bedroom light and a rush of iced chills surges through me. There Sabina stands, a flashlight and black panties in one hand and my journal in the other.

"Nora, I —"

"Why are you here!" I stammer. I'm startled to see her, even though, all along, I had felt her, suspected her. It's as if I'm astonished that my intuitions were so well-founded.

"This is the first time, I swear . . ." Sabina's eyes shift quickly. "In the past when you accused me of . . . well, after all, I simply would never actually break in or go through your things —"

I focus on the journal still clutched in her hand then back to her face. The energy around Sabina is both electric and wild. A reckless edge shimmers from her. Risk sparkles in her eyes. Surely, she missed me. Certainly, she cared.

She looks beautiful and dangerous, all at once. A knit cap is pulled low on her forehead and her clear blue eyes glimmer. I glance back to the journal. My words, my soul are held captive by her strong, capable hands.

"Have you missed me?" I step toward her. The fragrance from the pouch seems to radiate around me. *Come forth, Sabina.*

Sabina says nothing.

"Have you missed me?" I take another step — toward Sabina, toward the dream.

If only I could ensnare her before she fades. I'd make her remember, force her to remember — grab her wrist, not let go — until she remembered. *Sabina?* I'd say. *Sabina!* I'd insist. I'd stay there, grasp her and not back down. But she slips through my room with the slightest breeze, nudges me from dreams — whether day or night — only to evade me before I have a chance to convince her to stay.

Visions of how it could be swirl — on my knees

for her, face buried in the pillow for her. I'd spread my legs. I'd raise my ass.

Tease me, Sabina. Please me, Sabina. Release me. Unleash me. She'd strum me with her fingers. She'd drum me with her tongue.

Like this baby? And the dildo spear pushes deep. *Like this, baby?* And the dildo drags out. I'd jerk on it, squirm on it, roll on it, melt on it.

"Come forth, Sabina."

The Abbey

Barbara Johnson

Celia Rutherford approached the abandoned building with trepidation, despite the strong sunlight that splashed across its faded gray walls. What have I gotten myself into, she asked herself as she pushed the shiny new key into the old rusted lock. It took several tries before the key turned, and then she had to push against the resistant door. After several thrusts of her shoulder, the heavy wooden door finally inched open, its rusted hinges groaning in protest. She managed to squeeze her body through the small opening and was immediately assailed by the stench of animal droppings and stagnation.

She took a tentative step into the room and was entangled by a huge, old spiderweb. Frantically, she brushed away the fine threads across her face and neck. She staggered, momentarily blinded, into the room, her sneakered feet kicking up clouds of fifteen-year-old dust that swirled around her, settling onto her clothes and into her hair. She involuntarily opened her mouth to gulp in air and felt the fine particles of grit powdering her lips, tongue, and throat. She flapped her arms like a small bird, trying to dislodge the spiderweb before she opened her eyes. Coughing and choking on the thick dust, she lost her balance and fell over a broken chair, landing painfully on her knees and arms. The knapsack she carried slid across the floor, as if dragged by an invisible rope.

"Really graceful, Celia," she muttered as she rolled over into a sitting position, ruefully rubbing her throbbing elbows. A couple of splinters pricked her fingertips. Fortunately, her Wrangler jeans had prevented her knees from being scraped, but her Melissa Etheridge T-shirt had afforded no protection to her bare arms. She felt blood trickling down from a minor cut as she ran her fingers through her shoulder-length hair, which felt gritty and lank already.

With a sigh, Celia remained sitting and surveyed the room. She had bought the old building with the intention of turning it into a women's bookstore and cafe. The price had certainly been right, the building having remained empty these fifteen years. Now it was home only to crawling insects and rodents and the memories of times past.

Celia's eyes adjusted to the murky gloom. The two big front windows were mostly boarded up and covered with dirt, a couple of dilapidated tables under them silent sentinels of a time gone by. To her left, a soot-stained indentation was all that remained of a huge old fireplace. Directly in front of her line of vision was what appeared to be a dark pool, but she knew it was the opening to the stairs that descended to the basement. Any railing that might have protected the unwary had long since become termite fodder. To her right, a lumpy, threadbare couch perched at a ramshackle angle, tilted, as if someone had sawed off two of its legs. Her knapsack rested against the couch's flat right side, one shoulder strap caught on a protruding piece of wire.

As Celia scrambled to her feet, a strange, eerie sensation came over her. Goosebumps rose on her skin. She felt eyes watching her, and shuddered at leftover memories of her childhood fear of the dark. She glanced uneasily around the room. It was silent and still. Even the spiderwebs remained motionless.

"Don't be silly," she said aloud, and was startled by the sound of her own voice. There's nothing to be afraid of, she told herself, but decided to wait for the carpenter to arrive before continuing her exploration.

She walked quickly and boldly to the couch to retrieve her knapsack, which contained a flashlight and the blueprints of the building. As she reached for the knapsack, her foot broke through the rotted floorboards. She plunged screaming into the black abyss below.

* * * * *

Celia was acutely aware of a throbbing headache. An unexpected light blinded her. As she blinked her eyes open, she felt herself being helped to her feet.

"Are you all right?" a soft voice asked.

Celia found herself staring into the freckled face of a very feminine-looking redhead: her eyes were rimmed with black eyeliner, her lips glistened blood-red, and she wore a blue-and-white striped dress with a full skirt adorned with a black patent leather belt. Speechless, Celia could only look around her and register all the activity.

She stood near a large, wooden bar, its dark surface a polished mahogany. Music came from two speakers hanging high on the wall near the ceiling. She could hear the faint clinking of sounds of pool being played. The dim, smoke-filled room was crowded with women; several couples swayed lazily to the music of the Flamingos' "I Only Have Eyes for You." A harried waitress, carrying a tray laden with cola bottles and plates of food, appeared at the foot of the stairs and wound her way through the throng of laughing women.

Gaining her composure, Celia mumbled her thanks to the woman who had helped her up. The redhead gave her a strange look and then walked away toward the stairs, mumbling about women who couldn't hold their liquor. Celia stood still for a moment, wondering what had happened. Suddenly, the hairs on her neck prickled, and she felt someone's eyes watching her — the same feeling she'd had earlier. Cautiously winding her way between the tables, she glanced around the room. She pulled up short as she noticed the woman against the back wall.

A tall, dark-haired butch with broad shoulders, she leaned with her back against the wall, one khaki-clad leg bent so that her black-booted foot also rested against the wall. The sleeves of her white shirt were rolled up to her elbows to reveal muscular forearms, the starched collar closed tightly by a thin black tie. Her dark hair was slicked back but for a curl that dangled enticingly over her wide forehead. In one hand, she held a long-necked bottle of Pabst Blue Ribbon; in the other, a cigarette. Her full mouth curved in the hint of a smile, one corner tilting upward. Her shockingly brilliant blue eyes sparkled with invitation.

Slowly, like a cat stretching in the sun, the woman leaned away from the wall and approached Celia. She tossed her cigarette to the floor and crushed it with her boot. She deposited the beer bottle on a table. All sound faded from Celia's ears; she felt as if she and the woman were alone in the room.

"Would you like to dance?" the butch asked in a low smoke-husky voice as she held out one strong-looking hand. Her cologne reminded Celia of her father's aftershave.

Without a word, Celia melted into her arms. Their bodies fit together like pieces of a jigsaw puzzle. Celia rested her cheek against the shoulder of the tall woman, as if she'd always belonged there. The pungent odor of cigarette smoke mingled with the woman's cologne. One hand cupped Celia's buttocks;

the other grasped Celia's hand. As they swayed to the seductive music, the woman's leg thrust itself sensuously between Celia's legs.

"You didn't fool me one bit in those dungarees," the woman purred in her smoky voice. "I know a femme when I see one."

"Who are you?" Celia asked in wide-eyed confusion. Dungarees? Femme? These weren't terms she heard often.

The woman's throaty laugh sent warm shivers down Celia's spine. She felt helpless to resist, ensnared in a spiraling web of make-believe. Yet she knew that somehow, all of this was very real.

"I am your past and your future," the woman answered. "I've waited for you all my life."

The woman's grip on Celia tightened. She pulled Celia closer, molding their bodies into one. Their kiss was deep, intoxicating. The woman's probing tongue possessed her. She felt the heat spreading through her body, pulsing between her legs.

Celia splayed her hands across the woman's muscular shoulders. The fabric beneath her fingers was smooth and cool to the touch. She felt a whisper of air across her back as the woman untucked her T-shirt from her jeans. Then her calloused hands pressed against Celia's hot skin — possessive hands, insistent hands.

Celia's lips felt bruised by the kiss, but she couldn't pull away. She was being crushed, the air sucked from her lungs. Her heart beat against her ribcage. Her legs were on fire; she was burning and melting at the same time. Celia felt dizzy. Flashing colors swirled against her closed eyelids. She grasped the woman desperately, but felt herself falling into a deep void. She cried out, but heard only the woman's deep laughter booming in her ears. The dazzling colors gave way to jarring blackness.

Celia could hear her own moans, whether from pleasure or pain she could not immediately tell. She became aware of bone-crunching pain throughout her whole body. She took a deep breath and was wracked by a coughing spasm as thick dust invaded her nose and mouth. Hearing someone clattering down the stairs, she opened her eyes to darkness. Terror consumed her; her heart felt as if it would burst from her chest in one excruciating pulse.

"Oh my God! Are you all right?" a husky voice called out. "Can you move?"

The voice calmed her terror. Its cadence was somehow familiar, comforting. A flashlight beam shone directly in her eyes. She blinked and tentatively moved her arms and legs and turned her neck from side to side. More confident, she raised up onto her elbows.

"Let me help you," the voice said, and Celia felt strong arms encircle her shoulders and waist. "Careful now. I think I need to get you to a doctor."

Celia stood, feeling like a new-born foal on wobbly legs. "I'm okay, but I hurt all over. What happened?"

"You fell through the floor just as I came into the building," the woman said, pointing to the hole above them. Faint light streamed through the opening. She clicked off the flashlight.

Celia looked at her rescuer in the dim light and gasped. She moved out of her arms. The woman's brilliant blue eyes sparkled with concern. Her short dark hair was laced with dusty spiderwebs.

The familiar phrase tumbled from Celia's mouth. "Who are you?"

"I'm Randy Blake. You called me about doing some carpentry work."

Celia laughed nervously. "Yes, of course. For a moment, I mistook you for someone else. Let's go upstairs. We have much to discuss."

Randy stopped her and looked around, almost in awe. "Wow," she exclaimed, "this must be the Abbey. This place has quite a history, you know. I didn't recognize the address, but being here now brings it all back."

"The Abbey?" Celia inquired.

Randy nodded. "This was once a popular lesbian bar. A woman who called herself Randall established it after World War Two. Yeah, it was hidden down here in the basement. The place survived for nearly thirty years before the flashy new discos put it out of business."

It was then that Celia noticed they stood near a huge mahogany bar that jutted out from the wall. Its marred surface carried the scars of hundreds of cigarette burns, water rings, and deep scratches. Celia half-expected to see heart-enclosed initials carved into it as well. Several rusted barstools were still ranged in front, crowned by deep green vinyl, jagged with rips, the soft insides long ago disintegrated. Her falling body had just missed collision with one of them. Behind her was a stained wooden dance floor, the empty linoleum floor beside it still holding the faint outline of an object that could only have been a jukebox. To Celia's right was a pool table. On its faded, moth-eaten green velvet rested a pool cue and several balls, as if someone had left suddenly, intending to return and finish the game.

"I had no idea. That'll be great for publicity." Celia turned her attention to Randy. "What did you mean when you said being here brings it all back to you? You don't seem old enough to have patronized the Abbey."

Randy smiled, a sort of half-smile that turned up her mouth at one end. "Oh, I don't know. A figure of speech I suppose. Sometimes I feel I belong more to that time than my own. Come, let's go on up."

She put one muscular arm around Celia to help her up the stairs. Their bodies fit together like pieces of a jigsaw puzzle.

WHY YOUR FEET WILL ALWAYS FIND
WHAT'S LEFT OF THE MOUSE.

Apartment Seven B

Amanda Kyle Williams

I didn't know I was a stalker until I found them together. Then I couldn't stop. The extraordinary anger and passion, the anxiety, so powerful and so concentrated, the sting of betrayal every time I saw them — I was hooked.

It started when I pulled into the parking lot and saw the car. My lover's car. And the suspicion I'd wrestled with for weeks soared, burned into me, turned to rage, then fear. How long had they exchanged purposeful glances, flirted, teased, tried to impress, waited for time alone? How often had they found it?

I stepped out of the car and faced a row of town houses. Carol, my oldest and dearest friend, lived in Seven B, and I knew she wasn't alone tonight.

I let myself in — so quiet, so alert, rounding the corner and taking the stairs carefully, listening. There was something indistinct on the periphery of my hearing but I couldn't make it out. I felt the carpet crushing under my shoes, my jacket collar brushing against my neck, and I realized that I'd never been quite so calm, so sober, so lucid in my life.

I topped the stairs and saw them in Carol's bed, Natalie's small body on top of her, pressing, Carol's hands on Natalie's ass, rubbing, squeezing.

Walking towards the open bedroom door, my eyes never left them. I saw Natalie's tiny back, her red hair, the jeans in a pile on the floor, the unlaced boots next to them, and an odd sense of unreality grasped me. It was too fantastic, too bizarre — a movie, a script, someone else's story. Then I stepped into the bedroom and heard her voice, that smooth, sexy voice. The one she'd used in my ear, in my bed. All yours, she always said. Clearly we had very different ideas about what that meant, because tonight she was telling *Carol* how wet she was getting, that she touches herself and thinks about *her,* asking if Carol liked her pretty little pussy, telling her she'd waited so long, wanted her so much.

Time tends to distort when disaster strikes, but I think I stood there watching for a very long time. I wanted the calm to wash away so I could feel. I wanted to remember it always, though I have since questioned that judgment. Perhaps I watched too long, allowed it to mark my memory too distinctly. I could feel their urgency, their craving. I heard my own lover's breathing, heavy and staggered. *"Enough."*

Natalie's body stiffened, and Carol's strong hands moved to her back, patted her lightly. "Get up," she told her, and that pat, that tender, familiar, intimate pat carried with it the full magnitude of their disloyalty, and the force of it made me weak, makes me weak still.

I walked out that night, and when I reached my car I first noticed it — a blue-white blob on my shoulder. I stood frozen, horrified. *Fuck.* Did I actually stand in front of Carol's bed, defeated and outraged, with bird shit on my jacket?

I used a piece of tissue I found stuck to my shoe and cleaned it off.

"I've been so bad." It was Natalie's silky voice on my telephone. Natalie had many voices. I knew this one well, so steady, so compelling. "I need to be punished," she said, and I knew what she wanted. We had played this game before. She wanted me to strap it on, take her, force her.

She'd left the chain latched. A stiff boot, center door, popped it wide open and I stepped into the dark apartment. I didn't need light. I knew every inch of the place, knew where I was going.

The street light bled through the blinds and I saw her from the bedroom door, a small bundle barely visible under the covers.

She was crying softly. "I'm so sorry. Please, Daddy, don't hurt me." She sat up, and in one alluring moment swung her legs over the side of the bed and let the covers fall. She was so slight, so delicate, so wicked.

"I'll do anything you want," she whispered, and when I moved close to her, her expert hands traced the inside of my thighs, clutched at my crotch.

She whimpered slightly when she felt it. It was what she wanted, what she had asked for on the telephone. She'd take it out and put it in her mouth. She'd want me to hold her head and fuck her throat while I told her to suck on it, while I told her she deserved it, while I told her she was a whore. My whore. And she'd get so wet when I'd put her on her hands and knees and tease her pussy with the head, it would glide deep inside.

She wanted to be possessed, used, saturated. She wanted it hard. *Fuck me like a slut, like you don't care. Come all over me.*

And I did. I did. I took her without restraint, without consideration. I could deny her nothing. Not even then, barely two hours after I'd found them together.

But the game was finished as unexpectedly as it began, and the redhead was finished with me. "I want Carol," she told me simply.

I stood there that night silently, moronically it must have seemed to her, an enormous lifelike dildo hanging out of my jeans, sweaty, red-faced, utterly mortified.

Women always come to me this way it seems —
swiftly, stealthily. My romantic life till now had been
a succession of quick-strike operations, a catalog of
brave and heroic defeats in love. I'd been hammered
flat.

"What about us?" I managed finally, but I felt
like I'd swallowed a Kleenex.

Her cheeks were flushed. She was glowing, I
realized, absolutely fucking radiant. Natalie was at
her best when she was wreaking the most havoc. The
actor in her, the saboteur and subversive in her,
understood the power of drama and upheaval
instinctively. And she held on to it greedily,
flourished because of it, directed it with expert
efficiency.

"It's over," she said, and slipped into her panties
without remorse.

But I couldn't let her go. Not then, not ever. I'd
known that from the first moment I had seen her.
She was for me. Mine. I needed her, needed her
body, *required* it. I thought about Carol's hands on
her, Carol's fingers playing in her little pink pussy,
Carol's mouth on her. Carol my friend. Carol who
had taken her away with careless disregard. Carol
who could not yet begin to understand the
consequences of her actions.

I started calling. First Natalie, then Carol. So
desperate. Crying. Begging. "How can you do this to
me? How can you do this?"

But neither of them ever seemed to offer up a
satisfactory enough explanation, and soon they grew
tired of answering the telephone. That's when I
started watching.

From my car I could trace their movements inside — a lamp light here, a shadow there, the light from the television dancing across the blinds. I knew the floor plan, knew them, had watched their routines. It wasn't difficult.

I suppose it frightened me a little in the beginning — the desire to watch, to observe, that unyielding, almost essential need to see them. But on the first evening of my vigil, when a shadow passed the window and I felt a stab of adrenaline and exhilaration, I was engrossed, immersed suddenly in their private world. Watching was a way to hang on to them. Watching was control.

On the third evening, I saw Natalie's perfect body in silhouette against the living room window. She rose from the couch and pulled her sweater over her head. The long hair spilled over her bare shoulders. I saw her face in profile, her breast, watched her slow descent, and I knew what Carol must be seeing. I'd seen it a hundred times myself. I knew what Natalie looked like at that moment, her expression, her lips and her eyes, knew how she tasted, smelled. I felt a distinct moistening between my legs, an irresistible yearning to get closer, and the voyeur in me rose to the occasion daringly.

I left my car, and when I worked my way through the parking lot, when I crept silently around the shrubbery and gazed down through the crack in the blinds, the tension and fury that seized me when I saw them was unsurpassed — so strong, so bitter, yet so tantalizing.

I watched them kissing, saw their bodies tangled on the sofa, watched Carol's hands plunge into Natalie's jeans, watched the steady acceleration of their passion until a curious sense of power and of being utterly powerless seized me.

"But that's part of the hook, isn't it, Doctor? That discord, that unrest? It's part of the attraction, I think."

Dr. Childs looked at me thoughtfully. I was reclining on her couch, ankles crossed, smoking. "And you think that's what made you watch? That feeling of unrest?"

I nodded. "It's heady stuff, Doc. It's what drew me to that window night after night. To watch. To wait."

"What were you waiting for?"

"For Natalie to tire of Carol," I answered modestly.

It was true. Natalie always grew weary of lovers after the initial fascination had withered. And one night she would turn those soft blue eyes on that window and gaze out at me. She knew I was there, of course. It was why she liked to have Carol in the living room. In front of the big window.

It was all for Natalie from the beginning. I could deny her nothing. Not even my best friend.

We had played this game before.

The Reason Why

Hilary Mullins

Cathy is waiting for me at eight sharp, a figure in black behind the wheel. I step out from my building, brain vise-gripped with the headache I woke with earlier, sharp clanging behind my temples making me squint in the blank wash of winter light. Cathy pulls her car closer to the curb. "Hi," I say, climbing in. I can't look at her.

The inside of Cathy's car still smells new, the acrid plastic odor mixing with the steam of my coffee as I sip carefully through the hole in the lid of my cup. Cathy has her eyes on the road as she angles the car to the left, and I snatch a glimpse of her, all business as she cuts off the guy behind us. A take-charge kind of gal.

"How are you doing today?" she asks finally.

"I have a splitting headache."

"You want some aspirin? I have some in my bag."

"No thanks."

She aims a look at me that I don't meet. I know the face she wears for people in pain like me, the way her eyes go wet and soft at the same time her lips purse up. I know she means well, but I can't look anyway.

"So where is this funeral?" I ask, looking out as the car hurtles along Columbus Avenue, lights ahead of us turning green.

"I didn't tell you?"

"No."

"God, Jean, I should have told you yesterday. I would have except for that meeting and Victor breathing down my neck for the agenda — I couldn't stay on the phone."

"It's okay," I say, "I know what it's like for you there. But where are we going?"

Cathy turns left. "Long Island." She runs a hand through the stiffness of her perfectly permed hair.

"Long Island? The service is there?" I ask, incredulous.

"Sherry didn't tell you, did she?"

"Didn't tell me what?"

Cathy sighs. "She was going to church out there all the time."

"Sherry was going back to our old church?" The throbbing in my head picks up.

"Yeah, she took me once a couple of months ago. You wouldn't recognize the place. They've got this minister now who is fabulous. Everybody loves him, and the place is packed every Sunday. It's just great."

"But Sherry was going to church? Back there? She was going to church?"

"Well, she had that spiritual crisis —"

"What spiritual crisis?" I ask, feeling like we have strayed into territory I have no map for.

"Probably didn't want to upset the atheist in you, Jean." Cathy's voice sharpens momentarily, then goes husky. "Well, yes, she had that spiritual crisis, oh probably last winter she said it was, and then she started going back to church. She looked happier to me."

Cathy seems to be smelling the air, trying to sniff out my reaction. I shake my head, trying to re-orient myself. Sherry so long ago swore off the church and everything Christian that I can barely picture it. I try to imagine her taking communion, solemnly bringing a tiny glass of ruby liquid to her lips, chewing on the Host with her mouth closed and her head bowed, but my brain is like a TV that shudders into static. Back into focus comes the other Sherry I knew — or thought I knew — big-hipped pagan-artist woman, her thick red hair a tumble around her face, wide slope of her chest layered in necklaces of brightly colored baubles and small figurines. Quiet, as a young woman, she made up for it later. Sherry could fill a room with just her robust, booming being, and she often did. At parties you could feel it — the way a circle of people would draw in around her, her expansive gestures, her lively tongue and broad laugh projecting a light you could see quickening in the faces pointed toward the center she made. People loved her, and the fact that she was famous as "the wild flower painter" didn't hurt. And she thrived on all the attention, taking it in until she virtually radiated abundance, bursting like those stars in the firmament that throw off vast sparking sprays of light.

Never mind that she was neurotic, that she drank too much. Never mind that every man she loved treated her with smooth disdain. Suave and fatuous, they were always gunning after a bit of her limelight. And after they dumped her — and they always finally did — the other side of Sherry would come out, the side not too many people knew about, but that I knew well: those black holes where she collapsed in on herself.

Perhaps that is the wild card here, I think, remembering the two-week funk she fell into last winter, the worst one of its kind I had ever seen. When I saw that she was barely eating or sleeping, just sitting by her window for hours staring out, I started coming by every night to check on her. I suggested treatment, the new anti-depressants. I even tried contacting her family, but they never returned my calls. By the middle of the second week, I was getting very worried. And I did sense that somewhere underneath her wooden and muted heaviness, some part of Sherry was worried too. But once she had popped out of it with her usual cure — a new

obsessive relationship — she acted like it had just
been a bad case of the flu. This is the thing I need
to ask Cathy about, I think.

"What about that new boyfriend last spring?" I
ask her.

"What?" Cathy's head spins back toward me.

"I thought Sherry was happier because of that
new guy she started seeing last spring."

"What new guy?"

"Some businessman. That must be something she
didn't tell you. She told me she'd finally found The
One."

Cathy looks over at me as I deliver this
information, eyebrows going up. "That's weird. She
told me she was being celibate, that it was her way
of reconnecting with God."

"Celibate? Sherry?" I want to snort, but bend to
sip more coffee.

"That's what she told me. But what did she tell
you?"

"She didn't tell me anything until I ran into the
two of them in this cafe in Soho."

"So you met him?" Cathy asks. I nod. "Well, what
was his name? What did he look like? Do you think
he'll be there today?"

"God only knows," I say, popping the lid from my
cup.

"Well, maybe he would know something we
don't," Cathy says emphatically.

"Who? God?"

"No! That businessman! Maybe he knows more
than we do about what was really going on with
Sherry."

"I'm not sure I'd recognize him if I saw him.

Besides, I don't think I'd want to talk to him — he was too smooth for me. Greasy-smooth."

"You've said that about all of Sherry's boyfriends," says Cathy, her grip on the wheel tightening although there are no cars near us. "I'm sure he's hurting now too, just like the rest of us."

The edge begins to rise in me. "Don't try telling me he could be feeling half as bad as I feel right now, Cathy. Don't even try telling me that."

"Okay, okay. But look, if you see him, point him out to me, all right? And I'll talk to him myself. Will you at least do that?"

"All right. I'll point him out. But that's it."

"That'll be enough," Cathy says, letting out a heavy rush of air, her shoulders sagging.

I turn and try to look out my window, but it is no use; I've let the floodgate open and the images of Sherry that have been swamping me for the last day and a half surge up once more. I give myself over.

Sherry in 1968 at age sixteen, the quiet girl in long, pleated skirts I had never before noticed in the halls at school, the intense girl who came by to watch me play lacrosse on a hot September afternoon. I remember first noticing that she was watching only me as I ran, twirling my stick with the ball held loosely in its folds. And then I remember hurtling the ball forward, and how, with the arc of my arms through the air, I felt it, the way this girl on the sidelines was watching me with the keen eyes of a lover. I felt it in my arms, in my chest, her rapt attention.

I was already half on to myself by that fall junior

year, but right then, that afternoon, the other half
crashed into place, and I knew instantly the shape
my life would take. Suddenly I understood that my
long-simmering hunger was for the contours of
Sherry's hips, her belly, that what I wanted more
than anything in the world was to kiss her, to brush
my lips against hers, lose my tongue in her mouth.

So. I discovered myself. But along the way that
year I discovered Sherry as well, the joy she took in
the smallest things, the shiny stream-bed stones I left
in her locker, the last wildflowers of the season I
picked for her, delicate and streaked with color. I
remember hanging out with her for hours in the art
studio while she painted them, standing intent at the
easel, her thick red hair piled up under a
handkerchief as out from under her brush they
emerged, ethereal, their vibrant hues quivering.

"You know what?" I ask abruptly. Cathy, who has
clearly been in the midst of her own thoughts, turns
toward me. "She got that wildflower idea from me."
After all these years of never telling anyone, the
words come so casual now in this car with its plush
seats.

"Oh? So she gave you a cut I suppose?"

"What would I want a cut for?"

"Well, if I made a few million dollars on an idea
someone gave me, I'd think about sharing at least a
modest percentage."

"No. She deserved that money. Besides, it wasn't
that direct, me giving her the idea. It was more like
an echo. I mean, I was just the one who got her into
wildflowers in the first place."

"There's probably going to be some reporter there today who would love to hear that story."

"You think the press is going to be there?"

"I'm sure there will be at least a few. It's not every day a famous pop-artist kills herself."

I shake my head, thinking of the stories I could tell those reporters, of the times I sat with Sherry in the very same church we are heading for today, the two of us climbing the stairs to the choir loft, leaving her mother standing stiffly in the vestibule.

I eye Cathy, but she has turned away again, perhaps thinking about stories she could share herself. I close my eyes, thinking about Sundays with Sherry, how I looked forward to them all week, how my anticipation would mount as Sherry and I settled in our seats, safe from Mrs. Carlton's reproving eyes and thin-lipped, tight smile. We'd sit thigh to thigh, ignoring the ponderous, somnolent tones of the sermon, rolling our church bulletins into tubes, peering through them like spyglasses, scanning the hypocritical faithful from on high.

Finally, Sherry would point out one unwitting victim and launch into a long outrageous story of his sins of fornication, rambling and whispered fabrications that would set me giggling every time, earning us disapproving frowns from the frumpy matron who played the huge old organ. Sherry would smile demurely at her, approximating chagrin, but as soon as the old woman had turned away, I would feel the soft touch of my friend's lips at my ear again. As the year continued, fall into winter, winter into a sweet Long Island spring, her stories became more and more explicit, and my church attendance grew more and more regular.

Finally one Sunday she actually told me a story about the organ player and the choir director — another older woman, both single all their lives. "It's their way of getting closer to God," Sherry assured me, pressing her shoulder into mine. I couldn't look, the pulse between my legs pounding soft against the pew. I shifted, rearranging my weight, hoping I too would have a chance soon to get close to God.

I glance over at Cathy, but she is still gone in her own musings. I have an impulse then to fall into her lap, to burrow under the strap of her seat belt and cry there on the firm planes of her thighs. I turn away, back to the window. Cars are flashing by us on either side. I want to be another life in another car, zipping towards a sales meeting perhaps, or conducting a conference call on a cellular phone. I want to be anywhere but in this car, the next memory burning down toward me. I gulp down the last of my coffee, let my head fall back against the seat.

I can almost smell that night, my excitement. I was seventeen and the girl I loved like nobody's business was inviting me to her house for a sleep-over — something she had always refused to do before, citing vague excuses.

I remember how giddy we both were that evening as we boiled hot dogs and baked brownies, how Sherry kept finding ways to touch me, tugging at my arm at the stove. After dinner, we started in on a marathon Scrabble game, and before we were even halfway through, we heard her parents' car pulling up outside. In they came, her father weaving slightly, her mother ramrod-stiff as ever.

"You girls playing a game?" her dad asked, leaning over Sherry.

"Butt out Dad," Sherry said.

"Don't stay up late girls. You've got church in the morning." Sherry's mother's words were crisp as she hung her coat up on the rack in the hallway. I looked over at her, noticing the rough-hewn cross above her head — one of the many crosses throughout the house. I looked back at the table. Sherry's dad had leaned down closer over her and was moving her letter tiles around with one blunt finger, a strange chuckle coming from low in his throat.

"Dad!" Sherry pushed his hand, spilling little squares of wood across the table. He laughed, running a hand across her cheek, and for an instant I saw in her eyes a look that was one part fear, one part something else I could not recognize. He just laughed again and reeled off. I stared. Sherry would not look at me, just gathered up her tiles and neatly rearranged them in front of her.

I didn't dare say anything, and I didn't dare say anything later either when she got out the pitcher of orange juice and a bottle of vodka from her father's stash. She poured us up two brimming glasses and solemnly toasted me over the Scrabble board. We gulped, our moods growing giddy again. I couldn't think about it too hard, but I knew we were gearing up. I could feel it in her, a certain sharpening under the giggling, a certain purposefulness gathering. All spring I had been scheming on ways to seduce her, but that night I realized I wasn't going to have to do all the work myself.

And indeed, once we had climbed into our respective beds — me on the rollaway, Sherry in her frilly-topped twin — she was the one who started in, teasing me, talking about how cold she was in her bed alone, saying she needed me to warm her up.

"Warm you up?" My voice cracked.

"Warm me up real good," she said, "c'mon!"

"Yeah?" It was all I could get out, the churning in my crotch starting to streak through my whole body.

"Red Rover, Red Rover, send Jeanie right over!" A nervous giggle.

"Well, if Red Rover sends me, I guess I'm coming."

Her white T-shirt a dull glow in the dark, I crawled awkwardly over the gap between bed and cot and dove under the blankets. As I snuggled down, I realized with a sharp pang in my groin that the T-shirt was the only clothing she had on. And here I was, covered up in an old pair of boys' pajamas. I fumbled with the blankets, unsure of everything but the way I wanted to cover her body with mine, feel the wet of her mouth, taste her tongue. We lay there together for a couple of minutes, her breathing low, mine coming in big washes of air — when I remembered to breathe at all.

Then she giggled again. "Let's play Simon Says, okay?" I nodded. "Ready?" I bobbed my head, not trusting myself to speak. "Okay. Simon says Jean touch Sherry." A burst of feeling through me, all colors, like a great striking up of organ music, and I turned, tentatively stroked her arm with one finger, feathering up under the sleeve of her T-shirt, her skin so soft it was a revelation.

She turned toward me, wordless now, her eyes going deeper as I continued my halting exploration up into the hollow of her neck, across her cheek, along her lower lip and down her face, then along her other arm. I remember how I tried to touch her as lightly as I could, but my body was trembling so, what with the way I was propping my weight up on one elbow and swooning into the ocean of it all, her skin, the liquid wash of her eyes, the tightening and opening feeling in my cunt.

Sherry lay there beneath me, curiously motionless. I drew my hands down the curve of her hip, my brain exploding with the words, *I love you, I love you.* But I was too scared to say them out loud, too scared to look at her for more than a quick glance. Instead, I tried to let that swell of feeling pour out my fingers all over her.

I think I could have done just that and nothing more the whole night long, savored the textures of her flesh, the feeling of her hair like water in my hands. But when she turned her face directly toward mine with a look like wonder unfastening everything there, I thought she meant me to kiss her. And so yes, I moved on her, bent my face down. And it was just the way all my fantasies had been, that slow motion toward her. I brought my lips soft to hers and —

— She pulled back and the world stopped.

"I really need a cigarette," she said. She pulled out from under me and sat straight up, bedclothes falling from her. All my insides went frozen except for the burning in my crotch.

"Sher?" I didn't dare move. She was reaching for her ever-present cigarette pack, her body twisted away from me. She didn't answer.

"What did I do wrong?"

"Hey nothing, it's just a nicotine attack, okay?" She braced her back against the bed board, hair draping down the arms I'd just been caressing. I stared at her. She wouldn't look back. I rolled against the wall and watched her shaking fingers clench the cigarette, the sudden small flare of the match, the burnished point smoldering at the cigarette's end casting a vague glow over her mouth, the bottom of her nose with its fine-chiseled tip. How beautiful she was to me, and how far away. Gone for good. After a few minutes watching her blow smoke rings, I crawled back into the rollaway.

I shift, uncomfortable, in the seat next to Cathy. This is not the thing to be thinking about in a car with a woman who has never quite understood how two girls could kiss each other and like it. The windows have fogged, and I turn to scrunch my index finger through the moist cloudiness, leaving a murky trail. I round my shoulders to keep Cathy's opinions away, and go back inside to the place where Sherry still lives in me, alongside my love, my regret and sorrow.

I was right that night about Sherry — she wouldn't see me anymore, wouldn't return my calls.

Desperate, I tried waylaying her one morning after church, but she walked by like I wasn't even there. I remember standing on the sidewalk staring, invisible and devastated. Then came Senior year. The rest of the country spasming with war, music and revolution, I turned inward like a wounded animal, licking myself often and looking for corners. Sherry had arrived at school that fall transformed from bobby sock-artist girl to out-there hippie. Now I was the one who went unnoticed in the halls. Or so she tried to make it seem, from within the smokey swirl of her new clique of hippie kids. She went to protests in New York, smoked a lot of pot and fucked a lot of boys. That next summer she went to Woodstock. Me, I stayed home with my bitter handful of consolations: sports awards, good grades, and my acceptance to Barnard for the next fall. At least there in New York I was gradually able to find my way out of the closet.

In any case, Sherry and I finally ran into each other at a party in the Village in the mid-seventies. By that time, she was back to painting, but that was before she hit it big. After a bit of wrangling, we reconciled and fell into seeing each other every once a month or so, over drinks in the early years, and then later over dinner, usually at her place or mine, at which point I would no longer drink with her. We made for odd but loyal friends. Still, we never talked about high school, never really talked about that night in her bed. There were times I considered bringing up, but I knew she would consider it presumptuous of me. And I suppose I did not want to hear her say it had meant nothing to her, that it was just another night's dark groping, kinkier perhaps than her norm, but nothing more nonetheless.

"Everybody has a story, you know," says Cathy out of nowhere. I blink, rub my eyes. My headache is getting still worse. I squint and look at her.

"What?" I say.

"All these people who never knew her, even they have their pet theories about why Sherry did it. I overheard three people in my office in the lunchroom yesterday talking about her, saying what a shame it was that Sherry's alcoholism killed her."

"Maybe it *was* Sherry's alcoholism that killed her." I say this quietly.

"Oh no, it wasn't that bad yet, Jean. Alcohol killed my father, I know the difference. Just because it was an alcohol and drug overdose doesn't mean alcoholism killed her. Of course she drank a lot, everyone knows that. I think there were other factors, things happening we don't know about."

"But Sherry had those terrible depressions —"

"She wasn't that depressed! I keep thinking there must have been something about money —"

"Or her latest boyfriend was beating her," I suggest grimly.

"Do all lesbians think about men the way you do Jean?"

"Oh for Christ's sake Cathy!"

Cathy doesn't reply. We sit in awkward silence, and I close my eyes trying to block it all out — the pulsing in my head, the singular ache of loss and guilt. The thing that Cathy is not saying is that behind our speculation, each of us feels it is really our fault. If only we'd tried harder, had figured out the things she needed, known how to give them to her. With both of us knowing Sherry from high school — we should have been able to tell it was coming to this. We should have been able to save her.

"But don't you think there's got to be a reason why?" Cathy tries again, looking for common ground.

"I don't know if it's that simple," I say. "There could be a number of reasons — not just one."

"She seemed so much happier! Something terrible must have happened. Something she couldn't even tell us about."

Cathy shakes her head, and for an instant it's the girl in her I see, the young stubborn girl, the one who always had the answers, the one who always had her way. Ever since I've know her, it's never been any use talking with Cathy when she has her mind made up.

"I don't know, Cathy. I don't know if Sherry could tell us herself. But you know what, I've got to close my eyes for a while before we get there. This headache is killing me."

I fumble for the seat release down on my right, and the seat back jerks down. Cathy starts but doesn't say anything. I put a hand over my eyes and up wavers the image of Sherry sitting hollow-eyed at her window. Cathy doesn't really know about the depressions, I think as I turn my body away from her toward the door, but maybe she has a point. After all, don't they say that depression isn't just a chemical thing? That underlying causes also contribute? I'm no dope. I read history, I read

mysteries. I know there are always reasons for the
things that happen, always people responsible.

I lie motionless, suddenly struck with how much
despair Sherry must have felt, and then I feel myself
falling down into it, her pain, the unbearable infinite
anguish of it. I squeeze my eyes shut, take a deep
breath, try to bring myself to surface, but the weight
is dragging me down into the twisting heart of it, the
pulse in my head rapping louder as it tugs me
deeper, and it's like Sherry herself is tugging me on
my arm, and as I squirm against the soft synthetic
seat cover, I see her, and it's like she's under me
again, I'm lying on top of her, the two of us back on
her old bed back at her parents' house, and I think,
okay, I'm dreaming here. I look, seeing that Sherry's
seventeen again, stretching out below me, putting a
finger to her hair. Surely there are worse dreams
than this, I think, and then I am gone into it —
Sherry nodding at me while I trace the contours of
her face with the tip of one finger, the old wish to
kiss her growing in me. She is watching me, her eyes
following my finger then moving to my face, and I
see there in the way she squeezes her eyes shut
when I brush her lips how much she wants me to
kiss her. I lean down, happier than I have ever felt
in my whole life, but just as my lips graze hers, her
whole body seems to shudder, her eyes flying wide
with fear, like she's seeing something that wants to
eat her alive, and I twist around, but there's no one,
just a huge shadow on the wall behind us, long and
wide and looming, and the whole room seems to shift
and blur, and then rather than Sherry under me, I'm
lying on the floor, over against the wall, where the
shadow was. I look around, wild, and there she is,

kneeling in a nightgown beside the bed, looking even younger and muttering something I can't quite hear. I listen as her voice gets louder, but all I can make out is that it's some phrase, the same one she's repeating over and over in her earnest girl's voice. I call her name, but she doesn't answer, her voice getting louder and then louder, and I still can't make it out, but now it's as big as the whole room it's so loud, her voice, and the walls stretch to hold it, quaking out wider, and abruptly I see it's the church we're in, this expanded chalky-grey space, and way up front, Sherry is in the pulpit, still in her nightgown, still chanting, but now her face is older again, lines and features as sharp as her tone. She's shaking her arms up toward heaven, her voice rising and rising until it is the screech of a storm, and she looks right at me where I sit in the back, and I lean forward into the eye of the storm her screaming makes, the words so vast I am just a small ant slipping down their sides, unable to make out the whole, the cracking thunderousness a booming in my ears that bolts me upright in the seat, and I'm in the car careening along the highway and I'm babbling at Cathy, "Did you hear that? Did you hear what she said? Did you hear it?"

"Jean!" Cathy reaches over and grabs my shoulder. "What happened? Were you dreaming?"

I look around for Sherry, but she's not there. "You didn't hear her? She's not here?" I ask Cathy, frantic.

Cathy slows the car. "My God, are you all right? You must have fallen asleep. Here, lie back down. Take some deep breaths."

I do lie back down, my chest sinking. Gone, gone

again, Sherry's really gone. I cover my face with my
hands, wishing I could cry, wishing the hammering in
my head would finally cease. Cathy reaches over and
takes my hand for the rest of the way.

My headache still a baritone boom, I walk into
the church behind Cathy, eyes on the dark fabric
stretching across her back as I follow her to a pew in
the rear. We settle in, awkward, and I reach for a
hymnal, avoiding the glances of people around us. I
don't want to look up, knowing that if I do, I will
have to look at the casket up front that contains the
body of Sherry Carlton, the gleaming solid fact of it
more than I can bear. I leaf mindlessly through the
hefty book, and a gilded piece of paper falls out of it
onto my lap. It's the church bulletin. I pick it up
and turn it over, scanning the community notices — a
blurb about the church's annual rummage sale,
another about a meeting of the youth group the
minister's wife runs, and then two whole paragraphs
about the women's Bible study group, written by an
enthusiastic participant who waxes on about the
stimulating opinions of their minister who instructs
them.

The organ music strikes up. I turn the bulletin
over in my hands. Can I get through this whole
service without looking up once? I bend over as the
minister speaks some brief opening I don't listen to, I
am remembering sitting in the choir pews giggling
with Sherry. I cut a look toward Cathy, see her
dabbing at her eyes with a tissue as the organ music
swells up again, accompanied by a woman's alto voice

soaring out over us. My mind's eye flashes on a view
from the choir loft: Sherry and I watching summer-
time wasps floating over the heads of the congregation of old people, the long insect abdomens dangling
inches over shiny bald heads and ladies' gauzy hats.
Without thinking, I roll the paper in my hands up
into a cylinder and peer through it, first at the floor,
and then I make a quick sweep of the mourners,
catching snatches of jackets, hair, the glint of glasses.

I bow my head again, my headache rising with
the organ's crescendo, and then I feel it, the wispy
brush of lips against my ear, and it's as if she's
leaning into me again with the best story yet. I find
myself leaning sideways as if to hear better, and I
can't help it, a giggle chokes up from my gut, and I
bend down into my hands as if to stifle it, but it
struggles up and half gets out, a kind of gasp that
Cathy seems to interpret as a sob, because she crams
a ratty tissue into my hand. I start dabbing at my
eyes, but only for cover, afraid I'm losing my mind
as I press against my closed lids with the tissued tip
of my finger, watching the spurts of light that leap
up, funny sprays swirling across my vision. But then
what I see, all in a blow, is Sherry's lifeless body
sprawled in twisted sheets, her mouth gaped open
like an empty O, and this time, it's a real moan that
quakes out of me, and my eyes fly open, and I look
up and forward, my heart thudding as hard as the
ache in my head.

I look, I look, I look everywhere but at the
casket, and maybe a dozen pews forward, I recognize
Sherry's mother and father. Fighting for breath, I
look hard at their backs. They both are leaning
forward, and I try to focus on them, desperate for

the pounding in my head to leap whole out. I note numbly that Sherry's mother's hair has gone white but that she still has the same stiff thin neck. Her father, too, looks so much older, nearly bald, the fleshy roundness of his head a slight bobbing directly beneath the pulpit where the minister has just stepped forward.

"Friends, family —" He stretches his hands out to the mourners, "we are gathered here today to commemorate the brief but brilliant life of Sherry Carlton. I did not have the pleasure of knowing Sherry except for the last months of her life, but I stand before you today as a witness to her love for God and her devotion to his Living Word." He lilts smoothly on, listing the qualities of some demure woman I'm sure I've never met while my headache gets even worse yet: I have to squint as it clangs like a steam heater, and I lurch my head back down into my hands, the sharp echo in me growing edges now, sides, sounds, vowels and then the words themselves, great rocks heaving at the walls in my head, trying to get out. It's her. She's in there, throwing herself against the door, Sherry screaming the words. No, no, I can't, Sherry! Can't say those words. Not here! Not now!

I look up again, a whimper leaking out through my lips. I look, and there is the minister, arms outstretched towards us once more, his face wide and shining, saying something I can't hear for the shrieking in my head, and I look again, look at the square-faced man with his white collar, noticing, in spite of it all, something familiar about him, his long sideburns and brush of a beard conjuring up a vague memory of someone I know I've met.

I squint against the beating of sound in me as his features come into focus, and then I see his face, not over the ornate pulpit, but over a cafe table in Soho, the same swollen cheeks and jutting nose, the hand — now resting possessively on the Bible — last summer a splayed claw on the thigh of the red-haired woman sitting next to him. The words are a cataclysm now, a battering against my skull and I swear it is she who jerks me to my feet, frees my mouth, lets loose the words in a loud, raging torrent that runs roughshod over the minister's polished, greasy tones.

"You! You Father, you did it! The Father did it!" I see a shock wave rippling through the amassed backs in front of me, and then heads twisting around to see, eyes wide in pale faces. The words are not my own; they come pouring out again. "The Father did it! The Father did it!" Angry rumblings start up, hands wave me down. Cathy is staring up at me as if she has never seen me before in her life. I falter.

The minister's smooth tones rise up. "Sister, we know you are broken-hearted, we know how maddening grief can be. Would someone please comfort our sister?"

Cathy reaches up a firm hand to draw me back down in the pew. I look at her. "It's him, Godammit!" I hiss, shaking her hand off. Her brow knits together. "You told me to point the boyfriend out and there he is!" She looks up at me, astonished. I don't know what to say next, so I sweep my arm around, taking in the whole of the place, the angry and bewildered faces. I open my mouth. Out come the words. "This man is an adulterer and a liar! He had an affair with Sherry, and now he comes to bury

her, mouthing pieties! Do you hear me? He didn't
help Sherry find God! He's an adulterer and he used
her!"

"Someone please restrain this woman!" The
Father's face has gone harsh. "Let's show some
respect for the dead!" Men's thick-suited arms reach
for me, pulling me bodily toward the aisle.

"Liar!" I shout. "Adulterer!" The arms yank me
sharp into the side of the pew, and I double over, my
words falling to the floor. They are as thick as tree
trunks, these arms wrapping around my ribs and
dragging me. Angry voices clatter all around like a
swarm of pelted rocks.

"Let her go!" A clear tone, like a chime, like a
single church bell cleaving the air for miles on a
winter night. "She's telling the truth! Father Morris
is an adulterer!"

The arms release me, and I stumble to the floor,
still hanging to the timbre of this woman's voice,
scrambling back up as fast as I can to see a petite
woman in dark blue standing reed-straight in the
second row. "Father Morris had me too. Two years
ago, for a year. It ruined my marriage."

"Please remove these hysterical women!" Morris's
voice has gone hoarse. "This is a memorial service!"

People's heads are going back and forth. I grab
the pew to hold myself up.

"He had sex with me too!" A chesty woman in
the third row is pulling up against the clasp of a
man's hold around her elbow. "He told me I was the
only one, but I knew he was sleeping with Sherry!"
She wrenches herself free of the man's grip and
stands straight. "I confronted her! Three days later
she killed herself!"

The whole hall succumbs to uproar. Someone yells, "Get him out of here!" Morris's eyes are veering back and forth across his congregation, panic breaking out across his face. Suddenly he grabs the Bible and runs out, his feet thudding like stones across the floor, the door banging shut behind him. And then everyone is up and out of their seats, thronging in clumps in the aisles.

I totter, hanging on as people bump by me, but when I look back up to the front of the church, that's when I see her, standing up in the pulpit, it's Sherry, just like in my dream, but this time she is pointing out into the dense milling of mourners. I stare at her, blink. She points more emphatically, and I follow the line of her finger to the fleshy head of her father, sitting turned around in his seat, looking back at where Morris has disappeared.

I move slowly toward him, new bruises in my side tweaking as I go, and then I am standing there in front of him. He doesn't notice me at first, but then he looks up, his face blank of recognition.

"I'm Jean," I say. "Remember me?" He looks confused. "I just came to tell you that I know what you did to Sherry too. And I know what it did to her, you bastard." The confusion cracks off his face like plaster off a mask. He starts back, his bony old shoulder shoving into his wife's side.

"What's wrong, Wayne? Who is this girl?" Mrs. Carlton's voice wavers from behind him, but Mr. Carlton doesn't answer; he rushes to his feet and sweeps by me down the aisle, pushing his way out through the door Morris used.

I don't have anything to say to Sherry's mother. I turn and walk back toward my place, collapsing there on the cushioned seat. Cathy wraps a strong arm around my shoulder and draws me into the wide warmth of her side as the heaving sobs start, shaking me, a great wash of wet gushing from my eyes.

"We were both right!" she whispers into my ear, hugging me tighter. I nod my head yes, looking up through the blur of my tears to Sherry, and for one last time I see her, over the solid casket heaped with flowers, it's my bigger-than-life friend, red-haired and robust, nodding down at me for a job well done.

In the Dark

Elisabeth Nonas

I'm dreaming about a beach I've never been to.
In the dream, I'm lying on the deserted sand when
in the illogic of dreams someone is stroking my body,
touching me all over. Then reality intrudes and I
realize someone really is touching me all over.

I have my back to Lisa, but she has moved her
hands from my breasts down to my thighs, now
between my legs. She started slowly, persistent, until
she worked her hands into my dream and lifted me
out into the morning, off the beach and into our

bedroom, grey still because it's early, before seven, only the slightest hint of pink to the light.

I close my eyes again but she has to know I'm awake because I'm responding to her touches with my own. She tongues my ear and her fingers enter me and I surprise myself by coming hard, finding her at the same time. We come together, she moaning my name over and over, SarahSarahSarahSarah, and me calling out my love.

I'm in a stupor, but Lisa gets out of bed and right into the shower. She's the one with a structured job, regular hours and an office.

I'm still half-awake when she, dressed and ready for work, comes back to kiss me. "What time are we meeting?"

"Around two-fifteen."

"Don't be late."

I mumble something as she leaves. I'm notorious for being late. In the three years we've been together Lisa has learned to compensate.

We're going to meet at a dog park in the San Fernando Valley. I've got an assignment for a fluff piece that my editor wants to call "A Dog's Life." L.A. is now sprinkled with these neighborhood parks not just for kids to play in but for dog owners to bring their pets and let them run free — leash laws don't apply.

I prefer more serious work than this article, but a job's a job, and this won't be too strenuous. That's why I suggested Lisa rearrange her schedule to take the afternoon off so we can have a date. We're both so busy we have to make time these days to be together.

I do editorial photography mostly, for magazines

and newspapers. I'm not above a wedding or commitment ceremony, especially for friends. I've had a few shows. Straight photojournalism, nothing arty. I pride myself on capturing what's there. The camera never lies. It will pick up details we can't see, don't have time to notice. You can always go back to a photograph for memory, or truth.

I grumble to myself about this assignment all the way to the park. But it's a beautiful spring day and to have to be in a place like this on a day like this isn't a bad job.

I pull into the lot next to Lisa's red Miata. She's nowhere in sight. The park is nearly deserted because it's a school day and a little too early for the dog owners. But that'll give me a chance to get the lay of the land before I have to shoot.

The park is spoon-shaped, the bowl opening from the parking lot. A fenced-in play area with sandbox and jungle gym huddle at this end, and the rest of the area is a vast lawn. The grass alone must cover eight acres. Trailheads lead up into the hills. You can follow some of them to the coast.

I'm distracted by the trees bordering the expanse of lawn. I count twelve different shades of green. The pines are heavy with candles and little brown clusters that look like Rice Krispies.

When I turn back to the park I see Lisa about two hundred feet away from me, coming from one of the trails.

You know how you never get tired of some things? I'm talking things, possessions — a fountain pen, a watch, maybe a vase, a bracelet, even a photograph — something you really love and no matter how often you see it or use it, it never gets old for you, is always beautiful. People rarely affect me the same way. They're too changeable, mutable: good hair days, bad hair days, cranky days, blah days, a flattering color, a color that doesn't quite suit one's complexion. But Lisa takes my breath away. Always. Not just on days like today, after our coupling this morning. Every day for the past three years.

I was a long time coming to this place of unending appreciation. Not that I didn't always find her attractive, but the permanence of my affections, my willingness to commit to her for life took time, required that I learn to trust. I'd never been capable of fidelity before. Always wanted what I didn't have. I couldn't imagine not acting on my attractions. I got drunk on sheer love of women, their variety and beauty.

So what changed? Maybe at thirty-one I decided to settle down. I wanted to get past that initial thrill and into the routine of a real relationship. I wanted my life to have some of the depth I see in my photographs.

Or maybe I just fell in love with Lisa.

I watch her now. She seems as interested in the trees bordering the park as I was. Almost seems to be waving goodbye to them. I used to tease her about her rituals, little ceremonies she incorporated into our daily life, but now I find I maintain them even when she's out of town.

I turn my lens on her, start shooting as I approach. I call to her and she wheels around.

"Sarah, when did you get here?"

"Am I late?"

Lisa checks her watch. "You're right on time."

"Your good influence finally rubbing off on me." I take a few shots.

"Cut it out."

She tries to wave me away but I shoot off the rest of the roll, moving around her, hamming it up like a fashion photographer. "Beautiful, baby," I say in a phony Euro-trash accent, "just like that, a little more pout, good, we're done."

As the film rewinds our lips meet in a chaste kiss, for public consumption only, none of the passion of the morning.

I look around. No dogs yet. I point to the trail Lisa descended. "Anything interesting up there?"

"What?"

"Any of those trails worth exploring?"

"How would I know?"

"You were just on one."

"I didn't get very far."

"Come on." I take her hand and start walking.

She drags against me. "Do you really want to lug all your equipment?"

"I'm used to it."

We start up the trail, a dirt path that winds above the park. After only a hundred feet I spot a little clearing to the left. I head off the trail.

"Sarah, I don't think we should."

But I'm already in this natural alcove, leafy branches above and pine needles under foot. "Hey, a perfect little love nest." I put down my bag. "Come here."

"What about poison oak or something?"

"Come on." I bring Lisa in with me. I kiss her on the lips.

Somewhere outside our bower a twig snaps. Lisa jerks around. "What was that?"

"Just a squirrel or something. Calm down."

"What if someone sees us?"

"Who could see us?" And who could? You wouldn't even know there was a park below us. I place my hands flat against her chest, slide them down to pull her shirt from her pants.

"I'm scared," she says.

"I'm excited," I say. I am. I've never done anything like this before. Being with Lisa makes me unafraid. I unbutton my shirt, draw her hands to my body, unzip her jeans while she touches my breasts. I'm in a hurry now. My hand moves between her legs.

For someone so reluctant, she's very wet, slick as this morning. I pull back to look into her eyes. But she won't hold my gaze, instead reaches and finds me. She works herself inside me and I can hardly stand. She makes me come right there, my knees buckling a little, so I have to lean against her. She presses her mouth to mine to muffle my sounds. I take in her breath.

After I've caught my own I reach for her, but she gently pulls away to button her shirt. As soon as she's neatly tucked and presentable she heads back down the trail.

It takes me a little longer to pull myself together. My concentration is shot. My assignment is not due for another two days. I figure the dogs and their owners show up every morning and afternoon, I could

come back tomorrow. I want more time with Lisa.
"Let's go to the beach."

As I follow her car, I am amazed at my great
good fortune. To be loved and in love — and faithful
and still have passion. I never would have dreamed
this for myself.

We arrive while the sun still hovers inches above
the horizon, yellow still, and blinding. We lie on the
sand, eyes closed, fingertips barely touching. I'm so
content I fall asleep.

The chill wakes me. The sun has dropped, and
the sky is a bright salmon color. Lisa is already up,
looking out over the horizon. I put my hand on her
back. "What are you thinking about?"

"Stuff."

"What stuff?"

She shrugs. "Just stuff stuff."

I look up and down the beach, only a few people
in either direction, and quite far from us. "Melanie
stuff?" I know it's wrong as soon as I say it, but
hope she'll let it pass. I continue to nuzzle against
Lisa, working my way up to her face for a kiss.

"Not here." She stands and wipes sand off her
pants. Some of it blows into my face.

"Hey, cut it out."

"Pardon me for living." She strides toward the
water.

"I'm sorry. Lisa . . ."

But she won't turn around.

If anyone should storm off at the mention of that

name it should be me, not Lisa. For once I wasn't the one who was unfaithful. For once I hadn't been the one to sneak around behind my lover's back for three months.

I'd caught them at a party at a mutual friend's. In the bedroom, so wrapped up in their kiss they almost tumbled onto the pile of jackets on the bed. I can still see the back of Melanie's head: that short dark hair and bare neck, smooth and pale and empty. I wanted to plunge something dangerous and sharp into it. Mostly I was so stunned I let out a stupid little yip, followed by an incredulous "Lisa?" like maybe she was someone I hadn't seen in years and almost didn't recognize.

They were too muzzy to separate even then. Lisa just looked up, dazed. "Oh God," she said. And kept saying, "OhGodOhGodOhGod."

I grabbed my jacket and stood there. I'd always pegged myself as someone who would simply leave the room. But I froze. I couldn't cry. Couldn't drive home, either. Lisa had had to do that.

To her credit, she didn't make a lot of excuses. At least not that night on the way home, though she'd certainly been making excuses for three months. *I've got to work late,* she'd say, or *I've got to go in over the weekend.* I wondered how many of her business trips had been legitimate. And if she'd gone by herself.

I wouldn't talk to her that night. I just headed for my studio above the garage.

The darkroom's in the back. The print room is set up with a couch and table. I can meet with clients there and show my work. The place has all the comforts of home: a microwave, coffee maker, small refrigerator stocked with fruit and Oreos, and a cupboard full of teas, coffee and microwaveable soups.

I spent three days and nights there before I could even look at Lisa again.

Not that she didn't try to see me. She called on my business line, knocked on the door, once even ventured as far as the darkroom door, spoke to me through it. I didn't respond.

Lisa tried sending the dog out to me with notes — that trick used to work for little spats, but didn't break this ice. She left me a pert bouquet of daffodils that I made a point of ignoring.

I knew she felt terrible. I couldn't talk to her because I felt too many things. My emotions got in the way of my vision. We had a whole string of glorious winter days, warm but clear and sparkly like L.A. in the Fifties, and I saw them through a film, or like a photograph printed on the wrong paper — no snap or contrast. My hurt was physical. I ached all over, like I'd performed some strenuous activity I wasn't used to.

And through it all a little voice in my head said, *You did this to others, you deserve this.*

Maybe that voice got me back into the house, back into dialogue with Lisa. Eventually back into our bed and our life.

Has it been the same? Not quite. Whatever sent Lisa to Melanie was her own business, but I realized I had better work on my end of the relationship. Lisa and I came out of it stronger, resolved to stay together, to work through this.

And for three months we've done pretty well. But then every so often we'll have a moment like this one today.

Lisa's at the water's edge now, hurling pebbles out past the breakers.

I try calling to her again, but she doesn't turn around. I head back to my car to wait. I sit with the radio on, Miles Davis blasting across my frustration.

I don't know about forgiveness, whether or not I'm capable of it, whether it's mine to bestow. Or if there's even anything to forgive. What happened happened. I was the one who brought the whole thing up today. Out of nowhere, on a perfect afternoon.

By the time Lisa comes back, Dexter Gordon is blowing cool and blue and Lisa looks very beautiful, a light after those dark moments. I roll down my window. "I'm sorry," I say. "I shouldn't have brought her up."

We continue our date as planned, but even our favorite Italian restaurant doesn't completely cover the bad taste left from the beach.

The first time the lights go off in a darkroom you don't believe your eyes will ever adjust to the weak red glow of the safelight. Of course they do. Now I'm so used to the absence of normal color that daylight often seems garish by comparison.

I've made a contact sheet of the roll I did of Lisa. It shows me thirty-seven tiny images of my lover. She's at some distance from the camera, a minuscule figure dwarfed by trees. As the camera moves closer she assumes more of the frame. I settle on the image I want to work with.

In it, Lisa already knew I was there, but hadn't

started posing yet. She's turned to me, but at this size and without my loupe I can't make out the exact expression on her face.

I put the negative into the enlarger, frame and focus the image, then take out a sheet of paper and make the exposure.

I slide the paper into the developer, gently rocking the tray as I watch the hand of the timer sweep through the two and a half minutes. The dark of the trees shows up first, then Lisa's hair, until gradually the rest of the picture fills in.

The darkroom is magic. I slip what looks like a blank piece of paper into clear liquid and after about twenty-five seconds an image starts to appear. I associate the darkroom, and by extension the entire printing process, with truth. With a gradual emerging of truth. The magic of truth is revealed from this blank paper, whole stories out of pure white. And this truth has to be protected for a time from unfiltered light, until it's become part of the paper, deposited on the emulsion.

I keep rocking the tray. I can't quite read Lisa's expression. What on the contact looked like a smile at this size seems more startled, like I'd snuck up on her.

I move the paper into the stop bath. Thirty seconds. Then into the fix. After forty-five seconds I turn on the light and study the image.

I'm mesmerized by Lisa's expression — a combination of surprise and delight. This must have been right when she asked when I'd gotten there.

A white blur in the background distracts me. I'm very meticulous, and it's rare for dust or dirt that size to end up on a print of mine.

I check the negative. Nothing. Just to be sure, I clean every surface before I reprint the image. When the same white blur shows up, I know it's in the picture.

I raise the enlarger head, print again.

I remember the movie *Blow-Up,* David Hemming photographing Vanessa Redgrave and finding a dead body when he does his enlargements.

I still get an indistinct blur. I raise the enlarger a little more. I keep the print size the same — 11x14 — so all I'm getting is the blur and just a corner of Lisa's face, her right eye. Which at this size looks almost as if it could be following the blur.

I reframe the easel under the enlarger so the blur is in the center of the paper. Hard to tell with the reverse image, but this almost looks like a human shape. Oh God, could someone have been watching us? Was that the sound we heard? The thought might have excited me at the time, but now I'm more than a little embarrassed.

I slide the paper in the developer and wait for the image to come up. The blur at this size is discernible. At the smaller sizes it could have been a piece of paper caught on a branch. Unmistakable now: it's the back of someone's shirt. Maybe a raised arm. And maybe a head.

Now the top of the light box presses against the darkroom ceiling. I've never made a print this size, so it takes me a few tries to get the exposure right.

I count down with the timer. Two minutes and thirty seconds, twenty-nine, twenty-eight, twenty-seven, twenty-six. What was that person doing?

Coming or going? But we hadn't seen anyone. At least I hadn't.

Less than a minute now. Forty-six, forty-five, forty-four, forty-three. Time is its own truth. The blur has separated into the grain of the emulsion but retains enough definition for me to clearly make out the back of a shirt. I think I can make out an arm, swinging with the rhythm of walking.

Or could the arm have been raised in a wave, and now the person is turning forward to continue walking up the hill?

I remember Lisa's ceremonial wave to the trees.

I look at the other prints floating in the wash, study Lisa's eyes, her face turned to the camera, but her eyes still looking toward the bushes, toward that retreating shirt.

Which I go back to now. I study it longer than I need to, long after I've made out the vulnerable neck, recognized the short hair, just a dark blur really but once you've memorized something it doesn't go away, even through distortion and diffusion.

I remember kissing Lisa, touching her and being surprised to find her so wet so soon.

I glare at her picture and understand. Lisa's mouth isn't forming the half-smile as I'd thought at first, but an O of surprise. Any delight on her face is left over from the second before she'd seen me. The second before I called to her, when she'd just watched her lover disappear into the brush.

When she'd come down from the trail she'd just come from that same little alcove where in less than ten minutes she would fuck me.

I lean against the counter to catch my breath. I don't understand anything about trust or being faithful or forgiveness. I am blind with rage; I can't see anything. I grope my way to the wall switch.

I flip on the overhead light while the print is still in the developer, and in an instant the image bleeds to black.

A Murderer's Memoir

Susan E. Johnson

Anna and I had just finished making love when it came to me that murder was the only solution.

Our fear of the creep who'd been stalking Anna had allowed him to invade even our bedroom. Sex had become perfunctory, engaging our bodies while our minds were elsewhere. My elsewhere was polluted with all the horrible things this guy might do to Anna: he would attack and rape her, he would maim her, he would kidnap, torture and after a long time kill her.

Anna and I rolled away from each other, lying on our backs, barely touching, sweaty and satisfied on the surface. Underneath I felt more distant for having made love. Being sexual, once so consuming, so necessary to our connection, had deteriorated under the stress of anxiety to something we did out of desperation. So trapped were we in our separate fears that no intimacy could bring us together. Making love this way had become worse than not making love at all.

Perhaps it was my sexual disappointment that sparked the shocking idea, but whatever its emotional origin, my resolve to murder came unbidden to my mind: suddenly I knew without question that getting rid of this man was up to me. Alone.

Murder was not, of course, the choice of first resort. We had, as they say, considered other options.

At first Anna had just ignored him. Who even knew when he began stalking her? It was not until one frigid early January evening six weeks ago that she first noticed him.

The sun had set about 3:30 in the afternoon, putting an end to only five and a half hours of daylight. Winter in Alaska is not only cold but dark. The daily weather forecasts chart what time the sun will rise and set, how many hours, minutes and seconds of daylight we can look forward to, and how much change we can expect from the previous day. That particular day in January would have been about thirty seconds lighter than the day before, pitch dark when Anna left her office.

She was aware of a nondescript car idling its

engine next to hers, noticed it only because she had the fleeting impression the same car had been there the night before. She had figured the driver was picking someone up about the same time she normally finished her workday. She'd gotten into her car and driven off, forgetting about the whole thing.

Anna's office is in an historic building, the remodeled Alaska Railroad depot, built in 1942 and thus a survivor of our 1964 earthquake. The building has class — rust red tile floor and wainscoting, six-inch blond wood frames around the doors and multi-paned windows, beautiful details throughout — but it's isolated, set off by itself near the Port of Anchorage. The first floor waiting room and ticket booths are still used for passengers boarding the daily trains south to Seward and north to Fairbanks, but except for the hour or so around train arrivals and departures, few people are about. When Anna arrives for work in the dark of morning and leaves again in the dark of afternoon, she is often alone.

The same car, a dingy grey Ford Escort with rusting undercarriage and black exhaust, was idling near hers the next night as well. This time some premonition prompted her to write down the license number. The fourth night, the Escort was parked in the space just to the right of Anna's four-wheel-drive Subaru. She walked around her car, opened the passenger door, rummaged in the glove compartment, and looked up to check out the Escort's driver.

The stranger who stared directly back at her was young, in his twenties probably, thin-faced, with long scraggly hair and an unkempt skimpy beard. Like his car he was nondescript. Except for his eyes. These were a very light blue, intense and vacant at the same time, beautiful and terrifying, like the depths of an Alaskan crevasse.

Anna quickly got into the driver's side and without even thinking, locked all her doors. She arrived home considerably shaken.

We talked about the encounters, but wrote them off to chance contacts with a certain type of male over-represented here in Alaska. We have thousands of skaggy guys who have failed everywhere else but imagine they can make it on the Last Frontier. Attracted by oversold images of gold rushes and oil booms, they're also attracted by the distance Alaska puts between them and the disgusted people they've left behind. We reminded ourselves of the heterosexual Alaskan woman's lament: "The odds are good, but the goods are odd." We tried to dismiss the guy by giving him a low-life name, Hairball.

And we reminded ourselves of the excitement we'd felt moving to Alaska. Anna and I had wanted something entirely different: the austere beauty, the wilderness within walking distance, the chance to have moose in our front yard and grizzly bears in the neighborhood. The opportunity, as a friend said, for once in our lives to be second on the food chain. We had achieved our dream of adventure, and no weird and probably harmless guy should rob us of our pleasure.

It was our last innocent evening.

That night I awoke, my heart racing, my breathing shallow and rapid. Despite our brave resolution, I was profoundly frightened, my body rigid and alert. Something not good for us was beginning.

* * * * *

You'd like Anna. She is a loving, energetic, controlling extrovert. She meddles, though she would call it intervening. She believes the best of people and has an admirable faith in love and truth and justice. She even believes people can change. I accuse her of not being quite of this world. Naturally — given these qualities — she's a psychotherapist. She's also beautiful, especially her large blue-green-turquoise eyes that change color with the blouse she wears.

You might find me more distant. I'm a sociologist — on sabbatical right now from my university job — an observer, not a helper, more introverted than Anna. I pride myself on also being "realistic," more cynical, more sensitive to craziness and danger in the world and in the people I run into. I like to think I'm moderate, rational, even-tempered. Anna says this is ridiculous, that I'm moody, passionate, angry and implacable, but that I have a great veneer.

We've been together nearly ten years and routinely argue about our basic natures. I think we still barely know each other.

I know, though, that Anna believes in redemption. I believe in evil.

Anna's basic faith in the goodness of people helped her banish thoughts of Hairball from her mind. But the week following the car encounters Anna ushered her last client out of her waiting room and returned to her inner office to make some final phone calls. She can't remember if she heard the outside door open, but she became aware of an ominous presence beyond her door.

She took a deep breath, opened the door, and there was Hairball, sitting rigidly upright in one of the mauve chairs, his eyes focused on the nameplate on Anna's office door. He was holding a cigarette in the fingers of one hand, a match in the other. When Anna appeared he rose, placed the cigarette between his lips, lit the match and extended it toward Anna. He stared at the flame, then raised his eyes to stare fixedly at Anna. Just before the match burned his fingers he dropped it still burning on the rose carpet, turned and walked out. He'd never lit the cigarette.

Anna called after him, "What do you want?" but he never paused. She leapt back into her office, slammed and locked the door, called security downstairs, and had them escort her to her car. Hairball's car was no longer in the parking lot. She came home still shaking, and canceled all her appointments for the next day, afraid to go to work. I held her, stroking her hair, murmuring comforting words, reassuring her.

When Anna calmed down a little we began to make plans.

"We should call the police. Right now," she said, typically naive and quick to take charge.

"Okay, darling, but what are they going to do?" I replied, skeptical and slower.

"They'll pick him up."

"They'll also let him go."

We both knew stalkers were dangerous men. Anna's training had taught her this, and we'd seen a television special, comfortingly titled *Stalkers: The*

Assassins Among Us, that told about women stalked eight or ten years by the same man. Neither they nor the law were effective in discouraging these men. And sometimes the stalking escalated to murder. Newspapers all over the country, and Alaska is no exception, are full of articles about men who obsess about some woman, an old girlfriend or a total stranger, follow her and bother her and eventually work themselves up to killing her.

Without some form of protection what was to keep Anna's stalker from becoming her killer?

The next day we called all the friends we knew who could be of help. Fran, a police officer, used Hairball's license number to find out that he was just as creepy as he seemed. Richard Maxwell, nicknamed "Crazy," had a prior criminal record extending over the past ten years (before that he was a juvenile offender), for beating up his wife in Oakland, for assaults in Portland, for rape in Seattle. Apparently he was working his way north, leaving a trail of violence and damage.

Carol, an attorney, researched the new Anchorage anti-stalking law. The results were not reassuring. Confronting Maxwell with the police might scare him off, but it could also escalate the situation. If we survived long enough to persist, and Maxwell was convicted of stalking, we could expect a sentence that, given his prior record, would keep him off the streets and away from us for maybe three years, probably much less. As Carol said, "Just long enough for you both to find new jobs and move out of state."

The unbelievable had happened: our conventional, predictable life was being destroyed by a pathological person who had targeted us for misery and perhaps worse. And there was little that the organized forces of society could do to protect us. But I had no intention of running from Hairball, leaving the Alaska we loved because the law could not protect us from crazies. It was at this point that I began to realize that Anna and I were on our own.

The television special had ended with California police officers — "threat assessment specialists" — who dealt with stalkers all the time, explaining carefully that victims had to protect themselves. "It's their problem," they said calmly, abandoning us to our fate.

Anna was still in favor of alerting the authorities. I agreed, but just in case, we both began searching for things we ourselves could do at the same time. Several years ago Anna and I had taken an intensive women's self-defense course that taught us how to deliver blows with our feet that could render an attacker unconscious for anywhere from five to fifteen minutes — time to escape and call 911. We began practicing the moves we'd learned, refreshing Anna's memory so she could protect herself if he attacked.

I remember Anna replaying the scenario where an attacker has you on the ground: Bite his arm (so he lets go a little), turn toward him, gouge his eyes, and, as he pulls back, coil and kick him with your heel directly in the face. We learned the routines like a violent mantra: *Bite, Gouge, Kick, Kick Again!*

The catharsis of the exercise brought back the most important lesson we had learned: that a woman who intends to fight back has the strategic advantage of deception and surprise. She is not who her attacker has mistaken her for. He believes she is the victim, he the assailant. She will submit, he will control.

In fact, armed with her self-defense skills and her resolve, his "victim" is engaged in a radical role-reversal. Once she perceives his threat, she becomes in her mind the attacker waiting for her opening. And the opening always comes. Within seconds. The class called it becoming the huntress.

By the time Anna and I took the class, forty-two graduates had actually been attacked and had fought back. All were able to knock out or disable their assailant within an average of five seconds from the time the attack began. They remembered very little of the physical confrontation. One woman could tell the police nothing of her response to a mugger, but when they examined his hospital report the next day she had stomped both his insteps, kneed him in the groin, kneed him in the face, kneed him in the ribs, and kicked him in the head.

Without telling Anna, I decided to become Hairball's huntress, to stalk him as he was stalking Anna. At the same time I could provide some protection for Anna by being nearby.

I began the following Monday, waiting in my car outside Anna's office, armed with a can of "Counter Assault" bear mace, an eight inch canister of pepper gas, pressurized to shoot a blinding spray up to twenty-five feet. Hikers and hunters say it immediately reduces to tears any threatening grizzly. If you're upwind, of course.

Even though it was only 4:30 p.m., the Alaskan January afternoon was midnight black. Sure enough, there was the Escort, motor idling. He had parked between the building entrance and Anna's car. Just as Anna emerged from the building, Hairball got out of his car with something in his hand. I jumped from my car and began to run toward him. He walked to the front of his car, leaned his butt against the hood, and began cleaning his fingernails with a knife. He looked up, staring intently at Anna.

She stopped instantly, and fled back into the building. I too stopped and crouched beside a sheltering pickup truck. Hairball walked over to Anna's car and methodically gouged huge crosses in the paint of all four doors. He then closed the knife, slipped it in his pocket, got back in his car and drove away. He never gave me a look.

I dashed back to my car and followed him, leaving Anna to deal with her mutilated car. His other evening activities were perfectly normal. He stopped at a McDonald's and ate a Big Mac, fries and a Coke. So did I. He went to a shoot-'em-up film. I sat through it too, though I took a moment out to call Anna. She was home, with Carol and Fran visiting for support.

Hairball then left the theater and drove to a local downtown bar where he drank beer for a couple of hours. I sat outside freezing in the car. He emerged as the bar closed for the night, leaving by the back door into an alley and weaving his way along the street to his car. He drove home going too fast and ran one red light. I looked both ways and dashed through after him. He turned out his apartment lights fifteen minutes after he got in and I went home.

Hairball was a no-show outside Anna's office the next two nights, but we were under no illusions that he had disappeared for good. By now he was calling Anna regularly both at home and at her office, and hanging up when either of us answered, so there was no respite from his compulsive attentions. We had become so frightened that we moved about woodenly, in a state of on-going shock.

Wednesday evening we tried to make love, hungry for some color in a world gone grey. It was after this failed attempt to connect that I made my fateful decision. I simply did not trust the authorities to protect Anna in time all the time. What would protect her was Hairball's elimination. And that I could take care of. If I could bring myself to do it.

I thought about telling Anna my intention. But did not. I feared she would try to talk me out of it, cripple me just enough with reason that I would lose my resolve. I was on an adrenaline high, and did not want to be brought down.

Most of that adrenaline rush was fear. Fear of Hairball himself. Fear that I would further endanger Anna with my rashness. Fear that when the moment came I would choke, and myself become Hairball's victim. I never feared discovery because I believed I could avoid it with careful planning and preparation.

Now I am at the end of my preparations. It's been two weeks since the knife episode, and Hairball keeps showing up at Anna's office. He continues to call her, breathing into the phone for a few seconds and hanging up. I can sense him biding his time, enjoying the wait before he perpetrates some new intimidation. During that time I have followed him and know his routines. I feel I understand him by now, that as a fellow stalker I can almost identify with him. Except that he is a rank amateur compared to me. He has chosen Anna as his victim for personal reasons, reasons only his twisted psyche could justify; I have chosen him as my victim for the most objective reason, because he poses a threat to someone I love. He lies in wait for Anna for an hour every day at the most; I shadow him all day every day. He is groping in a disordered mind for some way to harm Anna that will feel good to him; I have thought about his death rationally, carefully planned its elements and will hopefully feel guilt-free at its completion, as if I have done a necessary task well.

Perhaps I am becoming a little crazy myself.

Last Tuesday the police served Maxwell with a restraining order that said he must not approach Anna at her work or home. Thursday she arrived at her office to find the waiting room open and her tropical fish tank smashed, water, glass and dead fish befouling the carpet. She cleaned up as best she could, alerted maintenance, posted a note to tell her clients she was home sick and left. She found the restraining order crumpled up and wedged in the handle of her car door. She hasn't returned to work.

This morning, Saturday, I put Anna on the plane to recuperate among friends in Seattle. Tonight I will seek out Hairball.

It's very cold this mid-February night, exactly ten degrees below zero when I left home. It's a perfect night for the aurora borealis, those displays of electromagnetic magic that light up the northern winter sky.

I don't even glance at the sky. I'm wearing a

loose-fitting pair of cotton pants and an old Anorak over my shirt, sweater and jeans. My high-top leather hiking boots were bought at least twenty years ago and haven't been worn since I moved to Alaska. I have on gloves, a wool cap pulled down over my ears and a scarf snuggled up around my neck that partially covers my face. I'm bundled up like every other man or woman who tonight has entered The Last Great Escape, Hairball's regular tavern.

No one looks up at me because the television is tuned to a University of Alaska hockey game, tied midway through the second period. I have exactly ten minutes and thirty-one seconds before anyone is likely to move. Hairball is sitting at the bar on his regular stool, the one closest to the ice and coffee machines, clear around the horseshoe-shaped bar from the back exit. I feel a surge of adrenaline at sight of him, then nausea pulls me up short. I take a deep breath and ease my way through the people standing to watch. Everyone is riveted on the game. Ten minutes five seconds to go.

I move over next to Hairball. I reach in my pocket and draw out a picture of Anna, taken last summer. She's in a black tailored skirt, electric blue blouse, and black blazer, looking cool and professional and gorgeous. I feel sick inviting Hairball to look at her, even though I know it's the bait he'll be unable to refuse. I haven't said a word. He stares at the picture and then slowly up at me. His eyes are indeed vacant — this is the first time I've confronted him up this close — but there's an edge of surprise in them. He clearly recognizes Anna; I don't think he recognizes me.

I force myself to look directly into his eyes, then

immediately turn and begin to work my way through
the crowd toward the back door. I do not look back
to see if Hairball is following. I have to trust that his
obsession will bring him to me.

I open the back door just as the play-by-play
announcer tells me there are nine minutes to go in
the period. I emerge into the alley that runs between
Fourth and Fifth avenues, connecting "G" and "H"
streets in downtown Anchorage. I have spent a lot of
surreptitious time in this alley, planning. Across from
the Great Escape's back door and along about ten
feet, there's a vacant area behind a defunct Chinese
restaurant. An old shed is built flush with the alley
on one side of this space, and behind it trash and
discarded lumber have been tossed. Alongside the
shed a car parks during the day, but not at night.
The whole area is maybe twenty-five feet deep and
twenty feet wide. No one looking down the alley can
see into the space, though the shed can be seen by
someone looking out the bar's back door.

I walk quickly across the alley, careful not to fall
on the icy patches, and stop three feet into the area,
close to the shed. I need to wait only about thirty
seconds before Hairball opens the bar's rear exit
door, spots me across the alley, and stumbles slightly
coming toward me. I was right, he couldn't leave the
bait alone.

"Who the fuck are you?" he says as he
approaches. I don't respond, but pull another picture
from my pocket, holding it out toward him as I back
into the secluded space. Hairball follows, reaching for
the picture. I turn it toward him so he can glimpse
Anna in shorts and a skimpy T-shirt leaning against
the lanai railing of the condo we rented in Hawaii

last year. Just as he is about to take the picture, I drop it between us. "Shit," I say and take half a step backwards, letting Hairball retrieve it. He hesitates, hearing the female voice, but bends slowly down reaching for the photo. I step forward, lock my hands behind his head and jerk his face down onto my up-thrusting knee. His nose breaks with a squishing and crunching sound. He grunts and collapses with his hands to his face, blood spurting from between his fingers. I step to the side and kick him in the temple. He pulls his hands away from his face and rolls to avoid me. I kick him again in the head. He lies now on his side, inert, curled up a bit. I kick him once more in the back of the neck, just below his hair line. There is no response.

I look around for Anna's picture, but do not see it. It must be under Hairball's body. I move closer to roll his body out of the way and nearly fall as his hand suddenly darts out toward my ankle. I stamp on his wrist, hear the crack of breaking bones, and jump away from him. He's not done yet for I see him struggling to his knees, the broken wrist held close to his side, blood streaming from his face. I pick up a discarded two-by-four and bash him over the head. He collapses, but I keep hitting him until an urge to vomit overwhelms me. I stagger a few feet away and throw up.

Wiping my mouth I look back to where Hairball lies, crumpled on the ice. I am terrified he is somehow not yet dead, but I must get close to him again to move his body. I take a deep breath of the frigid air, walk quickly the several steps to his body, grab him by the shoulders and drag him to a spot I've cleared behind the shed. I go through his pockets and take his wallet, leaving everything else. Then I pile lumber and trash over his body.

The pool of blood is steaming in the cold air, melting through the ice, and there's a trail of it that disappears in the pile of trash. I can see where I've dragged Hairball's body over about ten feet of icy gravel. I retrieve Anna's crumpled picture, the scene of paradise now fouled with dirt and blood. I'm careful not to step in Hairball's blood while I kick as much loose dirt over the trail as I can scrape away from the ice. I drag a sheet of old paneling over the pool. In the dim light I hope none of the disturbance will be noticed.

I take another deep breath, the cold air hits my lungs and I gasp audibly. The sound is a moan. Somehow I can no longer stand. I slump to the ground just as the back door to the bar opens. I can hear cheering from inside, and a patron exits. The second period of the hockey game must be over. Ten minutes have passed.

I lie still, fortunately in shadow. The guy pays no attention to me, but walks further along the alley and pees against the wall. He zips up and begins his walk back to the bar. I wait, immobilized by shock, unable to think what I should do if he notices me. He's in a hurry to return to the game, though, and moves back inside without more than a cursory glance my way.

I straighten up, take a shallower breath this time, and walk disjointedly down the alley away from The Great Escape and Hairball's body. I feel uncoordinated, my body unresponsive. Thirty feet along is a loading zone, recessed from the alley. I step in and with difficulty remove my Anorak and cotton pants. Both are heavily blood-stained. I take Hairball's wallet out of the Anorak's pocket and remove the money, which I put in my shirt pocket with the two pictures. My hands are shaking. I throw the wallet in a huge dumpster next to the loading zone, wrap up the clothes in a ball under my arm and walk carefully to the end of the alley. I look both ways, but the only car in sight is two blocks away. I walk deliberately down the sidewalk to the last parking spot where my car sits. I put the clothes on the floor behind the driver's seat, get in and drive slowly away.

At home I build a good-sized fire and burn the pictures, money and the blood-stained pants and jacket. I check for blood spots on the clothing I wore underneath and, finding none, throw everything in the wash. I clean the soles of the boots and return them to the garage. All my actions are slow and feel immensely difficult. I take a long, hot shower, put on a sweatshirt and sweatpants, and return to the living room where the fire is burning lower. I check the temperature outside and then sit for a long time staring into the fire, wondering dully if Hairball is really dead and, if not, how long it will take at fifteen degrees below zero for him to freeze to death. Not long, I imagine.

I feel empty.

Anna returned two days later, and I resumed guarding her since, as far as anyone knew, Hairball was still a threat. After three weeks with no appearance by him, Anna began to relax and we and our friends speculated that he had simply moved on, thank God. Two weeks later the paper reported an unidentified male found in the alley between "G" and "H" Streets. Apparently he had been mugged, beaten, robbed and his body hidden. Although the body had a broken arm and serious head injuries, the cause of death was exposure.

The next evening, which was last night, Fran and another police officer appeared to tell us the body had been identified from fingerprints on file in both Oregon and Washington. Anna and I expressed relief at having been delivered from Hairball by a mugger ex machina, and the four of us sank into an awkward silence. Fran, glancing at the other officer, broke the peculiar mood that was developing.

"There's something I do need to ask you both. Just for my own peace of mind, you know. Nothing official." She paused. "You don't, either of you, know anything about Maxwell's death, do you?"

"What could we possibly know about it?" Anna wondered.

"Just asking," reassured Fran. "What about you?" She turned to me.

"The only thing I know is I'm glad he's gone," I replied.

After a bit Fran and Sergeant Miller left, but they'd started Anna thinking. "Darling," she said as we were getting undressed for bed, "what did you spend your time doing that weekend I was gone, anyway?"

I surprised even myself with the casualness of my rejoinder. "Oh, nothing in particular," I said putting my arms around her. "Just cleaning up odds and ends."

* * * * *

The last few weeks I have felt on the edge of losing control; I desperately want to tell someone what I have done. And how I feel about it. Once the shock of the act itself wore off I knew how I *should* feel: horrified that I had killed another human being and guilty that I was getting away with it.

But I felt neither or these things. Once the fear that I would be discovered had passed, I felt relieved. Quieted somehow. It was as if murdering Hairball had set to rest demons that had plagued me for years. And with the same act I had rid the world of a violent and potentially lethal person. The truth is I felt deeply satisfied, almost joyous.

Of course, I cannot tell Anna or a friend what I have done. So I am telling you through this fictional tale, a memoir based presumably on imagination, not experience. I need to tell someone, you understand, not because I seek to be forgiven or punished, but because I want to be congratulated.

Amphibia

Penny Sumner

The first sign. Horse shit shall fall from the sky.

(Okay, so it didn't actually say horse shit in the fourteenth-century manuscript, but the "foule dounge" of various farmyard animals. Horse shit is close enough.)

The second sign. Women shall wear the clothes of men and men shall wear the jewels of women. Flames shall issue from their private parts.

(Remember, here's where you heard it first.)

The third sign. *Hedgehogs* ("hedgepigges" in the

original) *shall sing like nightingales and the frogges shall disappear from all the land.*

And there you have it, in number three, the formula required to turn a promising postgraduate student into self-employed genealogist into private detective. Metamorphosis, transfiguration, freedom; to my mind at least. "A great waste" is how my thesis supervisor, Dr. Veracity Emanuel, described it when I met her by chance in Trafalgar Square.

I turned to Beth, standing next to me, and kissed her full on her ruby-red mouth. "The best thing that ever happened to me," I replied. Following the doctor's hasty departure we continued to snog, soon attracting more tourists than either the statue of Nelson or the pigeons.

By now you'll be wondering what the hell's going on so I'll begin at the beginning, with the frogs. Not the prophecy frogs in an illuminated, fourteenth-century manuscript but the real thing: moist, shiny-green representatives of the genus *Rena*, as they are found (or, rather, *were* found because, and don't forget this, the frogs really are disappearing), in the land of my childhood, Australia.

Picture this, I'm six years old, a brown stick of a child with glasses taped together over the bridge of my nose and a thin plait reaching to my waist. My yellow cotton dress is tucked into my knickers and I'm squatting at the swampy edge of the creek that runs past the bottom of our garden. I'm clutching an empty Vegemite jar in my right hand and the jar is now full of semi-transparent sludge, the consistency of tapioca pudding. I'm collecting frogs' eggs.

So far there's nothing particularly surprising about this. The surprising bit comes a little later, when my father rounds the corner of our weatherboard house and finds me sitting on the bottom step, inspecting my catch.

"What," he demands, "have you got there?" And then, when he sees my haul of frog spawn, he doesn't empty the lot over the brown-baked grass, but instead gives a chuckle that sounds genuinely amused. "Well," he says, "frogs is it? You'll need something to keep them in." Five minutes later he returns from the garage with my old baby bath. "There." His voice is almost affectionate. "I'll fill it up with the hose and you call Mum out. Tell her it's a surprise."

Standing there on the top step, this was the only time I ever heard my mother swear. "You bastard." She spat it straight at him. I thought she was angry that we'd used the bath but after she ran back into the house Dad continued to laugh, saying people were like that about frogs. You either loved them or hated them. When he came home from the pub that night they had one of their really bad fights.

I told Beth this story the second time we met. I'd called round at her Clapham flat, ostensibly to drop off some work I'd done for her, and she invited me in for a drink. It was mid-June and hot in the way only south London can get hot. She poured Pimms and lemonade into two tall glasses, added ice, and we climbed out her living-room window onto the roof garden.

"Cheers." She raised her glass. "So tell me, Fran, how does a nice girl like you come to be working as a genealogist?"

Nice? What, exactly, did she mean by nice? I glanced down at my white cotton dress and school girl sandals: maybe I was creating the wrong impression.

When I looked up at her again she was grinning. I didn't, however, grin back. Instead I thought, "This could be it. This could be serious."

And so I told her about the frogs.

A year after the incident with the frogs' eggs the grown-up frogs came back to spawn. The first morning Dad found one he came out of the bathroom roaring with laughter. He'd lifted the lid and there it was, sitting in the bowl. "Here." He winked as I held out my hands. "Take that through to your mother. If you put it on her pillow she'll think it's her Prince Charming!"

In the excitement of it all I forgot how upset Mum had been before, and did as Dad suggested. Mum didn't swear this time though, she just went pale, here eyes dark against the sheets.

"It's fucking criminal." Beth clambered back through the window with a bowl of fresh strawberries. "It's fucking criminal, the petty cruelties that go on in families."

Dad was cruel, there's no doubt about it, although there's also no doubt he felt he was a victim. "A stinking, rotten crime," he'd say, shaking his head, "having to live in this bloody country." In other immigrant households it was the women who pined but in our family Mum insisted she was an Australian now while Dad, in his maudlin moments, reminisced about green, green grass and English skies. I once saw him weep over a Christmas card that showed a scruffy red robin sitting on a hillock of snow.

Frogs don't rate another mention in my family

saga until about five years later, when I was eleven years old. We'd moved north from Sydney to Townsville where, in the tropics, Dad's temper, and liver, deteriorated further. The last time I saw him was in the hospital. The man in the next bed complained that his wife never bothered to come. "A bitch," he said, and coughed phlegm into a stainless steel bucket. "That's what my old woman is."

"Well mine's a witch." Dad managed a rasping chuckle. "And so are you." He gripped my wrist with a claw-like hand. "It's in your blood. Don't you ever forget that. And don't you forget the frogs either." As Mum hurried me out of the ward he called after us. "Come by broomstick next time, why don't you?"

There wasn't a next time. He died that night.

Beth had a dinner engagement. "With a client," she explained, running competent fingers through her short, dark hair. "She suspects one of her managers is selling information to a rival company. I'll be working on this case most nights this week. But maybe you're free for dinner next Saturday?"

I'd already promised to have dinner on Saturday with Steve, and so had to ring him when I got home, in order to apologize. "I'm really, really sorry," I told him. "But this is important."

"Are we talking love or lust?" he asked.

This required about one second's thought. "Both."

"Good. And what does the lady do for a living?"

"She's a private detective."

"Good gracious. And how, pray tell, did you meet her?"

"She needed a search done for a death certificate."

"Well if I were you I'd sound her out for a job. You're heading for thirty, Fran, that's the big three, zero, and genealogy is never going to pay you enough to afford a mortgage. Besides, I can see you now, sitting behind a frosted glass door with *Detective Agency* stencilled across it. Very *film noire*, darling. If you don't mind my saying so, very you."

Come Saturday the weather still hadn't broken. In her small kitchen Beth's red silk shirt had clung to her back; out on the roof garden, however, there was a hint of breeze.

"So you're working as a genealogist." She popped a green olive into her mouth. "But you're trained as a medieval historian?"

"Sort of. I was actually doing my research through the literature department."

The fact that I wasn't really one thing or the other would always, Dr. Emanuel had warned me, be problematic. Staring at me through bifocals she'd explained that people like me aren't easily categorized. "You're, well *amphibious*. If you know what I mean." I had a pretty good idea.

Beth's eyes were a darker brown than mine. Almost black. Looking at me now they narrowed slightly. "So what happened to the academic career?"

"My mother died."

"And?" Her brazen mouth was as red as the silk shirt she wore. Red as the heart of a medieval heretic. In some medieval paintings, heretics' hearts are depicted as wormy apples. In my mind now I took a bite: the flesh of the apple was juicy, ripe.

"And her death made me start thinking about things. About the frogs for instance. Look, are you sure you want to hear all this?" Although as far as I was concerned there could be no going back.

"Tell me." Her fingers reached out to flick blonde fringe from my eyes. "Tell me about it."

My mother died unexpectedly and I'd rushed home for the funeral. A month later I was back in England, back in the library. And then I came across that prophecy about the frogs. What had my father meant, I wondered, about the frogs? About it being in the blood? I'd never got round to asking Mum, surprised as I was by the grief Dad's death caused her.

"You don't understand," she'd sobbed. "He didn't drink when he was young. Once upon a time he was a lovely man."

I had to take her word for that, finding it hard to imagine such sobriety myself. However, thinking about my father and his last words made me realize how little I really knew about either of my parents, especially about their lives before they left England. My father's parents had died when he was young and he didn't have any brothers or sisters. My mother's parents had also died years back, as had her younger brother. Who, I wondered, were these people? What had they been like? I knew my grandparents' names, but I didn't know where they'd lived, what they'd done with their lives . . .

"Hence the interest in genealogy," Beth observed. We were at the pudding stage of the meal — I'd

brought along a tub of passionfruit ice cream —
and, somehow, my head was resting in her lap.

"Yes." I looked up past her freckled face, to
where a thin wisp of cloud hung in a burnished sky.
"That afternoon I didn't go back to the manuscript
reading room but went instead to St. Catherine's
House, to start looking through the death certificates.
In fact I never went back to the manuscript room
again."

"It happened that quick?" Her fingers traced a
dreamy pattern on my forehead. "You simply walked
out of the library for ever?"

"I didn't know I wasn't going back, I only
planned to spend a couple of days working on my
family tree. But a couple of days turned into weeks
and, eventually, I realized I wasn't interested in my
academic work any more. I think I'd probably lost
interest in it a long time before, but was so into the
habit I hadn't noticed."

"Did you discover anything about your family?"

Far above us the solitary cloud tilts at its edges,
forming a lazy smile, and I decide that this is a story
best kept for tomorrow.

"Oh yes," I say. "Yes, I did." And then I reach
my mouth up to hers.

There was lightning the next morning, and low
rumbles of thunder. Beth gave me a blue cashmere
sweater to wear over my blue crepe dress and we ate
fingers of honeyed toast on the living room sofa.

"You're a natural," she said.

"I should hope so!"

"No, silly. What I was thinking is that you'd make a good detective. Genealogy is a form of detective work anyway. So tell me, what did you find out about your family?"

"I found out that my maternal grandfather was a carpenter, and my father's father was a traveling salesman. Both my grandmothers were housewives. They all hailed from the north." On top of the mantelpiece there were photos of three smiling children, who I knew to be Beth's niece and twin nephews.

"And what else?"

I took a deep breath. "My uncle, my mother's younger brother, died as the result of being impaled on a pitchfork." Wood and steel, through the heart.

When I'd told other friends this they'd looked suitably appalled. The look on Beth's face, however, could only be described as professional. "Do you know if he fell? Or was he pushed?"

"His death certificate didn't say."

"What year did he die?"

"Nineteen-forty-six. In a small village in the wilds of Yorkshire."

She nodded to herself. "It's possible there are still people in the village who remember him."

"I found one. A woman in her sixties."

"Do you want to tell me what the woman said?" Beth's voice was gentle. "Don't feel you have to, Fran."

"She told me that she'd been very young at the time, but she could remember hearing her parents say my uncle was killed as a witch."

* * * * *

That wasn't the real reason my uncle was murdered, of course, although that was the rumor going round the village at the time, and the more sensational newspapers featured *Ritual Murder* headlines. My uncle had been an amateur naturalist, with a special interest in amphibia, and after he died it was whispered that he'd been caught releasing frogs with carts tied behind them, in order to blight his neighbors' crops.

The more prosaic truth was that he'd been caught with a neighbor's wife. But that didn't come out till over twenty years later, when the husband who'd wielded the pitchfork stumbled out of a pub one bleak winter's evening, and into his local police station. His unexpected confession was widely reported in the English media at the time, but I guess that, in Australia, my parents didn't get to hear this particular piece of news.

So there you have it. The reason why my mother hated frogs. And the reason why my father, on his deathbed, made a crack about broomsticks.

From there you go to a medieval prophecy, to an interest in family history, to the office where I now work in central London. The door to the agency isn't frosted glass but painted pine, and the sign doesn't say *Detective Agency* but *Inquiry Agents*. Steve was right, however, about detective work paying the mortgage: Beth and I are now the proud owners of an end-of-terrace house in Streatham.

During the week we collaborate on cases together, and on the weekends we scour the markets and junk shops for old sepia prints for the living room, Edwardian jugs to fill with roses from the garden. Up in the attic I've got a study with oak rafters and a view over red-tile roofs. On the wall facing the window there are two framed posters from the British Library, showing pages from illuminated manuscripts, while over my desk hangs a small, nineteenth-century etching of a frog, Beth's first Christmas present to me. The message on the back reads: *To my favorite antipodean witch. Your father was right, you know. About it being in the blood.*

WHAT WE DO IN THE PRIVACY OF
OUR BEDROOMS.

The Last Time

Catherine Ennis

"Ellie, he done it agin'." The girl's shrill voice cut across the afternoon's stillness. "Ellie!" Again, louder, "ELLIE!"

The woman turned from the window, her hands clenched beneath the faded apron.

"Well, go get the bucket."

"Aw, why me?" The girl slammed her scissors down on the floor next to a stack of shredded magazines and rose, cross-legged, her mouth tight. "It's al'us me. Ever time, al'us me!"

The screen door slammed behind her, and the sound of her bare feet slapping against the wooden porch was loud.

The woman crossed the room and leaned in front of an old man in a rocking chair. The old man's head was nodding, his blue eyes, steady and unblinking, found the woman's face.

"You damned old bastard." Softly. "You did it on purpose."

Up close, the blue eyes were red-rimmed, yellowish, the flesh around them blotched and dry. The woman scowled at the sour odor of the old man's skin, the pungent odor of urine.

She straightened, looking down at him. His gaze didn't waver except that now it was centered somewhere near the apron pocket.

"You bastard." She hardly moved her mouth. "This time is the last."

They waited together in the dim room, listening to the sound of a tin bucket slamming into the metal pump, the dry squeak of a leather washer as the pump handle rose and fell and, finally, the splash of water gurgling into the bucket.

Beneath the old man's chair, a puddle began to drift across the uneven floor, finding channels in the worn linoleum. One wet finger reached out towards the woman's shoes, stopping short at a tear which had been rimmed with tacks.

"Here's th' pail, but I ain't gonna' do it a'gin." Water sloshed as the girl crossed the room and banged the bucket down near the chair. Her nose wrinkled. "Whew, it do smell!" She brushed a lank strand of corn-yellow hair behind one ear. Her eyes were the same blue as the old man's. She leaned to look at him.

"Gran'pa?" She searched his face. "Wanna go walk, Gran'pa?"

The woman shifted her weight. "That's good. Take him out, girl. Let him dry in the sun."

"Come on, Gran'pa." With an almost gentle touch, the girl took the old man's hand in hers.

He unraveled slowly, stood for a moment in a half-crouch, head nodding violently. As the girl pulled, he straightened, and began shuffling across the room. The wet area of his trousers, ringed with old stain marks, stood out clearly.

The woman watched until they crossed the road in front of the house and disappeared into the pine woods. With a sigh, she reached outside the screen door and yanked a mop from its nail in the door frame, her head turned towards the road as she listened for the sound of a car engine.

She thought, it's the waiting that gets to me.

She could remember how hard the waiting had been that first time. But then she had been waiting for an exact period of time to pass, and the sallow-faced lawyer had been very clear on that point.

"If he behaves, Miz Anderson, it won't be but three years, and that ain't so long considering what it coulda been." He had been shuffling papers into a little cardboard suitcase which he had kept on the table during the trial. She had stared at him through tears, she remembered, because three years had seemed like three centuries and she knew he couldn't understand how bad it was to be carrying a baby with the father going to jail and going to stay in jail until his child was over two years old.

"But you can go to the prison to see him," the lawyer was explaining, as if that made everything all right.

"Will they let me see him before he goes?" she had asked.

He snapped the case shut. "Well, you can go on back there." His head jerked in the direction of the judge's bench. "They'll probably let you."

But she had been timid then, too shy and afraid, so Billy had been taken away. Because he was the youngest, just married, and had never been in any serious trouble, they gave him eight years with time off if he behaved. If not for the gun, he would have been given a lighter sentence.

That was when the old man, Billy's father, had moved in on her. He was going to look after his boy's wife, he'd told everybody. So he moved into the house and, a couple of weeks later, he tried to move into her bed. She could still hear him blubbering, the shrill, drunken scream when she rolled from under him, ran to the kitchen, grabbed the iron frying pan, and brained him with it.

He'd slobbered the rest of the night, lying there by the stove, finally whimpering and drooling himself to sleep. She had listened to him from the porch where she sat until daybreak. If there'd been someplace for her to go, she'd have left right then, but there wasn't anyplace.

All her life there hadn't been anyplace for her to go. She always seemed to be waiting for things to happen to her, but she'd never had any say over what or when. Not having any say made the waiting so hard.

Even now, after so many years, it was hard to wait for what was going to happen. Even when this time she was the one to have the say. The thought caused her to smile. If I'm lucky, she thought, this will be the last time I mop that old man's pee.

Swishing the mop around under the chair, she rinsed it in the bucket then hung it back outside on the wall. The water she flung carelessly, slopping the sagging steps.

A look of expectancy on her face, she cocked her head listening, but there was no sound in the heavy afternoon.

Walking to the open window that faced the back of the house, she stared intently at a small garden plot. The short, clean rows were neatly hilled and the plants evenly spaced. Though not near to bearing, a few blossoms gave promise of a harvest if the greenery could outlast the blazing weight of the sun. She squinted as her eyes searched the red mounds, staring at each row, each plant as if for some secret symmetry that her scrutiny alone could detect.

Faintly at first, then louder like the drone of hornets excited in their nest, the sound of an approaching car came to her. She turned swiftly and moved to the front porch, impatiently pushing the door aside on its sagging hinges.

As the car came closer, her heartbeat began to quicken. She took in deep breaths, willing herself to be composed and unaffected by the excitement growing inside her. Her left hand touched and held the upright post that supported the sagging roof, her right hand clenched in the apron pocket.

The car, a trail of red dust in its wake, stopped on the road. Her eyes widened with sudden fear as she took in the meaning of the symbol on the door, the panel of red lights on the roof. Her hand tightened around the post, but her face remained expressionless; she was in control now.

"Howdy, Miz Anderson," the trooper called as he got out of the passenger side of the car. He turned and said something to the driver, then, politely removing his hat, jumped the ditch and walked across the dusty yard to the porch steps.

Keeping her face as still as granite, she made herself nod and allowed a faint smile to touch her mouth. "Howdy, Lisle. What are you doing out here on such a hot day? Don't tell me you've found Billy."

"No'm, we didn't. It's been months now since he broke out, and there ain't been no sign of him. The guard at the bank swore he shot him, so the sheriff figured Billy musta died in the swamp or else we'd of come 'cross him. We been lookin' but the dogs don't pick up nothin'. Tell you the truth, ma'am, we all but give up on findin' him."

"He's dead, do you think?"

"Yessum, that's about it. There's a reward out for the money he stole from the bank, but we figure the money sank in the swamp along with Billy. Least we ain't lookin' for him no more. Why we've come, the sheriff says to tell you that if Billy had insurance, you could probably collect. It'd help you out some if you did. The sheriff will speak for him being dead."

She shook her head slowly, as if she was thinking about what Lisle had told her. "No, there wasn't any insurance, at least that I know of."

"Well ..." He seemed embarrassed now. "If we can ever help, you get word to us, you hear?"

"That's kind of you, Lisle," she said, nodding to emphasize her thanks.

He seemed about to go, but stopped in mid-turn and looked up at her. "The social worker lady says Mary Jane's goin' to the home in Savannah."

It was a statement but the woman knew it for a question. She lowered her eyes for a moment, then looked at him again. The excitement was building, almost out of her control now, but she forced her face to remain still. "I can't keep her any more, Lisle. I don't have what she needs, but they say she can learn something, perhaps, if she gets to Savannah. There's simply nothing more I can do. I've tried for the last eleven years, you know."

"Yes'um. All the folks here admire you for takin' in Billy's sister and his father. You've done more than most would, what with your own baby dead of the fever, and Billy bein' in jail all these years. Ya' know, he coulda been paroled half a dozen times. We never could figure why he'd try to escape, then have time added onta time when he got caught. Billy wasn't stupid, he just did stupid things, I guess."

"I never could figure it either, I just know it's time for someone else to take over. Fact is, Lisle, I'm thinking I'll go away, too. I won't be getting any more money from welfare for Mary Jane, so I need to get back to work."

"Will you be teachin' again, do you think?"

"Heavens no. I haven't been in a classroom in years. Probably no one would have me now."

At these words, ripples of heat coursed through

her body. Someone has me now, she thought, and the image of their passion almost made her knees give way.

"Will you be takin' the old man?"

"No, he wouldn't leave here. He thinks Billy is going to get straight one day, and come home to stay. He can take care of himself, he doesn't need me. At least that's what he keeps saying."

Lisle's big hands fumbled with the brim of his trooper hat. "Well, Miz, you take care." He placed the hat firmly on his head, nodded, and walked back to the patrol car.

She watched the car maneuver back and forth as it turned in the road, leaving clouds of dust in its wake. It was not until the car was almost out of sight that she allowed her shoulders to relax.

It was two days later, on a Thursday morning, that the other waiting was finally over, too. She helped Mary Jane put on Sunday clothes, combed the freshly-washed yellow hair, and pinned it with a bow so it wouldn't hang in Mary Jane's face.

"Hit's today, ain't it?" The girl was anxious, her blue eyes wide with excitement. Mary Jane's memory was short at best, but the morning bath, the hair wash, and the good clothes and shoes had awakened some recall.

Together they folded clothes and laid each piece in a cardboard box from the grocery. Mary Jane carried the box to the porch, then she sat on the top step, arms squeezing her knees, eyes on the road. She would sit there all day if necessary. Waiting was, for Mary Jane, an accomplished skill. She could sit for hours, staring at nothing, not moving, not speaking.

The woman looked at the wind-up clock on the dresser. Time for her to get ready, too.

The peeling mirror made her look distorted and gray as she combed through short brown curls. She smoothed her dress over slim hips and peered at herself, then she walked into the central room and stood smiling down at the old man. His red-rimmed eyes peered at her suspiciously. "Git me 'nother cup," he quavered imperiously.

"Get it yourself, old man. It's time you learned to do for yourself."

"You take my check ever' month . . . I pay for what I git, woman." His eyes now showing fear, he clutched the cup, unmindful of the coffee slopping his hand.

"No more," the woman breathed. "No more."

She and the girl heard the car at the same time. It took only a few minutes to get the girl and her box of clothes into the station wagon.

"Here are the papers, Mrs. Anderson," the welfare lady said kindly. "You're not to worry about Mary Jane. She'll be just fine. They're going to take good care of her, and you can visit any time."

Mary Jane's enthusiasm had dimmed. She peered apprehensively at the welfare lady, then turned and opened the door, sliding her legs out of the car. "I ain't goin," she said, as if her wishes were the only ones to be considered.

The woman deftly turned the girl back on to the seat and closed the door. "Now, Mary Jane, it's time to go." She stepped back from the car and waved. "Bye, Mary Jane," she called. "Bye."

Mary Jane paused for a moment, then grinned

hugely at this new game. "Bye," she yelled. "Bye bye bye!"

The woman waved until the car was hidden by the dust that spewed out behind it. Then she turned and walked back into the house. Without a glance she passed the old man, his cup now overturned on the floor beside his chair.

In the bedroom she knelt by the bed, her hand searching underneath. With an audible sigh of relief, she grasped the handle of a black suitcase and slid it across the floor. Still kneeling, she unsnapped the locks and opened the lid, her eyes feasting on the orderly piles of cash that filled the suitcase almost to overflowing.

She lifted the case to the bed. Her movements now quick, she took five twenty-dollar bills from one of the piles and slipped them into her dress pocket. Then she wrapped a worn leather belt around the case and pulled it tight.

She had never counted the money, being afraid the old man or the girl would catch her at it. They said Billy had stolen over fifty thousand dollars, so she supposed that was what was in the case. No matter. Whatever it was, it was more than she had seen in all her life. More than enough, she thought, to take care of her needs in her new life. A life that would begin at three o'clock when the bookmobile came.

She had waited for the bookmobile on Tuesday, but it hadn't come, its progress along the route often delayed by unexpected stops. Today the converted bus would be on time. She wanted to be ready, waiting in the porch shade, when it arrived.

They would drive to the train station, first

stopping for a moment at a deserted stretch of road so that they could kiss. Kiss and touch. The touch causing her body to vibrate, her need so great that they often lay in the aisle between bookshelves, unmindful of the occasional passing car, and touched until the need was satisfied.

She grasped the suitcase handle firmly, then picked up a purse from the dresser. Her eyes alight, she walked past the old man, slamming the screen door behind her, and crossed the yard to the garden.

For a long minute, she stared at each wilted row. Then her eyes focused on the center hills of corn. They were greener, much taller than the rest, their stalks a sturdy contrast to the other spindly, yellowing rows. "Thank you, Billy," she nodded to the tallest rows, "Thank you."

The bus was early, roaring down the road, squealing to a stop in front of the house. Her heart beating furiously, she crossed the yard, climbed the steps, took the outstretched hand of the driver, and said, "There's no one here to see. Close the door."

The driver loosened the seat belt from her broad shoulders, and the two women, hands clinging, walked to the sheltered rear of the bus. They breathed into each other, the sound harsh as tongues touched, hands sought. The woman unbuttoned the driver's shirt, her warm mouth enclosing a hardened nipple. The driver freed slacks and briefs as the woman lowered her to the children's reading mat. Then the woman's fingers slipped through moisture into a dark well of engorged flesh, and she heard herself groaning as the driver thrashed to orgasm. Soon, her groans louder and quicker, she felt her own spasms begin.

Buttoned and zipped, now presentable, they headed for the station.

The woman turned to look behind her at the house she was leaving.

"Thank you, Billy," she whispered again.

Petals and Thorns

Molleen Zanger

This time it's pink.

Although the night is bitter cold I hesitate at the car door, keys fanned through my gloved fingers out of habit. Lot K is not as well-lit as it should be and by the time Professor Wong lets us go, most of the other night classes are long gone. Somehow the nearly empty lot seems more forbidding than a crowded one; even the occasional sweep of campus security does not reassure me.

Tonight there is no patrol car, only three other

cars in the dark lot and two at the exits. I stand beside my car and look down at the new snow for footprints but there are none. The snow was just beginning at 6:45 pm when I pulled into this space so I estimate it had to be shortly thereafter.

I unlock my car, stow my backpack behind the driver's seat and move the unwrapped rose to the passenger's side as I buckle in and start my car. I knew it would be here. Maybe hoped. It is the seventh Monday someone's left a rose in my car. As I wait for the engine to warm up I listen to the tape playing, and lift the rose and breathe deeply of it with my eyes closed, as if it were a kiss. Although still curious, I am no longer alarmed by the roses.

Whoever she is, she'll make herself known when she's ready. Then I'll find out about the key, too. Who can she be? Someone in my Shakespeare II class? Maybe the dark-haired older woman with the slow, lopsided smile? God, I hope it's not Sweatsuit with Dangly Earrings. Not Jane, either. Jane's so straight she doesn't know there is anything else. But the key?

As I leave the lot and start the fifty-minute drive home, my now ungloved right hand sifts through the petals that are left of the previous six roses. I hope it won't hurt my admirer's feelings but I pull the petals off the roses and leave them in the well between the bucket seats. I can't very well take them in the house. Some of the petals are leathery crisp, some are still pliable. Their scent pervades my cold solitude. I turn off the tape player so I can think, cutting off Melissa's plea for someone to bring her some water.

The first one was deep red, long-stemmed with the thorns still intact. It arrived during the first class of this semester. I can only manage one or two night classes each semester and at this rate I figure I'll finish in three more years. It is discouraging so I don't think of the period as years; "six more semesters" seems less formidable. Twice a week I stay in Saginaw after work, kill an hour and a half at the library, then go to class. I do temp work, word processing — WordPerfect, Microsoft Word, Display Write #3 — whatever. I'm on a job long enough to learn my way around, then on to the next. Often I'm offered permanent positions with companies, but refuse. I like change, need it, a trait that causes me no small measure of trouble. The roses for example, smell like sweet trouble to me.

I come to a complete stop, then turn right on Davis. I bury my nose in the heady, tempting pinkness and inhale deeply. Roses. Who would be leaving me roses? And how?

Again I think through the possibilities. Someone skilled with a jimmy bar? A cop? Penny? Nah, I'm not her type. How about Officer Beth of the campus police? Too cute, but taken. Shari? Nah. Haven't seen her in years. She wouldn't know where I am. A crook? Someone in between a cop and a crook? Cindy? Nah, she wouldn't drive three hours one way without compensation. Immediate compensation. Maybe it's someone with a car like mine whose key fits. I've heard of that happening. Rare but possible. The car was used when I bought it, so maybe the previous owner? Holly? Nah. Terminally straight if obviously intrigued. Besides, she's not the roses kind.

Someone with a key, obviously, but that doesn't narrow the field by much. I've given my keys as readily as my heart, my body, and haven't always had all of them returned. So maybe someone who wants me back? A shiver tingles through me and not only because the heater hasn't kicked on yet.

Left on Liberty. My last fling left me badly shaken, watching my back, not trusting my judgment. She has my keys, to my car and to the house. Another shiver. A shudder, really. Could Anne be back?

Suddenly I'm afraid, not only for myself but for Kay. Poor Kay. What I've put her through. Especially this last time. I don't know how our friendship survived Anne. There's no phone for miles. I can't call home to make sure she's safe. Why would Anne come back?

Under the overpass, over the underpass. Like loosely strung necklaces of northbound diamonds and southbound rubies, the traffic on I-75 seems leisurely tonight. On Fridays through all seasons the diamonds are tighter, faster, more urgent. On Sundays the rubies are.

Southbound. Anne was southbound when she shrieked out of my life. Snarling epithets, she left "this fucking state," my "fucking life." My fucking bed. And the dreams began.

Right on Adams a half mile, then up and around the loop to join the rubies over the Zilwaukee bridge. It always seems to me that at least one streetlight burns out as I pass under them, but I don't know if this is true or some kind of illusion.

Which was the real Anne? The shy, withdrawn, vulnerable Anne whose hesitancy so appealed to me?

The cunning, manipulative Anne who worked the system for a living? Or the threatening, dangerous Anne who left just in time to save my sanity? During those months with us, I never knew which Anne would walk in the door, up the stairs, which Anne would fall asleep beside me or wake up there.

In the dream I am at school, in the hall, about to enter a classroom. Someone calls my name, the nickname she uses for me although I asked her not to. I begin to turn toward the voice when suddenly she is beside me. Something pricks my side. She shows me a knife, an evil-looking hunting knife, brandishes it quickly, then puts it back to my side, pulls her quilted vest over it so no one can see. She hisses in my ear through a grimace of a smile, "You're coming with me." I see classmates, the professor, as she walks me to the stairs. They smile at me and say "Hi." I open my mouth to scream for help but no sound comes out. The knife pricks my side again, like the thorn of a rose.

Off 75 at the M-81 ramp and then left, eastward for the long, dreary, usually tedious final stretch home. But tonight there is an unaccustomed urgency as I depress the accelerator. Kay. I'm suddenly terrified for Kay.

Anne lived with us for four months one decade, is my usual bitter quip. Last winter, about this time. Another stray for me to save, to comfort, to house. But this one did more than shit in my shoes or sharpen her claws on the couch.

Kay never liked her, never trusted her, but tried to be civil. Kay's and my couplehood had ended several affairs before but we were still sharing the house, still cared about each other, were still family.

Kay seemed resigned to, if not accepting of, Anne's presence. It wasn't until Anne was gone that the truths began to trickle out: How Kay had found Anne removing the strikeplates to the doors because the sound of them shutting irritated her. How, after refusing to eat the cholesterol- or carbohydrate-laden dinners we eat of economic necessity, Anne would go to her room and eat a grocery sack of chocolate candy and wash it down with a six-pack of beer. How Kay caught Anne rifling her wallet one morning. How Anne offered to do anything for Kay, anything, even sleep with her. How she'd come on to our friend Leah, had gone to her to complain of my "abuses" — like going to work every damn day even when she needed company, like refusing to quit college for her, like refusing to leave Kay and move south with her so she could make me "really happy."

A rolling stop at the four ways at I-81 and I-15. I have to get home. I believe Anne is capable of anything. I believe that dream — that recurring dream — is a warning, a premonition.

I remember Kay's voice: "I was so afraid you were going to leave with her. I didn't know how I'd do it, but I would have found a way to stop you. She would have destroyed you."

We'd cried in each other's arms then, and many times since. Anne took something out of me, something primal, something vital. I clung to Kay as if she were a personal flotation device. And slowly we've worked to build a new relationship.

When I moved in with her I brought a beige leather couch, a long-haired calico cat and a fear of intimacy. I used to laugh when people said that to me. "How can someone who likes sex so much fear intimacy?" And when I read the definition of intimacy as a blending of identities with another person, I protested, "Why would anyone even want such a thing? That's appalling! Lose my identity? Take on someone else's? Never!" I did not understand blend as enrichment, I confused identity with identification. Without Kay I would still be a whole, complete, functional person, but I would not be the same one. Something special about me would be lost without her. What if I don't get the chance to tell her?

Slow down through Reese, dodge the drunk leaving the bar with his lights off and in my lane, note the cop parked at the other end of the village waiting for speeders behind a motor home at Reese RV Sales and Service.

I'm more than half way home and an ache to see that Kay is safe battles a sharp certainty that she is not. What had Anne said? *"If I can't have you, no one will."*

No one has. That whole part of me has shut down completely. I no longer flirt, no longer lust, no longer fantasize. I can't even bear to hear other people allude to their sex lives. I don't want to talk about it, don't want to read about it, don't want to think about it.

Kay and I sleep together. We have since the day Anne left. We cuddle, talk, rub or scratch backs, hold hands. But lovemaking is far from me. Anne scorched it out of me. God we fucked. I didn't know it was possible to fuck too much. There was not a fantasy we didn't share, didn't act out. We fucked each other empty, fucked each other dry. Then we woke up and she discovered she hated me and I discovered I was afraid of her.

A sudden vision flashes through my mind — Kay lying bloody and dead on the kitchen floor and Anne waiting for me behind the door with her knife. The horrifying weight and copper-tasting possibility of this image urges me to pull over to the side of the road. Instead I stomp down the accelerator, speed through Watrousville thirty miles an hour over the limit.

Kay would laugh, be amazed, if I got a speeding ticket. She's the brick-footed one. She frequently gets pulled over but somehow always gets off with a warning. I think it's her smile. I love her smile. When's the last time I told her that?

Don't let it be too late. Don't let anything happen to her. Ever. I pray to anyone listening.

Wajamega. I don't slow for the possibility of deer in the pine trees on the curve. The time we hit a deer I was in the passenger seat. Kay saw it and slowed. It turned away from the road and we relaxed, then suddenly it turned back again and dashed into our car, its face smashed against the glass inches from my face. I could see each coarse hair and its wide eyes full of terror. Blood smeared like finger paint across the window. I threw up the next day when I found the tuft of innocent hair stuck to the fender. For months I relived those seconds in my sleep and still react sharply to sudden movement at the side of the road. Tonight I don't care.

The pink rose now looks like a veiled threat. Its gentle fragrance is as deceptive as the words "I love you. How many women have said that to me? Or I to them? How many flowers have been given or

received? Roses. Daisies twisted into crowns. Mixed
bouquets. Armloads of gladiolus from the farm
market. The exotic spotted lily. The orchid. The birds
of paradise. Lilacs from the neighbor's yard. Tulips
from the park. Daffodils. Lilies of the valley. The
plate-sized night blooming cereus. The zany
sunflower. Trilliums. All those women, all those
flowers, saying "I want you," "I need you," "I'm
sorry."

The second light. Right one block, two, three. The
fire hydrant. Right into our driveway. Kay's blue
Gran Prix. No other, no bronze Impala. Hidden in
the garage? I park, turn off my car, hesitate, stomach
like a paint mixer. Be safe. Please. I leave my books
in the car but take the pink rose. If it's not too late,
I'll tell her everything, show her the rose, the petals.
Together we'll work it through. Trade cars? Change
the locks? I should have told her from the first one,
the red one. Or the white, or the yellow, or . . .

The house is dark. Eerie. No friendly porch light,
no kitchen light, no light from the living room. As I
reach for the light switch, I realize how quiet the
house is. The TV isn't on. Kay always kept the TV
on for company. It used to drive me nuts. I kept
turning it off, she kept turning it on. Past tense. I'm
thinking in the past tense. Through the moonlit
window I see dark spots on the pale vinyl floor, hold
my breath. Please. Please, no. I switch on the light.
Try to understand what I'm seeing.

Roses. Two pink ones, a foot and a half apart,
lead into the dining room. More roses on the wood
floor, the rugs, pink roses. I follow through the living
room to her door. I knock. There is no answer, so I
open it slowly. There are candles lit on her dresser

and more roses on the floor, on the bed, our pillows. Kay sits tailor-fashion in the purple satin nightshirt I bought her for her birthday. There is a question in her eyes, a smile on her lips.

I match it with one of my own.

Bunny

Carol Schmidt

You could say Bunny Robinson and I brought
ourselves out together when we were seven years old.

Back in 1951, our families had moved into a new
subdivision of cramped, white-shingled, one-story
square boxes in Warren, Michigan, and Bunny was
the only other child my age within blocks. Both our
fathers worked for Chrysler. We were both our
families' only children then, although each of our
families had another child soon after we moved to

Warren. The Robinsons had another daughter, while I got a baby brother.

Our families were soon wrapped up in the new babies, leaving Bunny and me to fend for ourselves. We spent just about every waking — and sleeping — moment together at one house or another. We were in her bed, giggling under the covers after repeated warnings from Mrs. Robinson to shut up and get to sleep, when Bunny told me the latest news about sex she'd learned from an older cousin.

"Let's play lesbian, it's kind of like playing doctor," she announced, and told me, showed me, what that entailed. I was horrified for only a moment. Then I let her slip off my flannel nightie and look at me down there, though we'd already checked each other out thoroughly in earlier versions of playing doctor. This time I felt a funny sensation and squirmed to get a look: she was licking me!

"What are you doing!" I yelped, and the loudness of my cry made us both jump up and get my nightie back on and pile the covers on and feign sleep. When it was clear Mrs. Robinson wasn't coming to check, we got undressed again and this time I forced myself to lick her. Even though we'd had a bath — together — before bed, I imagined I still could taste pee. But it was a different taste, still kind of salty, a heady smell that was immediately addictive. From that point on, every night we spent together, we "played lesbian."

Until the following year, when suddenly we didn't do that any more. We were a little distant for a while, and other kids our age moved onto our block to provide some variety to our play.

At ten we became best friends again, though she

insisted on playing with her Barbie and Ken dolls and cutting out paper dolls with fancy wedding dresses and ball gowns. I put up with it to be with her.

I was happier when I got her onto her bicycle and we explored the east side of Warren from Eight Mile Road to Twelve Mile Road, all the way from Van Dyke to Hayes Street, including the tiny town of Centerline which sat inside Warren, totally enclosed. The homes near the Eight Mile border to Detroit were like ours, tiny, framed and square, while the further north we bicycled, the houses became sprawling brick ranches with nice lawns. We got to know every kid, every dog, every pothole, every stop sign, in the sixteen square miles. Sounds incredible now, but we had that freedom to explore. Today I'd worry about a ten-year-old walking to school.

Kids had this need to identify with some singer or TV or movie star back then; I suppose they still do. When we transferred to middle school, our sixth grade classmates had raging arguments over who was more beautiful, Elizabeth Taylor or Doris Day.

Of course Liz was, everybody could see that, but in reality we were fighting over the popularity of Bunny Robinson, who was a bouncy cute honey blonde, versus Loretta DuShay, the cool Liz look-alike.

Me? Someone should have pointed out the resemblance to Kirk Douglas, but that was unthinkable back then; I got stuck as Debbie Reynolds because of my deepset eyes.

Boys started following Bunny and me home from school about then, and it soon became clear that I was being edged out. Bunny was a natural-born flirt.

I don't think she even noticed how I was hurting. I don't think she even noticed when I stopped walking with her altogether and took different routes to avoid seeing her and her entourage. The invitations to her house stopped.

Her mother let Bunny go on afternoon dates when she turned thirteen! I saw her kissing a boy at the Saturday afternoon matinee at the theater and almost gagged. We'd both been really smart in school, but while I continued to get all A's, her grades plummeted. Her parents divorced around then and her mother remarried, a hunk of a guy we immediately compared to James Dean.

In the eighth grade our school hosted a Bunny Hop, the culmination of a school year of well-supervised Friday night dances, seven to nine pm, with the sanitized white-bread versions of every rock and roll hit — Pat Boone instead of Elvis Presley, the Four Freshmen rather than the raunchy, sensual, very black sounds of the Penguins and the Satins. Bunny had gotten herself kicked off the dance floor a couple of times for doing the hip-shaking Chicken anyway. In the girls' bathroom she demonstrated for all of us how to do the shimmy, forbidden on the dance floor, while we choked on the Camels and Lucky Strikes we attempted to inhale with sophistication.

Bunny should have been the automatic choice for queen of the Bunny Hop, right? Instead, Loretta DuShay headed one line and Bunny headed the other, and all of us had to line up behind our choice. In the restroom Bunny had waved her new one-dollar, silver-toned, rhinestone-spangled friendship ring in my direction, a gift from her latest steady, and the

incident still rankled. I got into Loretta's line. I
wasn't sure Bunny noticed. Loretta won by three.
She got a rhinestone tiara to take home. Bunny made
a scene doing the shimmy on the dance floor and got
sent home early.

Once we reached Warren High, I was strictly
forbidden to go into The Hut, a smoky hamburger
joint a block from the school where older kids hung
around and anyone ditching school was likely to be
found. Of course I had to check it out a few times,
and on one of those times Bunny's new stepfather,
Jack Mullins, came stomping into The Hut with fury
in his eyes.

He waded through the crowd, tossing hefty
teenaged boys right and left, until he found Bunny,
and he dragged her kicking and hollering, out of
there, by her arm, her collar, her hair. At one point
he had her by her saddle shoes and tugged her along
the gritty wood floor, even though her tight straight
skirt was sliding up to her hips and showing her
white cotton underpants and she was screaming about
splinters. None of the boys lifted a hand.

He finally heard her, or noticed her exposure, and
he flipped her up and over his shoulder and carried
her out like a sack of potatoes, cursing at all of us.
He spotted me and gave me a particularly heinous
glare, as if it was all my fault. I never went back
inside The Hut, though I noticed Bunny entering or
leaving the hangout many times after that.

The second semester of ninth grade I signed up
for French, having decided that I really might have a
chance at college and ought to meet the college prep
requirements just in case I could get a scholarship.
To my surprise Bunny Robinson was sitting in the

first row, flirting with poor old Mr. LaPlante, who was obviously flustered by her cleavage revealed by a tight black sweater that had two too many buttons undone.

Bunny's hair was blonder, coarser — she had to be dyeing it herself. Her eyebrows were plucked and blackened, her eyes heavily lined, her lashes blobby black, and her lips fiery red in an emphasized bow shape.

Mr. LaPlante asked us to go around the room and give our names and the reasons we were taking French. Most of us said it was because four semesters of a foreign language were required in College Prep. Bunny said, Because it's such a sexy language, and changed postures in her seat so that her breasts stuck out in his direction. He turned even redder. She didn't come back the next day. Or the next. I was glad.

It was April, the semester nearly over, when I rushed into French class late and saw Bunny sitting in a back row seat. Her mascara was smeared badly and lipstick was on her teeth. Her blouse hung out over her skirt and was buttoned right up to her chin. She looked like hell. "Slut," I said to myself, angry at her very presence.

Mr. LaPlante did a double-take when he saw her, but he didn't say anything or ask for any explanation. Guess he figured she wouldn't be back again anyway, so why bother? That's about what I thought, too.

But in the middle of class Bunny raised her hand. Her skin was chalk-white against the black makeup. Yes, Bunny? Mr. LaPlante asked.

She motioned for him to come over to her. He tilted his head quizzically and walked over. She beckoned with her hand that he should bend over so she could whisper something to him. His face turned deep red and he stood up in a hurry, looking as if he'd been struck.

Finally he leaned back over and whispered something back to her. Her face was strained. Tears made fresh black tracks on the snow. She folded her arms and put her head down on her desk.

Curiosity was killing me. I'm ashamed to say it was only curiosity at that point. I'm sorry to say that I felt glad she was in trouble somehow. Served her right for being a slut. For dumping me. For not playing lesbian any more. My anger was a lingering burn that had been smoldering inside for years.

"Bunny, what's wrong?" I whispered loudly and repeatedly. She finally raised her head and gave me such a look of pain that it broke through my mindset. I felt a welling of pity, of caring, of love for my former friend.

And then I saw the clear yellow rivulets spreading from under her chair.

I got up and left the room with a nod at Mr. LaPlante. My locker was nearby, and I brought back my raincoat and a pair of dusty Levis that I'd left wadded up in the back after a Clean-Up, Paint-Up, Fix-Up day at the school. I stopped at the restroom and got a wad of paper towels, wetting some of them. When the bell rang at the end of class I slipped inside and wrapped Bunny in my coat and handed her the jeans.

"I'll meet you in the john when I clean up here,"

I told her. Mr. LaPlante looked so relieved that I was cleaning up under Bunny's chair. No one else in class had said a word or stuck around.

Afterward we went to The Hut, where else? In a rear booth she told me what had happened. She was pregnant. Her nerves were frazzled, and she couldn't seem to hold her bladder the past week, the thirteenth week since her last period. No wonder my Levis had fit her. She couldn't hide it anymore or pretend nothing was wrong. But she didn't know what to do.

Last I'd heard she'd been dating some hood named Tony. I asked, "Will Tony marry you?" She was only fifteen, but he was probably nineteen. The law would allow it, for the sake of the baby.

"It's not his," she whispered. She wouldn't say anything else.

I walked her home, my arm around her waist, her head snuggled against me, and she promised to get my raincoat dry cleaned. I told her not to worry about it.

She seemed reluctant to go inside her house. I kept asking her what was wrong, and who was the father of her baby. Finally she told me. The father was Jack Mullins, her stepfather.

She couldn't tell anyone else. She didn't know what to do except maybe kill herself. I made her promise not to do that, to let me think for awhile.

It was 1959; I'd never heard of such a thing as abortion, and neither had she, even if we'd had any idea how to find an illegal abortionist or the money to pay for it.

"Promise you won't tell," she insisted. I promised.
I told.

First thing the next day I asked Mr. LaPlante
what I should do. He was really good at turning red
but not so good at coming up with ideas. He told me
to see my counselor.

My counselor, to whom I'd been assigned
alphabetically, said that it was a home problem and
Bunny couldn't come back to school anyway, and
besides, she wasn't Bunny's counselor.

Bunny's counselor insisted that Bunny had to
come see her herself.

In desperation I tried the one counselor everyone
seemed to like, even though she was only supposed to
see Allen through Enright. At first she was too busy,
and then she tried to direct me back to places I'd
already been. But finally she listened, then sent a
page to get Bunny out of the class she was supposed
to be in that hour. Of course she'd skipped. "I have
to make some calls," the counselor said, and sent me
on to class.

I went through my classes in a daze, worrying if
I had done the right thing, worrying what was ahead.
At the end of the day the counselor got me out of
my last class and said we needed to talk to the police
and to a social worker, and I needed to be strong to
go through with it. I needed to be strong for Bunny.

The police took Jack Mullins away, and then they
took Bunny away. I was walking home from school
when I saw the green Macomb County official station
wagon pull up to her house and two men in suits
bring her out and force her into the car. She
screamed at me, hate in her eyes, reminding me I'd
promised not to tell. I felt as if I were the one who'd
repeatedly raped her. But I told the police and Social
Services everything.

Bunny never came back to school. Her mother would never talk to me. No one could tell me anything. I never saw her again.

I heard rumors at school, rumors that she'd been sent to Casa Maria Home for Wayward Girls, rumors that she was with an aunt in Missouri, rumors she'd married Tony. Nobody knew for sure. The counselor assured me I'd done the right thing. I wasn't at all sure. I thought of her constantly.

Eventually the memories faded. As we all learned more about child sexual abuse I finally forgave myself for breaking her confidence. I kept thinking about Bunny's kid sister who probably would have been next in line.

I got that scholarship to the University of Michigan and in Ann Arbor I discovered other women willing to "play lesbian." My first real lover turned out to be a four-year dyke who promptly went back in the closet upon graduation. I got a job with Parke-Davis Pharmaceuticals using my degree in chemistry, and when Parke-Davis moved out of Detroit I became a sales rep for a company distributing chemicals used in manufacturing. I met an art teacher at a lesbian bar and we lived together for twenty-three years, until she died of breast cancer.

Oprah Winfrey was on the tube one day that I was home sick with the flu, and she had on couples who had been high school sweethearts and then lost touch with one another, only to be reunited many decades later. Some of them were able to reestablish their romance, others had found they were hopelessly incompatible now. For the first time in years, I thought of Bunny again. She had certainly enjoyed "playing lesbian." It had been more than playing doctor, whether she wanted to admit it or not.

I looked up Private Investigators in the yellow pages and hired somebody to track down Bunny.

They found her, living alone in a trailer park in Toledo, Ohio, a hop and a skip down I-75 from Ferndale. She'd been married four times, the investigator reported, and all five of her kids were grown. None of the kids listed in the report was the right age to have been Jack's baby. She must have gone to live with that aunt in Missouri and given the baby up for adoption. Or maybe she'd miscarried. Maybe someone else had known how to get an abortionist, despite how far along she was.

Maybe she'll tell me what happened, maybe she won't. She did agree to see me again, and I'm driving down tonight.

I'm not too worried about her four marriages meaning she's heterosexual — too many marriages are as suspicious as never married, in my book. Maybe she was just playing, maybe not. I'm bringing her roses, in case not.

Grandma

Penny Hayes

1470 Elmwood Lane
Allentown, PA 17623
January 7, 1992

Dear Mom and Dad,

Last night I had the most frightening dream about Grandma. I won't go into detail, but the whole scene occurred during a terrible rainstorm much like the tornado of 'seventy-one that Daddy said killed Grandma. She was trying to tell me something, but the roar of the wind made it impossible to hear her.

I'd love to know what she wanted. She seemed terribly upset. I also wish I could have met her.

Winter break was one of the best I've ever had. I don't ever remember laughing quite so hard nor so often as you and Daddy and I did this time. Spring break seems so far away that I can't even imagine it ever getting here. I'm glad I'm a senior and have only a couple of years to go. It becomes tiring to study, which I must do now. Write soon.

Your loving daughter,
Sarah

R.D. 1
Lake Lillian, MN 56253
January 16, 1992

Dear Sarah,

It would have been splendid if you could have met both your grandparents. Your grandmother was a lovely lady and was taken from us so unexpectedly we could hardly get through the next several months without someone in total tears every day and sometimes several of us crying together.

Grandpa was always thought to be so stern and harsh toward her that it was an additional shock when, unable to bear his loss, he had a heart attack, dying not quite a year later.

It simply amazes me how much like Grandma you look with such fair skin, your thick brown hair and clear hazel eyes. I'd have to say you get your tall, thin frame from your mother. I always did enjoy being five feet-ten. By the way, do you recall that for a while your grandmother went to college? That was heady stuff for an eighteen-year-old Minnesota girl to do in the forties.

But this is old history. Tell me of your new housemate. That's what they're called now, isn't it? We used to call them roommates. I wonder if anyone still uses that term other than those who lived "way back then." Is she easy to get along with? Does she take her studies seriously, or is she a "college" girl looking for an M-R-S degree? Ha, ha.

I hope you two get along better than the last girl you roomed with. I'll send Daddy down there this time if I have to hear for the next six months about men being thrown out of your room at three in the morning.

With love,
Mother and Father

January 30, 1992

Dear Mom and Dad,

I'd forgotten that Grandma went to college. Wasn't she one of the "girls" who eventually went to Switzerland on an exchange program? I remember you saying something about it, but I don't recall the details.

My housemate looks a little like Audrey Hepburn, with long eyelids and eyelashes and chocolate brown eyes. Her hair is also a dark brown color. She walks with such grace she gives the impression of floating across the floor. Her elegance could put the Queen of England to shame. By the way, we aren't called "girls" anymore. We're women!

I find my housemate a big help. When I came in from jogging last evening, she gave me a fantastic backrub. It felt wonderful after having run through a thick fog for an hour. That lady has *hands*! I couldn't move for an hour afterward and didn't get to my studies for the rest of the night. She's something much more than a housemate when she can do that to me.

I forgot to mention. A couple of nights ago, I had another dream about Grandma. I wonder why she keeps cropping up in my sleep. I'm beginning to miss her. Is it possible to miss someone you've never met?

Your loving daughter,
Sarah

Dear Sarah,

You've asked an interesting question: "Is it possible to miss someone you've never met?" I believe so. I miss listening to Kate Smith, one of the greatest singers of this century. She's from the 'twenties through the 'sixties era and the one who sang "God Bless America" in such a powerful way that some people believed the song had become our new national anthem. Of course, I also miss Grandma. She was a wonderful mother-in-law who minded her own business.

I don't know why you keep dreaming about Grandma. I can't help you there, but I'm glad you do and hope your dreams have become pleasant ones.

It's as though I saw Grandma only yesterday. I can still easily recall her delicate wrists and hands. She was such a small-boned, fragile looking woman. I don't know how she bore a two-hundred-and-twenty-pound hairy hulk of a son like your father and two more giants after him. He mourns her so, he seldom speaks of her. He's waiting impatiently at the door to take me to town, so I'll close for now.

With love,
Mother and Father

P.S. It wasn't a college-based exchange program that Grandma was in, but a church-sponsored religious studies exchange program. That is, as long as the parents paid their child's way. At that time, her parents had plenty of money, and decided to send her over. They later regretted it, having had a terrible time getting her to come home. They eventually had to go after her.

Father's yelling now. I must run!

February 19, 1992

Dear Mom and Dad,

Mom, you're always so formal when you sign your letters Mother and Father. Dad's never written a word to me in his life. But it's nice of you to include him. He'd probably growl if you didn't and probably will anyway when he reads this. Hi, Daddy!

It was wonderful talking with you on the phone last week. I'm sorry I missed Daddy. I know you worry about money and phone bills, and you're absolutely right. College is too expensive, but hopefully the rewards will be worth the price. Biology seems to be a more costly subject than other courses offered.

I'm dying of curiosity about the contents of the small box you sent. It was such a coincidence it came at the very moment you called to stop me from opening it, or I would have for sure. However much my curiosity has been piqued, I've been honorably doing nothing more than hefting the package from time to time before putting it back into my drawer. My fingers burn each time I touch it. When may I open it?

What happened to all the money Grandma's family had? We've certainly never seen any of it.

Your loving daughter,

Sarah

February 23, 1992

Dear Sarah,

You are never to mention this letter to your father. *Ever*! He's asked me several times about the box. He doubts I'm telling the truth that what I sent you were cookies. He said he never smelled any cookies nor saw any baking going on when he got home from work. I've had to deceive him from time to time over the years, and I don't do it well.

In your next letter, could you *please* possibly mention your having received chocolate chip cookies? They've always been your favorite.

About the box — it'll be awhile before you open it.

Great-Grandpa lost his money horse-betting. Your father never mentions this part of his family's "darker" history. Being the first born of this generation, Daddy eventually became the family's next historian and keeper of all kinds of assorted junk from his distant past. I read about Great-Grandpa's fall from grace in some old letters tucked away in a moldy old trunk in the attic. Eventually, you'll be "keeper of these records." Hang onto them. They're wonderful history.

With love,

Mother and Father

P.S. I'm sorry, honey, I don't feel I can show your last letter to Daddy because of your mentioning not being able to open the box just yet and our phone call, although he'll find out about the call as soon as the bill comes in. I'll just tell him I missed you terribly — which I do! He wouldn't be particularly pleased to learn that you know about Great-Grandpa, either.

Love,
Mommy

February 27, 1992

Dear Mom and Dad:

I *loved* the chocolate chip cookies. You know they're my favorite. Did Daddy help bake them? If you did, Dad, you should take up baking instead of selling cars.

My housemate flew home to Florida this weekend, so it's terribly lonely around here. Her grandmother died a couple of days ago, and she's taking the loss extremely hard.

Grandma invaded my dreams again last night. I think she's on my mind because my housemate has talked about hers so much lately.

Time to study.

Your loving daughter,
Sarah

March 4, 1992

Dear Sarah,

Does your housemate have a name, or is that her name: "Housemate"? That's all you ever call her. What's she studying? You've only told me that she's lovely and has great hands. There must be more.

I'll be sending more cookies soon. Rum this time. They're better when they sit for a couple of weeks. Don't worry. They won't spoil. I made sure there were plenty for your Father, too, which seemed to pacify him since he didn't get any chocolate chip the last time.

We harvested the potatoes and squash yesterday. We gathered seven bushels of potatoes and three of squash. When I was a child, our family had a garden because of necessity. I remember hating to dig potatoes. Now I love it. I suppose we don't really need to plant anymore, but it brings back some wonderful memories of times when life seemed so much more simple.

With love,
Mother and Father

March 15, 1992

Dear Mom and Dad,

Thanks for the rum cookies. They arrived yesterday and are sitting in a drawer under lock and key along with some jewelry and a love letter or two.

Yes, my housemate has a name. Glorene shortened to Glo — which she seems to do. She manicures her nails, plucks her eyebrows and makes sure that her legs and underarms are meticulously clean of body hair. (Skip over this part, Dad.) Glo's a biology student.

She's back from her grandmother's funeral. Apparently it was an incredibly difficult time for her. She still cries every night. Last night I held her all night long. It's the first time I've ever slept with another adult. I suppose it should have felt quite strange, but I didn't feel a bit put out or crowded. I was little too warm from such close contact, but otherwise, comfortable.

Grandma visited me again last night. It felt as though she were standing beside my bed. In my dreams, she always looks just like that faded old photo sitting on the piano you have of her and Grandpa. She looks so young!

Your loving daughter,
Sarah

March 20, 1992

Dear Sarah,

Your father had a fit when he read your letter. You're going to have to come home if you write you've been sleeping with a woman. Those aren't my words. Those are his, and he means it! He's asked (told) me to tell you this. So don't sleep with this woman no matter how hard she cries. Your father says that's what shrinks are for — for tearful, weeping women. So respect how Daddy feels, and don't do it again. Please!

He's also troubled that you keep mentioning Grandma. It pains him to be reminded of his loss. He wasn't much better adjusting to his father's death.

Hope you're allowing the rum cookies to continue aging. Your father is chomping at the bit to try one. I keep telling him, no. He must wait. It doesn't please him very much.

I can't wait to see you over Spring Break. Daddy informed me that David Shultz will be joining us for dinner one evening.

With love,
Mother and Father

April 8, 1992

Dear Mom and Dad,

Vacation was wonderful. I wish it could have been

longer. It was especially pleasing to go skating on the pond with Dad just like we used to when I was a little girl. He often held my hand and saved me from falling. I hope he'll always be there for me like that, although I'm no longer a little girl.

The train ride back to school was exhausting this time. I've traveled the route so often, it's becoming old hat.

Glo and I had a very long talk last night. We've decided that after we graduate, no matter where one goes, the other will follow. We're not going to marry and have children. It's not in our stars. We'll be water lilies and float upon a saltless ocean until we die. Of course I'm talking like a silly schoolgirl, but recently I've felt exactly like one. Doubtless, my words will anger Daddy, but he'll adjust, I'm sure. I could have turned out to be something much different — like a serial killer.

I'll be trying the rum cookies tonight.

Your loving daughter,
Sarah

April 12, 1992

Dear Sarah,

Your father is in a rage. It was all I could do to keep him from calling you and ordering you home — now! I want you to continue with schooling. We fight all the time. He doesn't want me writing to you. He thinks he's lost his little girl. Of course he hasn't. He's acting like a damn fool, and I've told him so.

I'm happy that you enjoyed your vacation. It seemed exceptionally wonderful this year. How adult-like you've become. Even when that boring young man David Shultz poured red wine down your

white flannels, you were as cool as the day was
outside. Did Glo have a hand in your maturing? If
so, I like her and would one day enjoy meeting her.
Never mind what your father says.

With love,

Mother and Father

P.S. Your father sends his love whether he admits
it or not. He was very angry when his mother was
taken from him. He doesn't take loss of loved ones
well at all.

248 Oakland Lane
Minneapolis, Minnesota
August 15, 1945

Dearest Kirsten,

*It is with a grievous heart that I write you. I'm
thousands of miles from you, yet your face is vividly
etched before me. I see you in the clouds, in a flower,
in the ocean, the edge on which I stood a week ago
as I gazed toward lovely Switzerland.*

*I am to be wedded tomorrow. My father is forcing
this marriage. I've fought it as long as I could. My
mother is sick from the friction I feel I have created
between my parents. She is wasting away to nothing
and suffering so over my rebellion that I believe she
is dying. I wish I were only imagining such behavior
in a woman of her age and stature, but I'm not.*

*I dread this marriage. I dread tomorrow night
and all the morrow nights to come. To have this
man's hand on my breast where yours has rested is
unthinkable.*

*Oh, my darling, how will I get through life
without you? I'll never know such love and passion
with another. Please forgive me. If it is ever at all*

*within my power, I'll see you again before I die as I
once promised.*

> *Until death do us part —*
> *and beyond,*
> *Rose*

May 25, 1992

Dear Sarah,

You haven't written in weeks. I must admit to
anger when I continue writing faithfully and hear
nothing in return from you. Please don't forget your
mother.

Your father persists in his anger. I tell him he's
being foolish. He needs to understand that when he
sent you to college, he was opening your mind to all
kinds of new possibilities. He once told me that's
what happened to him in college. I reminded him of
once having said that to me, and he nearly blew a
gasket.

Please, please write and let me know you're fine.

> With love,
> Mother and Father

May 28, 1992

Dear Daddy,

Grandma is alive!

How could you and Mother have kept this
information from me? Obviously Mother has
maintained at least minimal contact with Grandma
over the years. Weeks ago, she sent me a small box
which, after putting a few things together in my
head, I finally opened not long after returning from

vacation. In it were Grandma's California address where she's been living for years and a very sensitive letter written the day before her wedding.

I'm guessing that Great-Grandpa either found the letter before Grandma had a chance to mail it or deliberately took it from her using it to "keep her in her place," then later, passing it on to Grandpa, assuring that she would stay there. And now, as our family historian, you received the letter, didn't you? Is that how you kept Grandma away from me all these years? Did you think I would love her less if I learned something about her that offended you?

How ironic it is that it was Grandma's life, not her "death," that killed Grandpa. It had to have been terrible for her, being blackmailed all her life, hiding all her life who she was, leaving Grandpa only because in the end, she had to, letter be damned!

Do you realize how honorably she behaved? She didn't leave before you boys were all grown up, before fulfilling her father's demands and her husband's, before providing grandchildren for her parents.

Grandma deserves a life after having had hers controlled and manipulated from birth until she moved away. I'm glad she grabbed hold while she still had time.

Glo and I are flying to California tomorrow. By the time you get this letter, we'll be there. I'm hoping against hope that when I meet Grandma, life has been good to Kirsten and that Grandma will be with her.

I love both you and Mommy very much. I also

love Glo. My place is with her. Whatever path we choose, we choose it together, and we choose it ourselves.

> Your loving and faithful
> daughter,
> Sarah

Finders Keepers

Dorothy Tell

Doris Hooper opened her door to find a frowning, nervous woman on her front step. She held a small cardboard box tightly with both hands.

"Yes?" Doris said.

"Um — you don't know me — I mean, at least I don't *think* you do ... oh boy, that's a dumb thing to say to a psychic." Upon saying this, the woman seemed to lose energy, like a top beginning to wobble in its orbit.

Doris never ever got used to the fact that being a

psychic and having the *finder's gift* in no way made her life easier. She didn't have a clue what was going on with her visitor, except for what she could glean from reading ordinary signs like body language.

The woman cleared her throat. Here it comes, Doris thought, still chagrined she had not seen it coming before she opened the door.

"My name's Natalie Stuart and I'm a school teacher and I live just down the street." She drew a deep breath and continued, "I read an article about you a few weeks ago that said you help the police find murder victims. Do you ever find *live* people?"

"Well, yeah. I've found a few live people." Doris made herself not ask why Natalie wanted to know. She had a plain old non-psychic hunch she was about to find out.

"Can I come in for a minute?" Natalie took a tentative step toward the open doorway. "There's someone I really need to find."

Doris led Natalie Stuart into the sitting room, where Natalie selected the plumpest chair and sat, smoothing her palms over her sturdy denim-covered thighs.

"Well — see . . ." Natalie seemed to search for just the right words. "I hope you aren't put off by what I'm about to say." She dropped her gaze for a second, then went on. "I'm a lesbian, see, and about eight years ago I did a real stupid thing."

Having once been a less-than-rocket-scientist-lesbian herself, and not about to re-visit that angst-filled place with her guest, Doris simply grinned and tried to make her visitor feel more at ease. "I'm hardly ever offended by stupidity ... I've done some pretty dumb things myself. What is it that you did?"

Natalie blushed but continued talking. "I ran out on the love of my life. I couldn't take all the pressure from my family, and the stress of having to hide my life from all my students and their parents did awful things to my personality."

She leaned forward and placed her hand on Doris's arm, apparently to convey her contrition. And before Doris could mount any defense, images of Esther crowded behind her eyes.

She hadn't allowed herself more than a momentary thought of Esther Bastrop in years. She'd been very successful in changing her life and staying away from women who attracted her the way Esther had. And now — here was that old dream, come to haunt her again.

She saw the two of them, herself and Esther, making love. That wonderfully gentle, woman-to-woman love that she would not let her conscious mind think about. But there they were, she and Esther coming together in wild abandon, hot and naked and ecstatic.

It was like she was seeing a movie. The whole scene from *Desert Hearts,* the both of them naked in front of the window, with Doris sitting in front with Esther's legs and arms wrapped around her. She could hear the music playing and feel Esther's mouth nuzzling her neck and Esther's voice whispering lovely, forbidden words in her ear. And then she was looking at the movie again and trying to hear what Cay was saying to Silver when they were in the

bathtub together. And then Cay was Natalie and
Natalie was telling Doris all about how she left her
lover, Ellen, and that she was wiser and older now
and *omygod* what would it take to get Doris to find
Ellen for her?

Doris straightened her back and tried to shake off
the effects of her momentary slide into the past.
"Have you tried to find Ellen yourself?"

Natalie threw her hands up in a gesture of
despair. "I've tried everything . . . even a private
investigator. There's just no trace after she went to
the Southwest. People at her last known address in
Albuquerque said she might have gone to New York
or Boston or San Francisco — she talked about all
those places." Natalie clasped her hands together and
wrung them. "Oh yes, I've looked. You're my last
hope. I don't have enough money to search all those
cities. I have some things that belonged to her,
though. I brought them with me. The article said it's
better if you have something like that to hold." She
looked at Doris with pleading brown eyes. "Maybe
you can at least get some idea of where I could begin
to look for her again."

Doris felt a little sigh of resignation escape her as
she studied Natalie. She guessed it wouldn't hurt to
hold the objects that lay nestled in the little box
Natalie had just placed on the low table in front of
her. Sometimes that was the best part of having the
gift. It always surprised her that the images could be
so distinct. It was like putting together the pieces of
a puzzle. Even when the police searches ended with
the discovery of a murder victim, she never
experienced the pain the victim had endured, she
only felt a pervasive sorrow and finality whenever the

images given her by her gift of psychometry led to a
sad conclusion.

She let her hand hover above the box for a
moment then curled her fingers around a shining
disk attached to a large chrome ring. Obviously a key
ring. The coldness of it leaked out and into her palm.
She closed her eyes and let her mind run free, like
an engine with no gears engaged, full of energy and
readiness, humming in place. She thought of what
Natalie had told her about her ex-lover. About how
cowardly Natalie had been when she'd run out on
Ellen.

The disk in her hand felt suddenly warm and in
a powerful rush of feeling that squeezed the breath
from her lungs, Doris was transported from the
reality of where she sat with Natalie to a place she
had tried for years to forget. The bed she had shared
with Esther.

And Esther was in the bed with Doris and they
were naked and Esther's hands were all over her and
Esther's tongue was bringing her to flashfires of
orgasm. She heard herself crying *no, no, nooo,* her
eyes flew open and immediately she was back in her
house and her loins were on fire and her swollen
clitoris was thumping in orgasmic relief.

Natalie was staring at her with alarm. "Are you
okay?"

Doris tried to stand but her knees were too weak.
She leaned forward instead and crossed her arms
over her abdomen. She was deeply embarrassed by
her runaway physicality but relieved as her brain
registered the obvious fact that Natalie didn't have
the slightest idea what Doris was feeling.

Control returning to her limbs, Doris nodded to

Natalie. "I just got some crossed messages, I guess . . . nothing bad. Some old stuff of my own got in the way."

She reached for the box. "I really need to do this alone. I'll call you in a few days and give you a report, okay?"

Natalie left after a few more questions and more reassurance that Doris was indeed okay and yes Doris would call with the very first information she had.

Doris spent the next few days in a stew of memories and images. She stumbled through the days, unable to concentrate long enough to complete the contract word-processing jobs which paid her rent and bought the eight-minute microwave meals on which she subsisted.

She had never before experienced a conflict like this. One moment the gift seemed to work fine, then the next time she tried to make sense of anything she was assailed with memories of her life with Esther. Past quarrels came back in total recall. Over and over the movie of their last time together would play in her mind.

"Go on then, Esther. You coward — leave! When are you going to identify yourself as what you *are*, not what you were? As long as you remain only an *ex*-nun, you can't be anything in the present."

And Esther had countered with, "I left all that *dee-dee dee-dee* mystical stuff back at the convent. Visions? No thank you — been there, done that! Why can't you just be a *normal* lesbian? How come you have to have some kind of spooky *gift*?"

And then Esther had gone. Had left Doris to close into herself and gradually despair of being a normal anything. To live with the chagrin of knowing she was doing exactly what she had accused Esther of. Being an ex-lesbian.

Over the years she'd seemed to live mostly in her head, allowing the physical side of her nature to atrophy until she came to think of herself as asexual. Not lesbian — not even woman — just *seeker*, finder of lost things for sad people. *Finders keepers, losers weepers.* The old child's poem had many meanings for her now.

Doris wrestled with her sudden inability to keep memories of Esther at bay. Why had they surfaced now? Because Natalie was a lesbian and hearing Natalie talk about her Ellen and giving Doris the box of Ellen's things to touch had opened a crack in Doris's old defenses? Had all this lesbian stuff come up from Doris's repressed little closet to get in the way of her psychic abilities?

She sat at her accustomed place for receiving images, her kitchen table, looking at Ellen's belongings. The key ring, a faded plastic Frisbee, a pair of driving gloves.

Doris composed herself and used both hands to pick up the Frisbee. She held it to her chest with her eyes tightly closed. The first image flashed through her mind. Quick and clear. She smiled as a big white dog leaped high and caught the red toy just as it began to arc up and away from it. The dog was obviously in a park ... but where, what city? Doris tried to see beyond the dog, to recognize the skyline that rose up in the distance. The dog ran by an equestrian statue of a Confederate soldier. *Robert E. Lee,* the bronze plaque read. The dog came and sat in front of Doris, dropping the Frisbee at her feet and looking up at her with expectation and curiosity.

Its intelligent brown eyes seemed almost human. Sunshine splashed over the scene in Doris's mind. Blue sky, lush flowers, green grass and . . . ah, the dog was wearing tags. If she could just get a look at its name — or maybe there was an address — she leaned forward reaching for the dog when *poof,* the scene changed and she recognized without a doubt where they were.

She was up over the city — a bird sailing over the endless maze of concrete streets and houses below, seeing everything just like the view from the Goodyear blimp. She recognized Texas Stadium with its hole in the roof so God could talk to His team, and in the distance that tall mirrored ball on a stick, Reunion Tower, the gaudy, electric dandelion that told her she was in Dallas.

Doris opened her eyes in relief. She could tell Natalie to start looking in Dallas for her Ellen and a big white dog in a park beside a statue of Robert E. Lee.

Doris leaned back in her chair and contemplated the worn Frisbee a moment before she replaced it on the table. Finally . . . the gift was back on track. She reached for the leather driving gloves and drew them on. An action which plunged her into a place she had never been before. A room full of diffused light where shimmering white curtains moved at the windows, stirred by a delicious breeze.

She saw herself on a soft bed, beneath a satiny coverlet, her naked body caressed and pampered by the silk sheets. And Esther was there. Doris knew by the smell of her shampoo. And from the sound of her humming coming from the bathroom.

"I miss you," Esther said. Her voice now very close to Doris's ear: "I need you."

"Me too you," Doris answered. As these words escaped her lips, something tight around her heart loosened and fell away. She turned to embrace Esther and saw past her, where, hanging on a chairback, was a monogrammed hotel towel. The big "R" braced by fleur-de-lis was the monogram of the Hotel Regis. Doris's eyes flew open and she was shocked to discover that she still sat at her kitchen table.

Her thoughts pinwheeled. The Hotel Regis was here, where she lived. Here in her own city. Here where Natalie lived. Not in Dallas, where Doris had seen the dog in the park. What did it mean? Maybe Ellen had driven to this city. And . . . what? Was staying at the Hotel Regis? And why was Esther always speaking for Natalie's Ellen? Why couldn't Doris see anyone but Esther?

Doris's next thought lit the inside of her brain like a traffic flare.

Maybe Ellen *was* Esther. Maybe she had changed her name. Maybe . . . oh no . . . maybe Esther had been Natalie's lover too and had been left behind by Natalie the same way Esther had deserted Doris. Maybe there was some kind of perverted justice at work in the world after all.

Doris sat for a moment, overwhelmed by her racing thoughts. Then she rose decisively and gathered her purse and car keys. There was one sure way to find out. The gift had not failed her before. It was time for a resolution to this present mystery.

A half hour later Doris stood in front of the sink in the Hotel Regis Ladies Room, around the corner from room three thirty-four where the clerk had verified that an Ellen Bennett was registered. Doris thoughtfully studied her reflection. Her color was high and her eyes were bright with nervous energy. She calmed herself, took a few deep breaths and entered the carpeted hallway.

One, two, three doors — around the corner — there it was. She had just raised her hand to knock, when the door opened slowly inward. A tall woman reached for her hand and pulled her gently into the room.

"What took you so long, Doris? I've been here almost a week."

Doris's heart raced and her tongue was frozen by the thousand things she needed to say but couldn't sort out. She let herself be led toward the bed and gratefully sat as her weakened knees touched the edge.

"Esther," Doris finally managed to utter. "Esther," she repeated as if her racing brain had lost its bearings. "Esther . . . it's you."

Esther sat beside Doris and took both her trembling hands. "Yes — it's me. I've been waiting for you to find me."

Doris's questions finally lined up and took a number, ordering themselves above the panic that threatened to overtake her. "How did you know I would come? You opened the door before I knocked — how did . . . how did you know I was looking for you? When were you and Natalie lovers? How did you find out Natalie was trying to find you? When did —"

"Whoa!" Esther gripped Doris's hands and shook them gently. "I'll tell you everything . . . but one question at a time, okay?"

Doris took a calming breath and felt herself being

drawn deep into Esther's dark blue eyes. Felt herself slide over the lip of that great emotional pool from which she had been so cruelly expelled long ago. It didn't feel wrong. Or scary. Just warm and free and erotic and somehow like coming home.

Esther's arms enclosed Doris in a strong embrace and held her for a long moment before she pulled away and began speaking.

"It's really all pretty simple ... Natalie is an old friend, not a lover. I knew you lived here. I read the papers too, you know." She grinned that old lopsided way that always made Doris acutely aware of why Esther had been asked to leave the convent.

Esther continued, "I've matured, I've changed. I've grown to understand your gift ... even discovered some talent in my own skeptical soul. I decided to try to send you psychic messages. I kept imagining you and me in a bright room with white curtains at the open windows. You and me naked in a soft bed of satin and silk. I kept sending you one message over and over until I got your answer. Last night I heard those words you used to tell me. The shorthand way you always said it, '*me too you.*' "

Doris felt her stomach begin a little slide toward a hollow place closer to her groin.

"I gave my things to Natalie to give to you. I needed you to find me. I made a terrible mistake when I left you. I've paid for it in so many ways ... Please — say you forgive me."

Doris looked at Esther. She nodded. A flood of feeling rose up and flashed from her in spurts of steaming energy, like storms on the surface of a faraway sun. She could see it bathe Esther, could see the light from it glowing around Esther's head and sparkling across the shoulders of the white dog she had seen in the park. The scene reminded her that Esther's story was still a little sketchy.

"But — the dog . . . Esther. What about the big white dog?"

Esther tossed her head in obvious delight.

"Her name is Finder . . . and she's waiting at home in Dallas to meet you."

Random Choice

Rose Beecham

Cathy Preston had never expected she would one day find herself answering intimate questions behind the heart-shaped doors of *Sappho's Companions*, Australia's pre-eminent lesbian introduction service. As luck would have it she had presented herself at the Melbourne office during a special incentive period.

"So, if you don't meet at least one likely candidate," explained her consultant, Arabella, a fair young woman wearing a pastel blouse with a label on the pocket which said *Fuzzy Peach*, "we will provide you with six extra introductions, absolutely free. Imagine it . . ."

She flicked a switch on her desk and the video screen on the far wall came to life. Two women sat at a candlelit table, glasses raised. When the dry ice cleared sufficiently, a beam of light splayed star-like from a diamond ring one woman slid onto the other's finger. It was so romantic and absurd Cathy felt like crying hysterically. She was only twenty-eight and she had sunk to this.

Noting her emotion, Arabella offered a tissue. "Don't be embarrassed," she advised. "Loneliness is the affliction of the twentieth century." For just three hundred dollars, Cathy could be spared a future destined to be shared only with a cat and a television set. She could meet Ms. Right.

To Cathy's horror, she could not write the check fast enough. Half an hour lager, back at work, she was still dumbstruck at her folly. In her satchel was a large pink envelope containing her first "Perfect Match Profile." Clinging to the conviction that she would wake up tomorrow, common-sense restored, she had not opened it. She would return it and get her money back, she reasoned. What was wrong with picking up a woman at the next lesbian tea-dance, anyway?

"You're very quiet today, love." In Cathy's doorway stood Noeline, her boss, the owner of Aphrodite Corsetry; the woman who had coined the matchless phrase *Bras for the Buxom* to describe her company's products. "Something on your mind?"

Cathy politely side-stepped the leading question. "Just a couple of hiccups with the balance sheet." Ever since Cathy had started six months ago as the firm's accountant, Noeline had done her best to extract a life history, with particular emphasis on relationships.

Noeline looked like she wanted to make conversation. "See the paper today?" she asked.

Cathy shook her head. In her view, reading the newspaper was a big mistake, a sure-fire invitation to feelings of battered hopelessness and clutching fear. But for some quirk of fate, yours could be the badly burned body pulled from a blazing motor vehicle, the home burgled, the telephone breathed into by some pervert who turned out to be your sister's husband.

"Well, he's done it again," Noeline announced. "The Bouquet Rapist. You'd think in this day and age women would be more careful . . . get some identification . . ."

"I guess they're just thrilled." Cathy tried to imagine someone besotted enough with her to blow thirty bucks on a bunch of flowers. The only time her ex-lover, Sharn, had ever bought flowers was when she felt guilty about something. Then she would pick up some three-day-old daffodils from the discount bin and expect Cathy to be overwhelmed.

"Mmmm. I suppose it's a big deal . . . for some." Noeline's tone implied that floral tributes were a routine event for her. "Poor things are completely taken in, the police said. It's not random choice, mark my words. He watches them. Picks the ones who live alone." Her brightly outlined blue eyes surveyed Cathy. "How's the security in your block, dear?"

Electronic locks on the lobby entrance, camera surveillance in the garage and the laundry, deadlocks on the doors. Windows that opened only three inches, steel mesh screens on the outside. I live in a prison, Cathy thought. Solitary confinement. "It's pretty good," she said.

But Noeline's interest in the subject was already flagging. Grasping a handful of the flesh that padded her hips, she demanded, "Liposuction — what do you think, Cathy?"

Cathy felt awkward. Publicly, Noeline was an outspoken advocate of fat pride, the success story paraded by women's magazines as a palliative to those who criticized the media's role in the diet culture. Noeline had built her fortune on big. She had a fabulous home in Toorak, a husband who looked like a male stripper, and she had written her autobiography — all before she was forty. Privately, she was a basket case over her ballooning weight.

"Liposuction is pretty drastic," Cathy said meekly. "I'm sure the company can afford some fitness equipment. It would be a tax write-off."

Noeline sighed. "Who's got time for that stuff? I'm going to talk to my doctor." She must have sensed Cathy's unspoken disapproval. "It's okay for girls like you. I'll bet you've never had a weight problem in your life. Christ — " She laughed without humor. "We don't make a cup size small enough to fit you."

Cathy was silent. She knew better than to argue with Noeline on the day of her *Jenny Craig* weigh-in.

"Well, I can't stand here listening to you all day. I have some calls to make." Noeline flounced off, closing her door with such a bang the flimsy partitioning quivered. A moment later, Cathy heard the rustling of cellophane. Noeline couldn't give up potato crisps. They kept her sane, she said.

* * * * *

In Albert Park, the great elms cast dense shadows. Few people passed within them, perhaps fearing hazards concealed — broken glass, dogshit, lurking psychopaths. Cathy guessed this was the reason she usually found herself alone as she trod the springy grass to her apartment building each night. It should have bothered her, she supposed. Indeed on some evenings her neck prickled and she fought off a compulsion to look behind her.

Lately this paranoia had become more pronounced. She had mentioned the sounds she heard to Ingrid, her therapist, who said it was probably the wind. Nature, weary of pillage, was exacting payment in kind from arrogant humanity. Hence Melbourne, like most of the world, was beset by unseasonable weather. This caused the trees to groan as though wounded, and the grass to whisper like the crazy people who slept at the bus terminal.

Having stopped by the supermarket, Cathy was now burdened with half a dozen grocery bags. She should have gone out later in her car, of course. But she wanted to watch *Shortland Street*, the soap opera her sister sent on video weekly from New Zealand. It had a lesbian character who got good lines and actually had a life on peak-time television.

Ignoring the prickling of her neck and the aching of her shoulders, she walked briskly and confidently. If anyone was watching her, they would see a sensibly dressed woman of medium height and build — if somewhat breastless — with short dark brown hair and a small silver labrys in her left ear. She was not exceptional in any way. She blended in.

Perhaps that explained why the women she fancied never seemed to notice her.

"Cathy!" Someone called from behind her.

Turning, Cathy saw a slender woman picking her way a little unevenly across the grass and twigs. Her narrow skirt and medium heels were unsuited for a grassy park and the wind whipped her light brown hair across her face. Plucking at a few long strands, May Lawrence, Cathy's neighbor, halted beside her, panting slightly. "Need a hand?" she offered.

Pleasantly surprised, Cathy thanked her and passed over a couple of grocery bags — the lighter ones with the cereals and the bathroom tissue. May was not the muscular type.

They exchanged smiles and walked the few remaining steps to their building in silence. Cathy could feel May watching as she ran her identity card through the security doors. Naturally, she fumbled.

"I do that all the time," May said. An unlikely story for someone who had lived in the building for three years, Cathy thought. But it was nice of her to be sensitive.

They took the elevator to the second floor where their apartments were side by side.

"I'll help you inside with these." Apparently detecting Cathy's hesitation, May added, "I do work out you know." As if to prove a point she swung the groceries aloft, displaying an expanse of lace-top stocking and a wide, infectious smile.

Grinning in wry appreciation, Cathy pushed her door wide and allowed May to go in ahead of her. Depositing the groceries on the kitchen bench, her visitor glanced around the apartment. "Well, this is looking cozy."

Read untidy, Cathy thought. May Lawrence's apartment was very designer. Her mother owned a store which sold hand-made quilts and leather chairs. By contrast Cathy's place was a shambles, furnished from garage sales, with various plants and ornaments bearing witness to the tastes of ex-lovers. The conversation piece was a loud rag rug her mother had made for her last birthday.

"Would you like a cup of tea?" Cathy said, fully expecting May to decline.

"I'd like that," May said brightly. "Sometimes it's such a bore to go home to an empty apartment." She sat on Cathy's tatty sofa, ankles crossed.

She was really very attractive, Cathy thought. As she often did. She and May had exchanged neighborly visits a few times since she had moved into the building and Cathy had contemplated asking her out. But May was not really her type. For a start she was the spoiled only daughter of trendy parents. And, if she was a lesbian, she was in deep cover. "Milk and sugar?" Cathy offered.

As if in proof that they had nothing in common, May replied, "Just lemon, thanks."

What madness was this? Cathy thought, rooting through the vegetable box for the single shrivelled lemon she knew she had. She was acutely aware of a pathetic gratitude that her neighbor was bothering to spend five minutes in her company. When had this loss of self-worth begun? she challenged herself. When she was born the wrong sex, the fifth girl in a farming family? When Sharn had thrown her over a year ago for a virtual child of seventeen? Or was it some creeping disease whose symptoms could be alleviated by alcohol, romance and chocolate, but which had no real cure? She handed May her tea, wondering if this charming, assured woman had ever suffered from self-doubt.

"I got a promotion," May said in a rush. Immediately she gave a self-deprecating laugh. "I'm sorry. I just had to tell someone."

"That's great." Cathy was flattered May had chosen to tell her. "What's the new job?"

"Chief buyer," May enthused. "We have sixty stores so it's — "

"Big." Cathy whistled. The job obviously meant a lot to May. "Congratulations."

"So, how's your job going?" May asked.

Terrible. I hate it. "Fine," Cathy lied. "You know how it is."

May placed her cup on the coffee table. Well, that's that, Cathy thought. They had covered the weather and their jobs. They would now say good-bye and each would spend half an hour cooking a one-person meal in her own apartment. Cathy would eat hers in front of the long-awaited soap opera and May would doubtless occupy a neatly set table and perhaps listen to Vivaldi on her stereo. For some reason Cathy felt like crying. Instead she carried the empty cups to the kitchen, tactfully signaling that May had discharged any social obligation she might feel.

May got to her feet. Awkwardly, she asked, "So . . . um, what are you doing tonight?"

Before Cathy could form an answer, the intercom buzzed. Through the receiver a voice that seemed very far off said, "Courier delivery for number three."

"I'm sorry . . . this is number four." She glanced at May. "It must be for you. A courier."

May seemed nonplussed. "Gosh ... er, Mummy must have heard about the job, after all. She knows my boss." She opened the door and Cathy followed her out into the hallway. "Well, thanks for the tea. Er ..."

She seemed about to say something else, when a gangly delivery man emerged from the elevator bearing a large bunch of flowers. He hesitated, staring at the two women before proceeding toward them. "Delivery for number four," he muttered.

Taking the flowers with an air of pained embarrassment, May said, "Tiger lilies and carnations. How lovely." It seemed obvious they were not from her mother.

With an edgy glance from May to Cathy, the delivery man gave a brief nod and headed down the stairs. There was something vaguely unsettling in the way he had looked at her and May, Cathy thought. She was being paranoid, she told herself. But, ignoring May's started stare, she scuttled impulsively down the stairs in his wake. From the lobby she saw him get into a small van parked a few doors along. Repeating the plate number beneath her breath, she returned to her apartment.

May was hovering in her doorway. "Cathy — "

"I just need to make a note of something." Cathy found a pen and paper in her kitchen and jotted down the registration number. "That delivery man was strange. I got his car registration — "

"Oh no!" May started to laugh. "You don't think it's him — the Bouquet Rapist? I'm sorry. Oh hell. What a mess ..." Catching Cathy's puzzled stare, she held out the flowers, her face bright pink. "Here. These are for you. It wasn't meant to be like this. I had it all planned. I was going to come over later and ask you to dinner. I wasn't expecting the delivery so soon . . . And they're not what I asked for . . . I guess I totally blew it."

"No, you didn't." Cathy shook her head. Her neighbor wanted a date? Wanted it badly enough to buy her a bunch of flowers? Hardly able to believe her luck, she followed May to her door. "Look, I know a great restaurant. Can you be ready in an hour?"

"Really? I mean, I'd love to. Don't feel you have to or anything . . ." She met Cathy's eyes and blushed. As they stared at one another, May's intercom sounded, and with a sharp sigh of frustration, she pushed open her door and grabbed the receiver. "It's the flowers," she said, the color seeping from her face. "The ones I ordered."

Cathy slowly released the breath she was holding. It was not her imagination. The delivery man had acted strangely. Recalling his uncertainty over the apartment number, she guessed he must have been watching the building, spying on her, or was it May? Shivering, she felt around in her pocket for the slip of paper she had crushed a few minutes before. "I guess I'd better call the police," she said.

As the genuine delivery boy approached, Cathy placed an arm around May's shoulders. Their heads rested softly together. May's hair smelled of jasmine. She had ordered roses.

Relatively Innocent
Claire McNab

After three years in New York I'd come back to Australia sadder, but not necessarily wiser. My career in the esoteric field of gourmet food photography had boomed, but my love life had had more peaks and valleys than the stock market, ending with a steep downward slide when Janice left for the second time. "I need to be me," she had announced around a mouthful of bagel, "and you're holding me back." She'd paused to swallow, then added in her nasal

New Yorker twang, "But I still love you, Eve, and probably always will."

"Fuck you," I'd responded, disdaining the scripted answer Janice expected, which should have been along the lines of how I'd wait for her (again) and/or I loved her too. I felt a certain grim satisfaction at her surprise — she was so used to the quiet, thoughtful me. "In fact, fuck you to hell."

During the long flight home to Australia I'd brooded about my conspicuous failure to maintain a rewarding love life. There'd be no more emotional doormatting for me. I was going to take control in my next relationship — if I ever had one again.

My family lived in the Deep North of outback Queensland, so living there was not an option if I was going to pursue my photography. Besides, although they accepted they had a lesbian daughter, my parents weren't terribly keen to publicize the fact to friends and neighbors. This is why I found myself standing in the Feminist Bookshop, in the suburb of Lilyfield, Sydney, gazing at the notice board. The exchange rate had meant my American dollars had translated into a very satisfactory sum in Australian currency, but I had to budget for a reasonable lead-time before I started earning as a free-lance photographer, so shared accommodation seemed the way to go.

One boldly lettered card caught my attention. *Half house, own bathroom, must be lesbian.* The address was in a neighboring suburb, Balmain. As I copied down the telephone number, the woman behind the counter smiled at me. "Find something?"

I pointed at the card. "This one looks promising."

An indefinable expression crossed her face. "That one? That's Lesley's."

"You know her?"

"Lesley Flemming . . . yes, I know her." She looked intently at me.

"Is she okay?" I suddenly realized they might be friends. "What I mean is . . ."

The woman took pity on my embarrassment. "Do you want to use the phone here? Lesley works from home, so she should be there."

Lesley gave me directions to the house in a voice that was dark-toned, almost husky. As I put down the phone, the woman behind the counter said, "Are you new to Sydney?"

"I feel like I'm new to Australia. I've been living in the States the last three years, and in Britain the two years before that."

She nodded as though I'd said something important. As I thanked her for the use of the phone and left the bookstore, I was aware that she was watching me with unusual attention. I couldn't understand it: I was dressed in my usual plain, conventional clothes; my blondish hair was conservatively cut. And I couldn't flatter myself that my looks were such that no red-blooded woman could keep her eyes off me. So why the interest? It must be something to do with Lesley.

My imagination, always skittish, presented me with various Lesleys: one very tall, one extremely wide, one abnormally short. Or perhaps she was misshapen in some strange, interesting way.

I found the address without difficulty. It was a small, freestanding building, unusual in a suburb where rows of semi-detached houses predominated. I approved of the freshly painted picket fence and the neat flower beds around the diminutive front lawn. The house itself was weatherboard, white with dark green trim on the window frames and front door. There was even a brass knocker in the form of a lion with a ring in its mouth. I knocked with more confidence than I felt.

I was both relieved and disappointed with the Lesley who answered the door. She was a little taller than I, and definitely thinner. She had short curly brown hair and a pleasant, intelligent face. I noticed her hands: strong, long-fingered, graceful. "You're Lesley Flemming?" She nodded slowly, watching me warily. What was it with Australians? Was this some national habit that had developed while I had been overseas? "I'm Eve Martini. I called you about the house . . ."

She stood aside to let me enter. The house was light and airy. Several skylights poured light into the agreeably furnished rooms. This was a place I could learn to like.

"We share the kitchen, but you have your own bathroom."

I raised an eyebrow at the queen-sized bed in the bedroom that would be mine. I could envisage myself tossing on that wide expanse through many lonely nights. I knew I was going to miss cuddling up to someone, but if ever Janice was to be replaced, it would have to be with someone I . . . well, loved. All right, someone I at least seriously *liked*.

As I wrote out a check, Lesley Flemming said, "You're sure?"

I grinned at her. "The place looks perfect. Don't

tell me this house has some dreadful secret. It's not haunted, is it?"

She frowned at me. "Not that I know of."

"And you don't do something unfortunate, like play the bagpipes?"

She smiled for the first time, transforming her face, and I felt a tug of attraction. *Careful! Don't even think of going to bed with the landlady.*

"No bagpipes."

I felt uncharacteristically bold. Usually I don't volunteer anything, but wait politely to be asked, although it often annoys me when people fail to ask the question I want to answer. "I've been living overseas for the past five or so years, so everything seems a little strange to me."

This one sentence transformed Lesley. As I listened to her explaining how she worked on her computer three days a week at home and spent the other two at the company, I puzzled over what I'd said that had caused her cheerful animation. Perhaps it was that I'd shared something about myself, though to me my whereabouts for the past five years didn't seem very much of a personal revelation.

When she paused, I mentioned that I was a photographer and needed to find a darkroom I could hire.

"The room off the laundry was once a darkroom. You might like to see if it'd be any use to you."

"You're interested in photography?"

She was solemn again. "No, my brother set up the darkroom . . . He used to own this house." There was a long pause, then she added, "I inherited it from him."

"Oh, I'm sorry." Damn it! "I mean, I'm not sorry

you inherited the house. I'm sorry about your brother."

"We weren't particularly close."

Her expression of bitter amusement put this subject off-limits, although I was curious. Perhaps he'd died in some bizarre way that had caused giggles at the funeral . . . I quashed my over-active imagination and searched for something to fill the silence that was rapidly becoming awkward. "I'm an only child," I said idiotically.

"Growing up, I felt like one," Lesley said, "because my brother was twelve years older."

Stopping myself from inquiring how he'd died took real will power. Instead I asked a couple innocuous questions about the running of the household and, disappointingly, we were on safer ground.

I moved in the next day, not an onerous task since I'd left most of my things in New York for Janice to dispose of. My luggage was mainly photographic gear and a selection of my well-cut, classic clothes. *Boring,* I thought when I once again surveyed the neutral colors I had always favored.

I eyed Lesley with some envy. She was one of those people who wear clothes with insouciant elegance. It irritated the hell out of me that even with a simple outfit like jeans and a shirt, all Lesley had to do was add a striking belt or a heavy bracelet, and immediately she would look subtly stylish.

Two uneventful weeks passed. I spent the time activating the contacts I'd had in photography before

I left Australia and hiking my portfolio around town. I had no doubt that I'd be able to make a living free-lancing, but it did take considerable effort to create the necessary network, and having to assume a gung-ho professional persona to sell myself was quite exhausting. And of course the market wasn't big enough for me to focus exclusively on food photography, and so, reluctantly, I'd had to broaden my scope.

I like photographing food. It doesn't talk or change expression or complain. It's all a matter of preparation — done by gourmet chefs — and the tricks of the trade I employ to make each item look both appetizing and aesthetically pleasing.

Lesley and I had agreed to share the cooking. Although I photographed the most exotic of foods, I was a pedestrian cook. I followed recipes slavishly, measuring each ingredient, while Lesley was an intuitive cook. She never seemed to worry about accuracy, but threw things together in approximate quantities, adding a pinch of this and a dash of that without any apparent idea what would happen. I was uncharitably pleased when a dish didn't quite work out, but I had to admit that most of the time she produced delicious meals.

We settled into a comfortable routine. She seemed to have no social life, other than contact with workmates. What Lesley actually did remained a mystery to me. Those days when she worked at home she would sit at her computer in total concentration, manipulating a bewildering array of symbols and numbers on the screen. On a couple of occasions, when members of her department dropped around, I gathered that they were installing a customized computer system for some important client, but since I was reluctant to ask a question when I was fairly sure I'd look a fool trying to understand the answer, Lesley's job continued to impress and puzzle me.

Lesley herself was an enigma. She would ask questions about New York and my career in photography, but my mild attempts to find out anything personal about her were always thwarted. What had happened to her brother continued to intrigue me, and that was not the only item exercising my imagination. I was feeling a growing attraction to my landlady, in part fed by my chagrin that my usual role of good listener wasn't working. Janice had once unkindly referred to my behavior as "being an auditory sponge," but I'd usually found people most grateful to have an attentive audience. Besides, listening had advantages: not only did I gain information, but, as someone wisely once said, "You can't put your foot in your mouth unless it's open."

It was after the kiss that I found out the truth. Actually, the kiss had nothing to do with how I discovered what had happened to her brother, but it marked a distinct change in me, not to mention my relationship with Lesley. This particular evening it had been my turn to cook and we'd had what my mother spoke of admiringly as good plain food. Since I'd produced the dinner, Lesley was cleaning up, a simple task. Unlike her, I was always very neat, washing up utensils as I cooked.

I only have to shut my eyes to see everything again. Lesley was standing at the sink rinsing our plates. She wore blue jeans and a scarlet silk shirt, and I blame that glowing color for drawing my attention to the way her breasts swelled provocatively under the fabric. I suppose I should also take some responsibility, since I'd willingly had two glasses of wine with dinner. Whatever contributed to the rush of warmth I felt, I admit it was my choice to do something about it — I walked up behind her and kissed the back of her neck as she stood at the sink.

She turned, frowning. I looked at her mouth, and was lost. For a moment she resisted, then her lips parted under the pressure of mine. I remember a fleeting satisfaction that I was an excellent kisser — I'm always willing to work at anything worthwhile — then pure sensation blinked out my higher thought processes. The center of delight was her mouth, her tongue. The simmering heat that had impelled me to kiss her boiled over into overwhelming need. Heady with joy, I took my mouth from hers to say, "Your bed or mine?"

"Neither."

"No?" I was still secure in her response to my kiss. "Are you playing hard to get?"

Lesley gently freed herself from my embrace. "I'm impossible to get."

"Oh." My flush of confidence drained away, to be replaced with embarrassment. What in the hell could I have been thinking of when I pushed myself onto the woman? It was worse than bad judgment on my part — it showed a lamentable lack of control.

We stood staring at each other. Lesley didn't look angry or offended. She looked somber. "Eve, don't say anything," she said. "I know it was just an impulse. We'll forget it, okay?"

I felt a sulky resentment. "You had the impulse too. It wasn't just me."

She gave me a faint smile. "No, it wasn't just

you, but . . ." She spread her hands in a "what can I say?" gesture.

Lesley went into her study to work. I went into my room to brood. The next day I had lunch with Cherelle Higgins.

Cherelle did not resemble her first name, being short, square and excellent at sports requiring hand/eye coordination. I knew this because she also came from the wilds of Queensland, and we had gone to the same girls' boarding school in Brisbane. We were not only in the same class throughout our school years, but Cherelle and I had represented the school on the A Grade tennis team, although she was my superior, both in technique and confidence. I always tended to play the percentages, and such safe play paid off enough to get me on the team, but left me far short of her tennis brilliance.

Astonishing to me, Cherelle had since become quite famous as a sports entrepreneur, and her company, Cherelle Enterprises, managed the careers and appearances of many sports stars. I was not blind to the photographic opportunities that might accrue from a little judicious base-touching, so I left a message with her assistant that I was in town and then responded enthusiastically when Cherelle called back to suggest lunch.

Except for the abundance of gold jewelry and the acquisition of an expensive wardrobe, my former classmate hadn't changed. She still ate with her mouth open and spoke in the same penetrating voice full of exclamations.

Excelsior was an exclusive restaurant filled with subdued conversation, except for our table. In a vain effort to provide a good example I talked very softly, but it was hopeless. Cherelle had only one volume. She was keen to discuss old times and what had happened to our classmates in the years since school. Of course Cherelle knew most details — she had always had an insatiable appetite for gossip and had been known, only semi-humorously, as Cherelle Guess What.

When it was time for her to update her information on me I complied gracefully. With her contacts she could assist my photography career considerably, and my imagination was already planning a series on famous sports women, perhaps playing a game other than the one that had bought them fame. I was discussing this when Cherelle said, "Where are you living, Eve?"

"Balmain." When she frowned, I added quickly, "It's very central."

"*Where* in Balmain?"

Clearly some areas were more desirable than others. "I'm sharing a house." I could see the next question coming, so I added, "With a woman named Lesley Flemming. She's in computers."

"Flemming!" Several heads turned. "Did you say Lesley Flemming? *Flemming*? You did say that?"

Some diners were now openly staring. I said quietly, "Do you know her?"

Cherelle sat back with a smile that combined incredulity and satisfaction. "Tallish? Thin? Dark curly hair?"

"Yes, that could be her."

"Of course it is!" She leaned forward. "Guess what!"

"What?"

"She's a murderer."

I forgot that people were staring at our table. "What!" My voice had risen in an undignified squeak. I cleared my throat. "It can't be the same person."

"She killed her brother . . . with a hatchet." When I gaped at her, she continued cheerfully, "She got off — they couldn't prove it beyond doubt, but everyone knows she did it." She waved imperiously at a waiter. "More coffee!"

Not Lesley. Not my Lesley. It had to be a mistake. "You'd better tell me about it."

Cherelle nodded wisely. "I certainly should . . . Lesley Flemming might go for *you* next."

I looked around the restaurant. Several people were obviously delaying their departure, and with a floor show like this, who could blame them? "Cherelle, perhaps we should discuss this somewhere else . . ."

She ignored my suggestion. "At the trial they never said there was incest, but it was *hinted at,* you know what I mean?"

"I don't know anything about a trial. Lesley's just a perfectly nice woman I happen to share a house with."

I came home with as full an account as Cherelle could give me. She had almost total recall of anything that interested her, and Lesley Flemming's trial had excited her keenest attention. "I don't understand why you didn't hear about it overseas. I mean, it was *sensational.*" I didn't bother mentioning that fratricide, even with an ax, would hardly be enough to excite an American public entertained by spectacularly grisly crimes much closer to home.

Lesley wasn't there. I stood in the kitchen trying to feel a thrill of fear by imagining that I was sharing a house with a murderer, but nothing happened. I just couldn't believe she could kill and then dismember her brother in his own garage. As I glanced at the rack of large cooking knives on the wall, my confidence wavered for a moment. Perhaps I'd been a heartbeat away from having a chef's knife plunged into my chest when I kissed her . . . No, that was ridiculous. But if she hadn't murdered her brother, who had? Cherelle had made it clear there were no other suspects and that brother and sister had quarreled bitterly before George Flemming had been dispatched.

When the not guilty verdict had been announced, Lesley's sister-in-law had denounced the judge, the jurors and the ineptitude of the police. "Murderer!" she'd shrieked as she pointed at Lesley. Marjorie Flemming had even contested her husband's will because, although it left the bulk of his estate to her, the small Balmain house that had been his first home was given to his sister. When the ruling had gone against her, she had again been carried out of the court room shrieking "Murderer!" She sounded tiresome.

As did George and Marjorie Flemming's eighteen-year-old son. Some time after his father's death, Tony Flemming had been arrested with cocaine in his possession and had blamed his drug habit on his Aunt Lesley, who'd ruined his life by murdering his father. Tony had obviously put on a winning performance, as he'd got probation even though, according to Cherelle, there were rumors he'd previously been expelled from his exclusive private school for drug dealing.

The front door slammed. "Hi," said Lesley. "Have a good day?"

"Interesting."

"You were going to meet an old school friend, weren't you?"

"We had lunch." I looked at her graceful fingers and visualized them curled around the handle of a hatchet. Blood must have spurted everywhere . . .

Cherelle had said that one of the main points in Lesley's favor was that the police hadn't been able to find any bloodstained clothes. "If you ask me," she'd announced to the restaurant, "she did it stark naked like Lizzie Borden!"

I could imagine Lesley naked without any difficulty at all, but Lesley covered with the blood of her brother was another matter. I looked into her dark eyes and said, "I know about the trial."

She looked curiously relieved. "Who told you?"

"My school friend, Cherelle, during lunch."

"That would be enough to give you indigestion." She paused, rubbing her forehead. "Do you want to move out?"

"Of course not," I said stoutly.

"Don't worry, I'll understand if you want to go. Lots of people still think I did it."

She turned away so that I couldn't see her face. What I'd thought was physical attraction plus affection suddenly assumed a wider dimension. "Don't expect me to ask if you killed your brother, I *know* you didn't."

"You *hope* I didn't." There was a tremor in her voice.

This was an emergency, so I excused myself from my usual cautious consideration of what to say and do. I put my arms around her and held her tightly. "I don't hope anything. I know *you,* and that's enough for me."

Her breath sighed past my ear. "Thank you."

Kissing her neck generated a surge of intoxicating assurance. "Lesley, we have to go to bed, now. I can't wait any longer."

"If you insist."

I slid my hands under her shirt, thinking assertiveness had a lot going for it. "I insist."

Her eager mouth overwhelmed me. I pulled her to the floor — the bedroom was too far away. We undressed each other with clumsy urgency and when Lesley's gorgeous naked length flamed against me I willingly drowned in passion. I could hear the loud noises of pleasure I was making, and I didn't care.

Jolted by the electricity of her touch, I opened to her as her fingers brushed my thighs. "Oh, yes . . ." I was ascending, one dizzy step at a time, to meet a fiery ecstasy that had never been completely mine. Teeth clenched, back arched, flooded with molten sensation, I trusted her not to stop, not to let me fall. Reaching the summit, I groaned with the sweetness until she launched me into exultant flight.

Panting, slippery with sweat, I turned until Lesley was beneath me, her breast in my mouth, my hand sliding into the wet warmth of her, the rhythm of my fingers matching the pulse of her hips. My thudding heart seemed to burst as she called out her delight.

We lay entwined, our breathing slowed. I opened my eyes and saw the room from an unexpected perspective. The rough mohair rug tickled my skin. It was going to be difficult to extricate myself from this position with dignity.

Lesley kissed my shoulder. "It might be nice to try the bed next time."

Next time sounded good to me. I propped myself on one elbow and surveyed our clothes strewn all around us. "I think this is called Swept Away by Passion."

She gave me a slow grin. "Want to be swept again?"

The next morning I took a break from networking and investigated the darkroom Lesley's brother had set up. It was surprisingly well-appointed, including electric steel shutters to black out the windows. I went inside to find Lesley before she left for one of her work days in the city. "The darkroom's in very good order," I told her.

"George often used it. He was a very keen amateur photographer and Marjorie refused to let him have a darkroom in their house." She grimaced. "After George died, Marjorie thought I might try to sell the equipment, so she sent Tony around while I was out. I had the locks changed before he stripped out the sinks, but he took the rest of the stuff."

"Marjorie sounds like a real sweetheart. Maybe she killed him."

Lesley's face closed. "Maybe . . . but we'll probably never know."

This wasn't good enough for me. "As long as it's a mystery, some people are always going to think you got away with murder."

My blunt tone angered her. "Don't you think I know that, Eve? What do you expect me to do — play Sherlock Holmes?" She grabbed her briefcase. "I'll see you tonight."

I had another look at the darkroom and made a list of what I would need to get it into working order. Then I went off to the nearest public library to research George Flemming's murder. The sensational nature of the crime — respected businessman killed with a hatchet, body roughly dismembered and packages of parts dumped around Sydney — guaranteed that newspaper accounts were extensive.

I studied the press photographs before I began reading accounts of the arrest and trial. Unlike many suspects, Lesley had never tried to hide her face, and in most of the photographs she stared blank-faced at the camera. George Flemming, the victim, had a family resemblance to his sister, but his face was puffy and he had a weak mouth.

Marjorie Flemming, pointedly dressed in black, had attended every day of the trial. Her photographs showed a rigid hairdo and a self-righteous expression.

Most of the time she wore dark glasses, but when photographed without them she proved to have large, faintly bulging eyes and thin, arched eyebrows that gave her a look of supercilious surprise. Not surprisingly, I took an instant dislike to her.

Tony Flemming had a doughy, unformed face, and had been unfortunate enough to inherit his mother's eyes and his father's mouth. I took an instant dislike to him, too.

A reporter's in-depth profile of the Flemming family revealed that George and Marjorie's marriage had been the standard model with some conflict and a lot of boredom. Their son, Tony, had caused enough trouble for his parents to polarize, with Marjorie defending him and George reacting with baffled irritation. One other thing was clear: Marjorie Flemming detested Lesley and resented any time George spent with his sister.

Why had Lesley been accused, when Marjorie and Tony seemed to me to be perfectly adequate suspects? During the trial the prosecution had made much of a violent quarrel between Lesley and her brother on the day he died. George had visited his sister to tell her that Marjorie was demanding that Lesley move out of the Balmain house immediately, even though she paid market rent and had made considerable improvements at her own cost. In the past George Flemming had withstood similar pressure from his wife, but this time he was giving in — not only because Marjorie was continuing to rail about Lesley's "abnormal sexual appetites," but also because Tony needed accommodation. Marjorie had announced that their son was in constant turmoil because of unfair criticism from his father, and therefore needed to have somewhere of his own so he could "grow".

This reminded me so much of Janice's self-indulgence that for a moment I felt a murderous rage.

There was other evidence, of course. Not only had they quarreled loudly enough for the neighbors to hear, but Lesley had then stormed over to her brother's home to confront Marjorie. George, whose staid Volvo couldn't keep up with Lesley's furious driving, had arrived to find the two women yelling at each other — and he had snapped. I could sympathize: I knew what it felt like to keep everything under tight control until the pressure was so great that a searing emotional explosion was the only relief.

George's uncontrolled rage had reduced his wife to unaccustomed silence. The interior decorator Marjorie had hired to redesign the decor in the room next door had made an enthusiastic prosecution witness: "Mr. Flemming just lost it, absolutely lost it. He was screaming that his sister was to get out of his home and never come back. And that she had to leave the Balmain house, too, or he'd throw her out himself."

It didn't help that Lesley, in the decorator's words, "Just chilled me when she said to her brother, calm as you like, 'I could kill you for this.' I mean, you could tell she meant every word!"

There was no one to support Lesley's claim that after the fight with her brother she'd gone for a long drive into the country, returning late that night. And, although no blood had been detected on Lesley's clothes or in her car, the thoroughly cleaned hatchet, found by children in a bushland reserve, was identified as hers by the initials burned into the polished wooden handle. The prosecution case was that Lesley had brought her own weapon to the garage later that evening, rather than trust to luck that she'd grab a suitably lethal implement from the workbench. It was fortunate that her defense barrister was able to prove that George Flemming had borrowed the hatchet some weeks before his death to take on a camping trip with Tony that was, as Lesley's barrister had said with meaningful scorn, "apparently an attempt to bond father and son."

I nodded as I read this. Surely excessive male bonding might lead to violent macho acts — though dismemberment was a bit extreme...

I spent the rest of the day chasing up equipment and chemicals for the darkroom and came home late to find Lesley moodily staring at the television screen. She looked up as I came in. "Tony's just called. He wants to come round this evening."

"Why?" I was secretly pleased to be meeting one of my two suspects, but it was obvious Lesley didn't want to see her nephew.

"He said he'd tell me when he saw me, but he did ask if it were true I was living with a photographer." She scowled at the screen where a beefcake-type was flogging soft drink by taking off his shirt for an audience of twittering females. "I told him to forget it. I don't trust the little bastard and I don't want him here."

"He did his best in the trial to nail you, and failed, so what could he do to you now?"

Lesley looked at me narrowly. "How do you know what he did in the trial?"

If I'd just kept quiet, as I usually did, I wouldn't

be rushing to explain now. "I went to the public library and read through newspaper accounts of your trial."

Her mouth tightened. "Worried I might be guilty?"

"No. And I didn't think you'd have kept a scrapbook." I ran my hand down the back of her neck, making my fingers tingle. "You didn't, did you?"

"Of course not." She looked astonished at my question.

I shook my head. "Shortsighted, darling. Once the real killer's found you'll be wanting to write a book. Everyone does. And then there's the television rights . . ."

Lesley didn't smile. "George's murder won't be solved, Eve. It's in the too hard basket now, especially as the cops think I did it, but the dumb jury let me off."

"What about hiring a private eye?"

She threw her hands up. "I used every cent I had paying for my defense. Why do you think I rent half this house to you? I'm broke."

"I've got some spare money."

"No." Her flat tone made it clear there was to be no debate on this matter.

The photographic equipment I'd ordered was to be delivered later in the week, so I devoted the next morning to cleaning the darkroom. If there's one thing I do, it's clean thoroughly. It's not that I'm obsessive, but I take it as a personal crusade to remove every trace of debris, dirt, or dust. There's no corner too difficult, no ledge too high, no nook or cranny safe from my ministrations.

After the initial clean-up of surfaces and floor, I zealously attacked those areas that other people always treat as out of sight, out of mind. I crawled under the developing trays with a flashlight to check the plumbing and generally investigate the grime situation.

At the very back of the frame holding the trays a small packet tightly wrapped in black plastic was jammed into the space between the wall and the metal.

I levered it loose and shuffled my way backwards to see what I had found.

The packet contained at least thirty negatives, and, although I looked at each one carefully, it was difficult to see what was going on, except that most contained several people sitting in cars or meeting in the street. The film used was thirty-two hundred ASA, which would take reasonable shots without a flash even in poor light conditions, and it was my guess that most of the photos had been taken with a telephoto lens.

I needed to have prints made to see exactly what I'd found, but somehow I hesitated to go to a commercial photographer. It took several cajoling phone calls to get early delivery for the darkroom equipment. "I'll make prints of the negatives as soon as I get set up tomorrow," I explained on the phone to Lesley, who was at work. "This could be important, darling. Your brother must have hidden them there for some reason."

She wouldn't allow herself to be as excited as I was. "Probably pornography," she said dismissively.

"It's not pornography — everyone's fully clothed. I

think it's a set of surveillance photos, but we won't know for sure until tomorrow afternoon."

Next morning the delivery of my equipment was late and then it took me some time to get the darkroom into working order. Lesley hovered around getting in the way until, exasperated, I sent her off to work at her computer terminal. It was mid-afternoon before I finished the last print, but I already knew that Tony Flemming featured in most of the photographs, all of which had been taken in a variety of suburban streets and car parks. And I had a fair idea what was going on.

"Hold them by the edges," I commanded as Lesley seized the first print.

Using my magnifying glass, she began to study each print. "It's Tony, but I don't recognize anyone else . . . Wait a minute!" She pointed to a well-dressed man with a complacent heavily jowled face. "That's Victor Sharp."

"Who's Victor Sharp?"

"The media politely calls him 'the well-known business man,' but everyone knows he's into drugs and prostitution. Victor Sharp might not yet be the Mr. Big of Sydney crime, but he's working at it. He's been arrested a few times, but nothing ever sticks — witnesses mysteriously develop amnesia and it's rumored he's got cops in his pocket."

I showed her extra prints I'd made. "These are enlargements. Your brother was a pretty good photographer — he got some great shots of drugs and money changing hands. I'd say he was keeping Tony under surveillance and he got lucky."

Lesley looked at me soberly. "Lucky? He's dead."

That wiped the smile off my face. George's murder was almost certainly tied to these photographs, and I had the negatives and probably the only prints. "We'd better call your attorney."

"Solicitor," she corrected me. "Why not go directly to the police?"

"If this Victor Sharp has anything to do with the murder, we don't want evidence disappearing. It's much better if we have your lawyer involved as insurance. I'll make another set of prints and put them in a safe deposit box." I was quite proud of my foresight — there was no way I was going to let anything happen to evidence that would exonerate Lesley.

"What if it was Tony who killed George because these photos would land him in jail?" She didn't look happy.

I was impatient. It was a bit late to start worrying about relatives. "So what if it is Tony? Doesn't he deserve to be punished?"

As it turned out, it hadn't been Tony who'd killed his father — that had been accomplished rather messily by one of Victor Sharp's thugs — but Tony had been forced to help dispose of the body, thus guaranteeing his silence. Lesley's brother had taken the ill-advised step of contacting Victor Sharp to say that, if he ever used Tony again to deal drugs, George would take the set of incriminating surveillance photographs to the authorities. That incautious threat ensured it was Goodbye, George.

On the stand as a prosecution witness at Victor Sharp's trial for murder, Tony had been alternately sulky and defiant. "Mr. Sharp told me to find the negatives of the photos and get rid of them. When they weren't at home I thought Dad must have left them in the darkroom at Aunt Lesley's place." Tony glared at her where she sat beside me in the courtroom. "But she told me to get lost before I could do a proper search. I was frightened of Mr. Sharp so I told him I'd found the negatives and burnt them." He shrugged when asked why he hadn't persevered. "I forgot about it. I figured if anyone found them they wouldn't know what they were, anyway . . . Until that photographer turned up . . ." This time the glare was for me.

Months later, when Victor Sharp was appealing his guilty verdict and Tony was serving a substantial sentence as an accessory before the fact, a news magazine ran a lengthy story about George Flemming's murder, his sister's trial and the solving of the case. The heading above Lesley's photograph declared: INNOCENT OF BROTHER'S AX MURDER!

She laughed as she took me in her arms. "I know one thing — I'm guilty of loving you."

I grinned at her. "Other than that," I said, "I'd say you're *relatively* innocent . . ."

On the Authors

ROSE BEECHAM is a pseudonym of Jennifer Fulton, author of *Passion Bay, Saving Grace* and *True Love*. A New Zealander, Jennifer divides her time between two cities — Wellington, NZ, and Melbourne, Australia. The Amanda Valentine series includes *Introducing Amanda Valentine, Second Guess* and the forthcoming title, *Fair Play*. Under her real name, Jennifer Fulton, she had stories in this series' first two volumes, *The Erotic Naiad* and *The Romantic Naiad*.

RHONDA DICKSION, 34, is a resident of Washington state. She is the author of The Lesbian

Survival Manual (1990), *Stay Tooned* (1993), and a contributor to numerous books, publications, and art shows. Living with her partner of six years, five cats, two dogs, and a stuffed armadillo named Boerne has helped her formulate her mantra: "Keep laughing, damnit!"

LAUREN WRIGHT DOUGLAS was born in Canada in 1947. She grew up in a military family and spent part of her childhood in Europe. Several years ago, Lauren moved from her home in the Pacific Northwest to the American Southwest where she now lives with her partner Martha and their cats. *A Rage of Maidens* is her eighth book for Naiad Press and the sixth in the Caitlin Reece series. *Ninth Life,* the second Caitlin Reece novel, won the 1990 Lambda Literary Award for Best Lesbian Mystery. Lauren's short stories have appeared in *The Erotic Naiad, The Romantic Naiad* and *The Mysterious Naiad.* At present, Lauren is at work on another novel.

CATHERINE ENNIS lives on the outskirts of a small southern town. She and her lover of seventeen years share their rural haven with creatures that fly, hop, run, swim and slither.

Often included in her gourmet cooking hobby are the growing things that survive their gardening efforts.

Catherine has long owned a 1930 Model A Ford coupe which she restored, and enters in shows and parades.

JENNIFER FULTON (See Rose Beecham)

PENNY HAYES was born in Johnson City, New York, February, 1940. As a child she lived on a farm near Binghamton, New York. She later attended school in Utica and Buffalo, graduating with degrees in art and special education. She has made her living teaching in both New York State and West Virginia. She presently resides in Ithaca, New York.

Ms. Hayes' interests include backpacking, mountain climbing, canoeing, traveling, reading, gardening and studying early American history. She picks up abandoned animals along the road and takes them home and keeps them.

She has been published in *I Know You Know, Of the Summits & Of the Forests* and various backpacking magazines. Her Naiad Press novels include *The Long Trail, Yellowthroat, Montana Feathers, Grassy Flats,* and *Kathleen O'Donald.* Her sixth book, *Now and Then,* will be published by Naiad Press in 1996. She has also published short fiction in *The Erotic Naiad* and *The Romantic Naiad.*

BARBARA JOHNSON's love for writing began when she was eight and had her winning essay, *What It Means To Me To Be a Good Catholic,* published in the church bulletin. Though she kept on writing, her next published work, *Stonehurst,* came almost 30 years later. She lives in Maryland with her lover of 20 years and is working on her next novel, *The*

Beach Affair, which will be published by Naiad sometime in 1995.

SUSAN E. JOHNSON is the author of *Staying Power: Long Term Lesbian Couples* (Naiad Press, 1990), *When Women Played Hardball* (Seal Press, 1994) and the forthcoming *For Love and for Life* (Naiad Press, 1995), a collection of intimate profiles of lesbian couples who have been together ten years or more.

Susan is fifty-five years old, a writer and sociologist who lives in Anchorage, Alaska. Her partner does indeed have blue-green-turquoise eyes. Susan herself would never harm a soul.

KARIN KALLMAKER was born in 1960 and raised by loving, middle-class parents. From a normal childhood and equally unremarkable public school adolescence, she went on to obtain an ordinary Bachelor's degree from the California State University at Sacramento. At the age of 16, eyes wide open, she fell into the arms of her first and only sweetheart. Ten years later, after seeing the film *Desert Hearts,* her sweetheart descended on the Berkeley Public Library determined to find some of "those" books. "Rule, Jane" led to "Lesbianism — Fiction" and then on to book after self-affirming book by and about lesbians. Works such as *All True Lovers, Curious Wine,* and *Faultline,* were the encouragement Karin needed to forget the so-called "mainstream" and spin her first romance for lesbians. That manuscript became her first Naiad Press book, *In Every Port.* Now a full-time financial manager in the nonprofit sector, she lives in Oakland with that very same sweetheart; she is a one-woman woman.

Karin is also the contributing editor of Uncommon Voices, the bi-monthly publication of the Bay Area Career Women, which is the largest lesbian social organization in the United States. Her essay "When I Grow Up I Want To Be a Lesbian" appears in Multicultural America: A Resource Book for Teachers of Humanities and American Studies. In addition to *In Every Port,* she has authored the best-selling *Touchwood, Paperback Romance* and *Car Pool.* Her fifth Naiad romance is *Painted Moon.* After that, look for *Wild Things.* Since Karin considers her lesbian readers to be the only mainstream, she intends to write many more.

JAYE MAIMAN is the author of three romantic mysteries featuring the private investigator Robin Miller: *I Left My Heart,* the award-winning *Crazy for Loving,* and *Under My Skin.* Her fourth book in the series, *Someone To Watch,* will be published by Naiad Press in 1995. A Halloween baby, she was born in Brooklyn, New York, 1957, and raised in a Coney Island housing project where she spent Tuesday nights consuming blueberry cheese knishes and watching fireworks from a beachside boardwalk. She now lives in Park Slope, Brooklyn, with her two puppy cats and her partner, playmate, editor, co-neurotic, and magic-maker Rhea.

CLAIRE McNAB is the author of the Detective Inspector Carol Ashton mysteries, *Lessons in Murder, Fatal Reunion, Death Down Under, Cop Out, Dead Certain* and *Body Guard.* She has also written two romances, *Under the Southern Cross* and *Silent Heart.* While a high school English teacher she began her writing career with comedy plays and textbooks. After she became a full-time writer she wrote for television soap opera. In her native Australia she is known for her self-help and children's books.

For reasons of the heart, Claire is now a permanent resident of the United States. She lives in Los Angeles, which she says is, "Exciting — but absolutely nothing like Sydney!"

PENNY MICKELBURY, novelist and playwright, is a former newspaper, radio and television reporter who currently lives in Washington, DC. She conducts writing workshops for women in Washington and in Baltimore.

Her mystery novel *Keeping Secrets,* was published by Naiad in 1994, and her second novel in the Giana Maglione/Mimi Patterson series, *Night Songs,* will be published in January, 1995.

Penny was born and raised in Atlanta, Georgia and is of African- and Native American ancestry.

HILARY MULLINS wrote her first mystery at the tender age of eight, self-illustrating and publishing "The Mystery of the Secret Tunnel," a serialized adventure starring a boy named Will and an anonymous orange cat. Her first novel *The Cat*

Came Back, published by Naiad Press, also featured a strong, though more subtle feline role and was awarded a 1993 Lambda Literary Award for Young Adult Fiction. Hilary is a Vermont transplant who now lives in Oakland, California with her partner April and their three cats. She is currently at work on her first screenplay.

ELISABETH NONAS has written three novels, *Staying Home* (1994), *A Room Full of Women* (1990), and *For Keeps* (1985) all published by Naiad Press. *A Room Full of Women* has been optioned and is being made into a motion picture. She has also written articles for "The Advocate" documenting lesbian and gay life in America, as well as the screenplay adaptation of Paul Monette's novel *Afterlife.*

Elisabeth teaches fiction writing at UCLA Extension, and developed and taught the first lesbian and gay fiction writing classes offered there. She also teaches lesbian and gay fiction writing workshops at The Institute of Gay and Lesbian Education in West Hollywood.

She and Simon LeVay are co-authoring an introduction to lesbian and gay culture to be published in 1995 by MIT Press.

She lives in Los Angeles with her lover, photographer Carole Topalian. They have two dogs, Annie and Oakley.

CAROL SCHMIDT and Norma Hair, her partner of fifteen years, live in an old country church they've converted to a home in rural Michigan, and spend much of the year camping throughout North America. Both in their early fifties, they moved back to their native Michigan after many years in Los Angeles, where Carol had written a column, "Country Womyn/City Dyke," for the *L.A. Lesbian News,* and co-owned a small business called Words & Numbers with Norma. Schmidt's first two novels of suspense published by Naiad are Silverlake Heat and *Sweet Cherry Wine,* which will be followed by *Cabin Fever* (1995) and *Stop the Music* (1996).

ROBBI SOMMERS, best-selling author of lesbian erotica — Pleasures, Players, Kiss and Tell, Uncertain Companions, Behind Closed Doors and *Personal Ads* — was born in Cincinnati, Ohio in 1950. Now residing in Northern California, she divides her time between motherhood (three sons), writing and dental hygiene. "It's odd how similar dentistry and lesbian erotica are . . ." Robbi has often been heard remarking. "Whether in the dental chair or deep in erotica research, I am always compelled to do a complete oral exam." So be it.

PENNY SUMNER was born in Australia in 1955 and moved to England to undertake postgraduate studies at the University of Oxford. She has worked as a waitress, librarian, photographer at a dolphin pool, and as a seller of antiquarian books. She currently teaches feminist theory and contemporary writing at a university in the North-East of England. Her mystery novels, *The End of April* and

Crosswords were both published by Naiad Press. She has a story in *The Romantic Naiad* and is currently working on the third Victoria Cross mystery.

DOROTHY TELL and her partner Ruth (since 1972) live in Texas where Dot has another year and a half at the job from hell. But Dot won't retire, she will just change jobs. After a couple of carefree vacation months in the high desert of Arizona she will write full time. And go fishing on the Texas coast and spend more time with her daughter and granddaughter, both of whom she is teaching to shoot sporting clays. And even though Dot was born in San Francisco, she hasn't been back but once (courtesy U.S. Marine Corps) in the fifty years since. She thinks she will visit her home state and get to know the women who live there. And just maybe she will find time for that big yellow dog she's always wanted.

Her works published by Naiad Press include *Wilderness Trek, Murder at Red Rook Ranch* (Poppy Dillworth), *The Hallelujah Murders* (Poppy Dillworth), *Certain Smiles,* and the forthcoming *Promises.* She also has stories in *The Erotic Naiad* and *The Romantic Naiad.*

PAT WELCH was born in 1957 in Japan. She spent most of her childhood in the south before relocating to California. A current resident of Oakland, Pat has published three books with Naiad Press in the Helen Black mystery series. Her fourth book in the series, *Open House,* will be out in 1995.

AMANDA KYLE WILLIAMS is the best-selling author of *Club Twelve, A Singular Spy, The Spy in Question* and the Lambda Literary Award nominated *The Providence File* — all espionage thrillers featuring the very sexy and capable Madison McGuire. Contributions to this series include stories in *The Erotic Naiad* and *The Romantic Naiad. Apartment Seven B,* her story featured here, is dedicated in loving memory to Deb.

Amanda Kyle Williams lives in Atlanta, Georgia, loves the South, holds a senior belt in Martial Arts, and is currently working on her next thriller.

MOLLEEN ZANGER lives in the thumb of Michigan with her mate, her son, two dogs, two cats and a collection of cacti and succulents. She was born in Panama C.Z. and raised in Michigan. Among other things, she has worked as a postal carrier, bartender, real estate sales associate and staff writer-photographer on a weekly newspaper. Other Naiad publications include short stories in *The Erotic Naiad* and *The Romantic Naiad* and two novels, *The Year Seven,* and *Gardenias Where There Are None.*

A few of the publications of
THE NAIAD PRESS, INC.
P.O. Box 10543 • Tallahassee, Florida 32302
Phone (904) 539-5965
Toll-Free Order Number: 1-800-533-1973
Mail orders welcome. Please include 15% postage.

THE MYSTERIOUS NAIAD edited by Katherine V. Forrest & Barbara Grier. 320 pp. Love stories by Naiad Press authors.
ISBN 1-56280-074-4 $14.95

BODY GUARD by Claire McNab. 208 pp. A Carol Ashton Mystery. 6th in a series.   ISBN 1-56280-073-6   9.95

CACTUS LOVE by Lee Lynch. 192 pp. Stories by the beloved storyteller.   ISBN 1-56280-071-X   9.95

SECOND GUESS by Rose Beecham. 216 pp. An Amanda Valentine Mystery. 2nd in a series.   ISBN 1-56280-069-8   9.95

THE SURE THING by Melissa Hartman. 208 pp. L.A. earthquake romance.   ISBN 1-56280-078-7   9.95

A RAGE OF MAIDENS by Lauren Wright Douglas. 240 pp. A Caitlin Reece Mystery. 6th in a series.   ISBN 1-56280-068-X   9.95

TRIPLE EXPOSURE by Jackie Calhoun. 224 pp. Romantic drama involving many characters.   ISBN 1-56280-067-1   9.95

UP, UP AND AWAY by Catherine Ennis. 192 pp. Delightful romance.   ISBN 1-56280-065-5   9.95

PERSONAL ADS by Robbi Sommers. 176 pp. Sizzling short stories.   ISBN 1-56280-059-0   9.95

FLASHPOINT by Katherine V. Forrest. 256 pp. Lesbian blockbuster!   ISBN 1-56280-043-4   22.95

CROSSWORDS by Penny Sumner. 256 pp. 2nd Victoria Cross Mystery.   ISBN 1-56280-064-7   9.95

SWEET CHERRY WINE by Carol Schmidt. 224 pp. A novel of suspense.   ISBN 1-56280-063-9   9.95

CERTAIN SMILES by Dorothy Tell. 160 pp. Erotic short stories.
ISBN 1-56280-066-3   9.95

EDITED OUT by Lisa Haddock. 224 pp. 1st Carmen Ramirez Mystery.   ISBN 1-56280-077-9   9.95

WEDNESDAY NIGHTS by Camarin Grae. 288 pp. Sexy adventure.   ISBN 1-56280-060-4   10.95

SMOKEY O by Celia Cohen. 176 pp. Relationships on the playing
field.   ISBN 1-56280-057-4   9.95

KATHLEEN O'DONALD by Penny Hayes. 256 pp. Rose and
Kathleen find each other and employment in 1909 NYC.
                                      ISBN 1-56280-070-1   9.95

STAYING HOME by Elisabeth Nonas. 256 pp. Molly and Alix
want a baby . . . or do they?   ISBN 1-56280-076-0   10.95

TRUE LOVE by Jennifer Fulton. 240 pp. Six lesbians searching for
love in all the "right" places.   ISBN 1-56280-035-3   9.95

GARDENIAS WHERE THERE ARE NONE by Molleen Zanger.
176 pp. Why is Melanie inextricably drawn to the old house?
                                      ISBN 1-56280-056-6   9.95

MICHAELA by Sarah Aldridge. 256 pp. A "Sarah Aldridge"
romance.   ISBN 1-56280-055-8   10.95

KEEPING SECRETS by Penny Mickelbury. 208 pp. A Gianna
Maglione Mystery. First in a series. ISBN 1-56280-052-3   9.95

THE ROMANTIC NAIAD edited by Katherine V. Forrest &
Barbara Grier. 336 pp. Love stories by Naiad Press authors.
                                      ISBN 1-56280-054-X   14.95

UNDER MY SKIN by Jaye Maiman. 336 pp. A Robin Miller
mystery. 3rd in a series.   ISBN 1-56280-049-3.   10.95

STAY TOONED by Rhonda Dicksion. 144 pp. Cartoons — 1st
collection since *Lesbian Survival Manual.*   ISBN 1-56280-045-0   9.95

CAR POOL by Karin Kallmaker. 272pp. Lesbians on wheels
and then some!   ISBN 1-56280-048-5   9.95

NOT TELLING MOTHER: STORIES FROM A LIFE by Diane
Salvatore. 176 pp. Her 3rd novel.   ISBN 1-56280-044-2   9.95

GOBLIN MARKET by Lauren Wright Douglas. 240pp. A Caitlin
Reece Mystery. 5th in a series.   ISBN 1-56280-047-7   9.95

LONG GOODBYES by Nikki Baker. 256 pp. A Virginia Kelly
mystery. 3rd in a series.   ISBN 1-56280-042-6   9.95

FRIENDS AND LOVERS by Jackie Calhoun. 224 pp. Mid-western
Lesbian lives and loves.   ISBN 1-56280-041-8   9.95

THE CAT CAME BACK by Hilary Mullins. 208 pp. Highly praised
Lesbian novel.   ISBN 1-56280-040-X   9.95

BEHIND CLOSED DOORS by Robbi Sommers. 192 pp. Hot, erotic
short stories.   ISBN 1-56280-039-6   9.95

CLAIRE OF THE MOON by Nicole Conn. 192 pp. See the movie —
read the book!   ISBN 1-56280-038-8   10.95

SILENT HEART by Claire McNab. 192 pp. Exotic Lesbian
romance.   ISBN 1-56280-036-1   9.95

HAPPY ENDINGS by Kate Brandt. 272 pp. Intimate conversations
with Lesbian authors.   ISBN 1-56280-050-7   10.95

THE SPY IN QUESTION by Amanda Kyle Williams. 256 pp. 4th
Madison McGuire.   ISBN 1-56280-037-X   9.95

SAVING GRACE by Jennifer Fulton. 240 pp. Adventure and
romantic entanglement.   ISBN 1-56280-051-5   9.95

THE YEAR SEVEN by Molleen Zanger. 208 pp. Women surviving
in a new world.   ISBN 1-56280-034-5   9.95

CURIOUS WINE by Katherine V. Forrest. 176 pp. Tenth
Anniversary Edition. The most popular contemporary Lesbian
love story.   ISBN 1-56280-053-1   10.95

CHAUTAUQUA by Catherine Ennis. 192 pp. Exciting, romantic
adventure.   ISBN 1-56280-032-9   9.95

A PROPER BURIAL by Pat Welch. 192 pp. A Helen Black
mystery. 3rd in a series.   ISBN 1-56280-033-7   9.95

SILVERLAKE HEAT: A Novel of Suspense by Carol Schmidt.
240 pp. Rhonda is as hot as Laney's dreams.   ISBN 1-56280-031-0   9.95

LOVE, ZENA BETH by Diane Salvatore. 224 pp. The most talked
about lesbian novel of the nineties!   ISBN 1-56280-030-2   9.95

A DOORYARD FULL OF FLOWERS by Isabel Miller. 160 pp.
Stories incl. 2 sequels to *Patience and Sarah.*   ISBN 1-56280-029-9   9.95

MURDER BY TRADITION by Katherine V. Forrest. 288 pp. A
Kate Delafield Mystery. 4th in a series.   ISBN 1-56280-002-7   9.95

THE EROTIC NAIAD edited by Katherine V. Forrest & Barbara Grier.
224 pp. Love stories by Naiad Press authors.   ISBN 1-56280-026-4   12.95

DEAD CERTAIN by Claire McNab. 224 pp. A Carol Ashton
mystery. 5th in a series.   ISBN 1-56280-027-2   9.95

CRAZY FOR LOVING by Jaye Maiman. 320 pp. A Robin Miller
mystery. 2nd in a series.   ISBN 1-56280-025-6   9.95

STONEHURST by Barbara Johnson. 176 pp. Passionate regency
romance.   ISBN 1-56280-024-8   9.95

INTRODUCING AMANDA VALENTINE by Rose Beecham.
256 pp. An Amanda Valentine Mystery. First in a series.
                                         ISBN 1-56280-021-3   9.95

UNCERTAIN COMPANIONS by Robbi Sommers. 204 pp.
Steamy, erotic novel.   ISBN 1-56280-017-5   9.95

A TIGER'S HEART by Lauren W. Douglas. 240 pp. A Caitlin
Reece mystery. 4th in a series.   ISBN 1-56280-018-3   9.95

PAPERBACK ROMANCE by Karin Kallmaker. 256 pp. A
delicious romance.   ISBN 1-56280-019-1   9.95

MORTON RIVER VALLEY by Lee Lynch. 304 pp. Lee Lynch at
her best!   ISBN 1-56280-016-7   9.95

THE LAVENDER HOUSE MURDER by Nikki Baker. 224 pp. A
Virginia Kelly Mystery. 2nd in a series.   ISBN 1-56280-012-4   9.95

PASSION BAY by Jennifer Fulton. 224 pp. Passionate romance,
virgin beaches, tropical skies.   ISBN 1-56280-028-0   9.95

STICKS AND STONES by Jackie Calhoun. 208 pp. Contemporary
lesbian lives and loves.   ISBN 1-56280-020-5   9.95

DELIA IRONFOOT by Jeane Harris. 192 pp. Adventure for Delia
and Beth in the Utah mountains.   ISBN 1-56280-014-0   9.95

UNDER THE SOUTHERN CROSS by Claire McNab. 192 pp.
Romantic nights Down Under.   ISBN 1-56280-011-6   9.95

RIVERFINGER WOMEN by Elana Nachman/Dykewomon.
208 pp. Classic Lesbian/feminist novel.   ISBN 1-56280-013-2   8.95

GRASSY FLATS by Penny Hayes. 256 pp. Lesbian romance in
the '30s.   ISBN 1-56280-010-8   9.95

A SINGULAR SPY by Amanda K. Williams. 192 pp. 3rd Madison
McGuire.   ISBN 1-56280-008-6   8.95

THE END OF APRIL by Penny Sumner. 240 pp. A Victoria Cross
Mystery. First in a series.   ISBN 1-56280-007-8   8.95

A FLIGHT OF ANGELS by Sarah Aldridge. 240 pp. Romance set at
the National Gallery of Art   ISBN 1-56280-001-9   9.95

HOUSTON TOWN by Deborah Powell. 208 pp. A Hollis Carpenter
mystery. Second in a series.   ISBN 1-56280-006-X   8.95

KISS AND TELL by Robbi Sommers. 192 pp. Scorching stories by
the author of *Pleasures*.   ISBN 1-56280-005-1   9.95

STILL WATERS by Pat Welch. 208 pp. A Helen Black mystery.
2nd in a series.   ISBN 0-941483-97-5   9.95

TO LOVE AGAIN by Evelyn Kennedy. 208 pp. Wildly
romantic love story.   ISBN 0-941483-85-1   9.95

IN THE GAME by Nikki Baker. 192 pp. A Virginia Kelly
mystery. First in a series.   ISBN 1-56280-004-3   9.95

AVALON by Mary Jane Jones. 256 pp. A Lesbian Arthurian
romance.   ISBN 0-941483-96-7   9.95

STRANDED by Camarin Grae. 320 pp. Entertaining, riveting
adventure.   ISBN 0-941483-99-1   9.95

THE DAUGHTERS OF ARTEMIS by Lauren Wright Douglas.
240 pp. A Caitlin Reece mystery. 3rd in a series.
                                                  ISBN 0-941483-95-9   9.95

CLEARWATER by Catherine Ennis. 176 pp. Romantic secrets
of a small Louisiana town.   ISBN 0-941483-65-7   8.95

THE HALLELUJAH MURDERS by Dorothy Tell. 176 pp. A Poppy
Dillworth mystery. 2nd in a series.   ISBN 0-941483-88-6   8.95

SECOND CHANCE by Jackie Calhoun. 256 pp. Contemporary
Lesbian lives and loves.   ISBN 0-941483-93-2   9.95

BENEDICTION by Diane Salvatore. 272 pp. Striking,
contemporary romantic novel.   ISBN 0-941483-90-8   9.95

BLACK IRIS by Jeane Harris. 192 pp. Caroline's hidden past . . .
                                                   ISBN 0-941483-68-1   8.95

TOUCHWOOD by Karin Kallmaker. 240 pp. Loving, May/
December romance.   ISBN 0-941483-76-2   9.95

COP OUT by Claire McNab. 208 pp. A Carol Ashton mystery.
4th in a series.   ISBN 0-941483-84-3   9.95

THE BEVERLY MALIBU by Katherine V. Forrest. 288 pp. A
Kate Delafield Mystery. 3rd in a series.   ISBN 0-941483-48-7   9.95

THAT OLD STUDEBAKER by Lee Lynch. 272 pp. Andy's affair
with Regina and her attachment to her beloved car.
                                                   ISBN 0-941483-82-7   9.95

PASSION'S LEGACY by Lori Paige. 224 pp. Sarah is swept into
the arms of Augusta Pym in this delightful historical romance.
                                                   ISBN 0-941483-81-9   8.95

THE PROVIDENCE FILE by Amanda Kyle Williams. 256 pp.
Second Madison McGuire   ISBN 0-941483-92-4   8.95

I LEFT MY HEART by Jaye Maiman. 320 pp. A Robin Miller
Mystery. First in a series.   ISBN 0-941483-72-X   9.95

THE PRICE OF SALT by Patricia Highsmith (writing as Claire
Morgan). 288 pp. Classic lesbian novel, first issued in 1952 . . .
acknowledged by its author under her own, very famous, name.
                                                   ISBN 1-56280-003-5   9.95

SIDE BY SIDE by Isabel Miller. 256 pp. From beloved author of
Patience and Sarah.   ISBN 0-941483-77-0   9.95

STAYING POWER: LONG TERM LESBIAN COUPLES
by Susan E. Johnson. 352 pp. Joys of coupledom.
                                                   ISBN 0-941-483-75-4   12.95

SLICK by Camarin Grae. 304 pp. Exotic, erotic adventure.
                                                   ISBN 0-941483-74-6   9.95

NINTH LIFE by Lauren Wright Douglas. 256 pp. A Caitlin
Reece mystery. 2nd in a series.   ISBN 0-941483-50-9   8.95

PLAYERS by Robbi Sommers. 192 pp. Sizzling, erotic novel.
                                                   ISBN 0-941483-73-8   9.95

MURDER AT RED ROOK RANCH by Dorothy Tell. 224 pp.
A Poppy Dillworth mystery. 1st in a series.   ISBN 0-941483-80-0   8.95

LESBIAN SURVIVAL MANUAL by Rhonda Dicksion.
112 pp. Cartoons!   ISBN 0-941483-71-1   8.95

A ROOM FULL OF WOMEN by Elisabeth Nonas. 256 pp.
Contemporary Lesbian lives.   ISBN 0-941483-69-X   9.95

THEME FOR DIVERSE INSTRUMENTS by Jane Rule. 208
pp. Powerful romantic lesbian stories.   ISBN 0-941483-63-0   8.95

LESBIAN QUERIES by Hertz & Ertman. 112 pp. The questions
you were too embarrassed to ask.   ISBN 0-941483-67-3   8.95

CLUB 12 by Amanda Kyle Williams. 288 pp. Espionage thriller
featuring a lesbian agent!   ISBN 0-941483-64-9   8.95

DEATH DOWN UNDER by Claire McNab. 240 pp. A Carol
Ashton mystery. 3rd in a series.   ISBN 0-941483-39-8   9.95

MONTANA FEATHERS by Penny Hayes. 256 pp. Vivian and
Elizabeth find love in frontier Montana.   ISBN 0-941483-61-4   8.95

LIFESTYLES by Jackie Calhoun. 224 pp. Contemporary Lesbian
lives and loves.   ISBN 0-941483-57-6   9.95

WILDERNESS TREK by Dorothy Tell. 192 pp. Six women on
vacation learning ''new'' skills.   ISBN 0-941483-60-6   8.95

MURDER BY THE BOOK by Pat Welch. 256 pp. A Helen
Black Mystery. First in a series.   ISBN 0-941483-59-2   9.95

THERE'S SOMETHING I'VE BEEN MEANING TO TELL
YOU Ed. by Loralee MacPike. 288 pp. Gay men and lesbians
coming out to their children.   ISBN 0-941483-44-4   9.95

LIFTING BELLY by Gertrude Stein. Ed. by Rebecca Mark. 104
pp. Erotic poetry.   ISBN 0-941483-51-7   8.95

AFTER THE FIRE by Jane Rule. 256 pp. Warm, human novel
by this incomparable author.   ISBN 0-941483-45-2   8.95

THREE WOMEN by March Hastings. 232 pp. Golden oldie. A
triangle among wealthy sophisticates.   ISBN 0-941483-43-6   8.95

PLEASURES by Robbi Sommers. 204 pp. Unprecedented
eroticism.   ISBN 0-941483-49-5   8.95

EDGEWISE by Camarin Grae. 372 pp. Spellbinding
adventure.   ISBN 0-941483-19-3   9.95

FATAL REUNION by Claire McNab. 224 pp. A Carol Ashton
mystery. 2nd in a series.   ISBN 0-941483-40-1   8.95

KEEP TO ME STRANGER by Sarah Aldridge. 372 pp. Romance
set in a department store dynasty.   ISBN 0-941483-38-X   9.95

IN EVERY PORT by Karin Kallmaker. 228 pp. Jessica's sexy,
adventuresome travels.   ISBN 0-941483-37-7   9.95

OF LOVE AND GLORY by Evelyn Kennedy. 192 pp. Exciting
WWII romance.   ISBN 0-941483-32-0   8.95

CLICKING STONES by Nancy Tyler Glenn. 288 pp. Love
transcending time.   ISBN 0-941483-31-2   9.95

SURVIVING SISTERS by Gail Pass. 252 pp. Powerful love
story.   ISBN 0-941483-16-9   8.95

SOUTH OF THE LINE by Catherine Ennis. 216 pp. Civil War
adventure. ISBN 0-941483-29-0   8.95

WOMAN PLUS WOMAN by Dolores Klaich. 300 pp. Supurb
Lesbian overview. ISBN 0-941483-28-2   9.95

THE FINER GRAIN by Denise Ohio. 216 pp. Brilliant young
college lesbian novel. ISBN 0-941483-11-8   8.95

OCTOBER OBSESSION by Meredith More. Josie's rich, secret
Lesbian life. ISBN 0-941483-18-5   8.95

BEFORE STONEWALL: THE MAKING OF A GAY AND
LESBIAN COMMUNITY by Andrea Weiss & Greta Schiller.
96 pp., 25 illus. ISBN 0-941483-20-7   7.95

OSTEN'S BAY by Zenobia N. Vole. 204 pp. Sizzling adventure
romance set on Bonaire. ISBN 0-941483-15-0   8.95

LESSONS IN MURDER by Claire McNab. 216 pp. A Carol
Ashton mystery. First in a series. ISBN 0-941483-14-2   9.95

YELLOWTHROAT by Penny Hayes. 240 pp. Margarita, bandit,
kidnaps Julia. ISBN 0-941483-10-X   8.95

SAPPHISTRY: THE BOOK OF LESBIAN SEXUALITY by
Pat Califia. 3d edition, revised. 208 pp. ISBN 0-941483-24-X   10.95

CHERISHED LOVE by Evelyn Kennedy. 192 pp. Erotic
Lesbian love story. ISBN 0-941483-08-8   9.95

THE SECRET IN THE BIRD by Camarin Grae. 312 pp. Striking,
psychological suspense novel. ISBN 0-941483-05-3   8.95

TO THE LIGHTNING by Catherine Ennis. 208 pp. Romantic
Lesbian 'Robinson Crusoe' adventure. ISBN 0-941483-06-1   8.95

DREAMS AND SWORDS by Katherine V. Forrest. 192 pp.
Romantic, erotic, imaginative stories. ISBN 0-941483-03-7   8.95

MEMORY BOARD by Jane Rule. 336 pp. Memorable novel
about an aging Lesbian couple. ISBN 0-941483-02-9   9.95

THE ALWAYS ANONYMOUS BEAST by Lauren Wright
Douglas. 224 pp. A Caitlin Reece mystery. First in a series.
ISBN 0-941483-04-5   8.95

PARENTS MATTER by Ann Muller. 240 pp. Parents'
relationships with Lesbian daughters and gay sons.
ISBN 0-930044-91-6   9.95

MAGDALENA by Sarah Aldridge. 352 pp. Epic Lesbian novel
set on three continents. ISBN 0-930044-99-1   8.95

THE BLACK AND WHITE OF IT by Ann Allen Shockley.
144 pp. Short stories. ISBN 0-930044-96-7   7.95

SAY JESUS AND COME TO ME by Ann Allen Shockley. 288 pp. Contemporary romance. ISBN 0-930044-98-3   8.95

LOVING HER by Ann Allen Shockley. 192 pp. Romantic love story. ISBN 0-930044-97-5   7.95

MURDER AT THE NIGHTWOOD BAR by Katherine V. Forrest. 240 pp. A Kate Delafield mystery. Second in a series. ISBN 0-930044-92-4   10.95

WINGED DANCER by Camarin Grae. 228 pp. Erotic Lesbian adventure story. ISBN 0-930044-88-6   8.95

PAZ by Camarin Grae. 336 pp. Romantic Lesbian adventurer with the power to change the world. ISBN 0-930044-89-4   8.95

SOUL SNATCHER by Camarin Grae. 224 pp. A puzzle, an adventure, a mystery — Lesbian romance. ISBN 0-930044-90-8   8.95

THE LOVE OF GOOD WOMEN by Isabel Miller. 224 pp. Long-awaited new novel by the author of the beloved *Patience and Sarah*. ISBN 0-930044-81-9   8.95

THE HOUSE AT PELHAM FALLS by Brenda Weathers. 240 pp. Suspenseful Lesbian ghost story. ISBN 0-930044-79-7   7.95

HOME IN YOUR HANDS by Lee Lynch. 240 pp. More stories from the author of *Old Dyke Tales*. ISBN 0-930044-80-0   7.95

PEMBROKE PARK by Michelle Martin. 256 pp. Derring-do and daring romance in Regency England. ISBN 0-930044-77-0   7.95

THE LONG TRAIL by Penny Hayes. 248 pp. Vivid adventures of two women in love in the old west. ISBN 0-930044-76-2   8.95

AN EMERGENCE OF GREEN by Katherine V. Forrest. 288 pp. Powerful novel of sexual discovery. ISBN 0-930044-69-X   9.95

THE LESBIAN PERIODICALS INDEX edited by Claire Potter. 432 pp. Author & subject index. ISBN 0-930044-74-6   12.95

DESERT OF THE HEART by Jane Rule. 224 pp. A classic; basis for the movie *Desert Hearts*. ISBN 0-930044-73-8   10.95

TORCHLIGHT TO VALHALLA by Gale Wilhelm. 128 pp. Classic novel by a great Lesbian writer. ISBN 0-930044-68-1   7.95

LESBIAN NUNS: BREAKING SILENCE edited by Rosemary Curb and Nancy Manahan. 432 pp. Unprecedented autobiographies of religious life. ISBN 0-930044-62-2   9.95

THE SWASHBUCKLER by Lee Lynch. 288 pp. Colorful novel set in Greenwich Village in the sixties. ISBN 0-930044-66-5   8.95

MISFORTUNE'S FRIEND by Sarah Aldridge. 320 pp. Historical Lesbian novel set on two continents. ISBN 0-930044-67-3   7.95

THE LATECOMER by Sarah Aldridge. 107 pp. A delicate love
story.   ISBN 0-930044-00-2   6.95

ODD GIRL OUT by Ann Bannon.   ISBN 0-930044-83-5   5.95
I AM A WOMAN 84-3; WOMEN IN THE SHADOWS 85-1;   each
JOURNEY TO A WOMAN 86-X; BEEBO BRINKER 87-8. Golden
oldies about life in Greenwich Village.
JOURNEY TO FULFILLMENT, A WORLD WITHOUT MEN, and   3.95
RETURN TO LESBOS. All by Valerie Taylor   each

These are just a few of the many Naiad Press titles — we are the oldest and
largest lesbian/feminist publishing company in the world. Please request a
complete catalog. We offer personal service; we encourage and welcome
direct mail orders from individuals who have limited access to bookstores
carrying our publications.